Mannerism and Renaissance Poetry

Agnolo Bronzino, *Portrait of Laura Battiferri*. Florence, Palazzo Vecchio.

Mannerism and Renaissance Poetry

CONCEPT, MODE, INNER DESIGN

JAMES V. MIROLLO

YALE UNIVERSITY PRESS
NEW HAVEN AND LONDON

Designed by Sally Harris
and set in Garamond No. 3 type by
Northeast Typographic Services, Meriden, Connecticut.
Printed in the United States of America
by Vail-Ballou Press, Binghamton, New York.

Library of Congress Cataloging in Publication Data

Mirollo, James V.
Mannerism and Renaissance Poetry.
Bibliography: p.
Includes index.
1. *Mannerism (Literature)* 2. *Petrarchism.*
3. *European poetry—Renaissance, 1450–1600*—History and criticism.
4. Mannerism (Art) I. Title.
PN605.M3M57   1984   809'.91   84-40199
ISBN 0-300-03227-7

The paper in this book meets the guidelines for
permanence and durability of the Committee on
Production Guidelines for Book Longevity
of the Council on Library Resources.

10   9   8   7   6   5   4   3   2   1

Alla sacra memoria dei miei genitori

Contents

Illustrations

Preface

At the gates of this book the reader has already encountered two signs, one visual and the other verbal, that together announce its subject, intent, and scope. The *Portrait of Laura Battiferri* by the mannerist painter Agnolo Bronzino depicts a contemporary poet, herself named Laura, pointing to a volume of Petrarch's verses. It imitates an earlier *Portrait of a Girl Holding a Volume of Petrarch* by Andrea del Sarto that serves as the visual proem to my third and fourth chapters on imitative Petrarchism as a type of literary mannerism. The verbal sign is my title, the phrase "inner design" *(disegno interno)* being borrowed from the late sixteenth-century theorist of mannerist art, Federico Zuccaro (1549– 1609), who used it to distinguish the artist's superior aesthetic conception from his subordinate sensory experience of external reality.

My use of the term *mode* is not intended to invoke Northrop Frye, nor, despite the echoing of his several titles, Earl Miner. I have in mind something more modest and more suited to my theme, since the mannerist artist is less likely to be preoccupied with the self, others, and the world than with other works of art. The common dictionary meaning, "a way of doing something," what the sixteenth-century Italian word *maniera* could minimally signify, is closer to my purpose, as it, like *maniera,* can also connote a literary, artistic, or social style. For reasons that will become clear later, to speak of a mannerist lyric "style," another alternative, would be to say more than I wish to claim. Given the obvious infelicity of "sub-style" or "mannerist manner," then, I have had recourse to and ask the reader to keep in mind a meaning of *mode* that portends no more than the hypothesis of a mannerist variant of Renaissance lyric style.

This book, therefore, is primarily about literary mannerism as it may be evidenced in Petrarchism. And since the poetry of Petrarch engendered not only an Italian and European literary movement but also a broader cultural phenomenon, especially in Italy, it offers an appropriate and promising point of departure for discreet interdisciplinary soundings of the notion of a literary mannerism. At the same time, concentration on the literary facts and artifacts of the lyric production of Petrarch and his followers ballasts an analysis that might otherwise soar into the aery realm of impressionistic intermedia musings. It also skirts the equal danger of total absorption in the "problem" of mannerism. Obviously there would be no need to speculate about its literary variety were it not the case that the concept of mannerism, about which there has only recently begun to emerge a glimmering of a possible consensus, has been for most of this century the topic of one of our notoriously controversial debates—or, as some might argue, of one of our scandalous intellectual games! One must therefore approach the literary facts with this debate in mind, yet determined to test its assumptions as hypotheses, or propose new ones, with eyes glued to relevant texts.

As to the particulars of my plan and method, I have had in mind from the start an ideal general or academic reader, a student or scholar of English and comparative European literature and art who is also curious about the sister arts. To this end I have tried to accomplish the admittedly difficult task of providing simultaneously an introduction to the subject of mannerism, an updated account of the conceptual controversy it has stirred, and a discussion of one of its literary manifestations that may contribute to and advance the debate. As will become evident in the following comments on the structure and parts of this book, I have also imposed several restrictions on, and employed several foci within, the materials I discuss in order to achieve this multiple purpose in the face of a theme whose size and scope would otherwise dictate either a sweeping flight high above its landscape or a tedious probing of one small area of its surface.

The overall division of the book into what the sixteenth century would have called *teorica* and *pratica* allots the first two chapters to the theory and the next two chapters to the literary evidence of mannerism, with the second chapter, on Benvenuto Cellini's *Vita,* serving both to document the mannerist aesthetic sensibility and, as a literary work in its own right, to provide a transition to the studies focused on lyric Petrarchism that follow. The Postlude is a pastoral detour that brushes lightly the related problem of the relationship between literary mannerism and literary baroque. Finally, the Selected Bibliography on the concept of mannerism completes the first chapter by listing conveniently the primary and secondary works mentioned therein or otherwise of interest.

Because of its length and detail, the first chapter on the controversy over mannerism in relation to Renaissance literature needs some explanation here. Although a number of valuable surveys of this controversy have been published, there is none in English or, as far as I am aware, in any other language, that combines such features as, for example, a comprehensive chronological survey that begins with the sixteenth century and continues to the present (1983), concise commentary upon or evaluation of certain crucial items, special attention to studies in English, and inclusion of relevant selected art theory and criticism from Vasari to the present. These and other features of this opening chapter will, it is hoped, enable it at least partially to fill a gap that still exists insofar as no individual and widely available survey of the controversy over mannerism has yet found the kind of acceptance still accorded by scholars to René Wellek's authoritative essay on the concept of the baroque (1946, 1963). In addition, for those dipping a toe into the troubled waters of mannerism for the first time, the chapter should provide a helpful crash course in what the fuss is about.

The painting by Vasari of *St. Luke Painting the Virgin* that prefaces the first chapter, where the artist depicts himself as the Evangelist in turn depicting the Virgin (posing like a real model, but on clouds floating above a box of brushes and a palette), is fairly bursting with mannerist aesthetic self-consciousness. As such, it signals the importance of Vasari's *Vite* (still not as well known as they should be to students of mannerism) and is a fitting visual prelude to the survey that follows. As a kind of compressed pictorial autobiography, Vasari's painting also anticipates the second chapter, on Cellini's *Vita*, in which the attitude toward art it manifests is also shown to permeate the literary autobiography and sculptural works of his boisterous Florentine contemporary. The other illustrations I include reinforce the argument of the succeeding essays on Petrarchism, which are essentially thematic studies focused on the lyric topoi of visage and veil, hand and glove (*bel viso* and *bel velo, bella mano* and *bel guanto*). My focus on Italian and English Renaissance texts in these essays, while not ignoring other European sources, inevitably reflects the particular comparative interest that has long dominated my research and teaching.

All translations are my own and for my purposes as literal as I could make them. To avoid endnotes of a jungle density and a monster general bibliography, I have committed the lesser sin of inconsistency. I cite in abridged form all primary and secondary sources in the notes to chapter 1 that are listed with full publication information in the Selected Bibliography. However, any sources cited or referred to in the notes to chapter 1 and subsequent chapters that do not appear in the bibliography I give in full as they occur. An asterisk next to an item in the bibliography indicates those few instances where I was not able to peruse the source myself but have reason to believe it is significant.

During its overly long gestation, this book has incurred more debts than Panurge. The many scholars and critics who have preceded or labored alongside me in the vineyards of mannerism will find their efforts duly mentioned below, and if I do not acknowledge here my indebtedness to specific works it is only because there are too many, and I would be unable at this stage to sort out those that have been more or less influential on my research during the last decade. I can affirm, however, that my work is in some important ways a product of the graduate division of Columbia's Department of English and Comparative Literature, and especially its Renaissance "wing." In that eclectic atmosphere, where English and American as well as comparative literature and interdisciplinary studies proceed apace, one never lacks an audience of interested students and colleagues. To the students who over the years have made my seminar and lecture course in comparative Renaissance the joy of my professional life I am especially grateful, as they well know. I also appreciate and happily acknowledge here the intellectual stimulation and warm friendship that I have been fortunate to enjoy over those same years, thanks to the following colleagues in the Renaissance: Maurice J. Valency, Joseph A. Mazzeo, Edward W. Tayler, Anne L. Prescott, and Richard A. Katz. If an ideal editor may be defined as one who stalks and nurtures a manuscript with genuine interest and care, then I know of none who deserves the title better than Edward Tripp, who never doubted and thereby contributed mightily to the completion of my project.

In the crucial final stages of its preparation, the book was also the fortunate beneficiary of some timely practical help from Joseph Gibaldi, a wonderfully acute reading by William J. Kennedy, and the superbly diligent editing of Barbara Folsom.

In a more personal vein, I have dedicated my work to the memory of two loving parents, though such a tribute could not begin to commemorate properly the immensity of their affection and concern. Because of her passionate desire that it be finished and the unstinting practical help she provided to that end, my wife Julia is the only begetter of this book. The contribution of our progeny, Renato and Gabriella, evokes a typically mannerist paradox: I remember how often they distracted me from my work, yet also how often those intrusions of reality had the salutary effect of jarring a mind absorbed too deeply in the past, recalling it to an equally nourishing and rewarding present.

Acknowledgments

Preliminary versions of chapters 1 and 3 have previously appeared in *The Meaning of Mannerism,* edited by Franklin W. Robinson and Stephen G. Nichols, Jr., published by the University Press of New England, © 1972 University Press of New England (Hanover, New Hampshire), pp. 7–24, and in *Comparative Literature Studies* 9 (1972): 31–43, edited by A. O. Aldridge, published by the University of Illinois Press, Urbana, © 1972 by The Board of Trustees of the University of Illinois. I am grateful to the editors and publishers of these volumes for permission to recycle some portions of those versions.

I also wish to thank Viking–Penguin Inc. for permission to quote from John Ashbery's poem, "Self-Portrait in a Convex Mirror," in *Self-Portrait in a Convex Mirror: Poems by John Ashbery.* Copyright © 1972, 1973, 1974, and 1975, by John Ashbery.

Mannerism and Renaissance Poetry

Introduction
Mannerism as Term, Concept, and Controversy

*annerism* is a term now widely used with reference to a stylistic current in the arts within the broad cultural stream known as the Renaissance. It also refers to a controversial concept elaborated by art and literary historians and critics to describe the phenomenon and explain its causes. In addition to several different general theories to account for the cherished particulars, there exist at present several conflicting lists of particular works alleged to have inspired or to prove the theories. There is continuing doubt that a concept nourished within the confines of the history and theory of Italian Renaissance art can survive in the adjacent territories of literature and music, especially when its scope is argued to be European rather than merely Italian. As to temporal limits, some scholars place mannerism, whatever it is, squarely and only within the sixteenth century; others see it as an attitude or style in a cyclical scheme of recurring taste in verbal or visual art. A vocal few even question whether we need the term at all.

As E. H. Gombrich suggests, the best one can do is to juxtapose theory and particular, to check each out against the other in a continuing process of verification. At some point, however, the historian or critic has to pause and report his findings, to decide upon the best "set" of facts and explanations available or to come up with a new and more satisfactory combination. Thus, in these introductory pages I hope to prepare the reader to draw his or her own conclusions from the more particularized chapters that follow by reporting my own findings and offering some theories that have both shaped and been shaped by my analysis of literary particulars. In doing so I have also tried to ask myself the same questions that a curious reader might

Giorgio Vasari, *St. Luke Painting the Virgin*. Florence, SS. Annunziata, Capella di San Luca.

ask about *mannerism:* what does the word mean, how did it become the sign of a controversial concept, and finally, is it worth using?

Before trying to answer those questions, it might be helpful to remind the reader who may begin with serious doubts about the ultimate worth of all terminological and conceptual wrangles that we can all take heart from an earlier and similar controversy that arose over the term and concept of the baroque. In fact, much as Gombrich describes it, study of particular works of art, music, and literature went hand in hand with general theories, generating inevitable debate and confusion. And while the term continued to be used at an increasing rate, dissatisfaction with its vague meaning grew in intensity. Now we have reached a point in time when hardly anyone bothers to argue the meaning of *baroque* anymore, whereas only a short time ago every book that dealt with any aspect of the baroque opened with an obligatory review of the status of the question followed by counterarguments and definitions. Some would say that this cessation of debate is proof that, especially in literary history and criticism where skepticism about the baroque has been particularly stubborn, inertia sets in and allows sloppy terminology to darken further our already clouded understanding. While I certain agree that the term is here to stay, I am not convinced the reason is solely inertia, or a state of exhaustion about trying to define it more precisely, or spent anger at its abuse, especially in popular parlance (the term *baroque* currently being used as a synonym for *grotesque* or *excessive* in size, ornament, or complexity). I would argue, more positively, that we have reached a general consensus, not so much out of frustration and despair as from an enlightened conviction that all such debates end in a truce of convenience, an acceptance of limited utility. Indeed, one could argue further that the only real remaining *problem* with the baroque is its intricate and still somewhat perplexing relationship to mannerism, and therefore that once the question of mannerism progresses (or retreats, as the skeptics would have it) to a similar state of relative clarity and acceptance, one can see the problem of the baroque referred to increasingly as the "so-called" problem, and ultimately as the "once problematical" baroque.

This semantic scenario is actually drawn from the history of the term and concept of *Renaissance*. As with *Renaissance,* it may be that terms like *mannerism* and *baroque* prove their utility by their very survival, maintaining their tattered existence not because of our inertia but because they make do for us in some satisfying way. Long after we have ceased to use them for good or bad reasons, empirical or modish, they surprise and defeat our skepticism by proving at last that they *do* have referential value of sorts, blurred though it may be. For rigorists, this is not an acceptable state of affairs. But what can we do if the terms will not go away? If they have proved to have enough usefulness to claim survival rights? My answer would be that we let them be, while simultaneously going forward with the work of tidying up their field of meaning, imposing greater clarity and precision on their messy semantic selves. Surely the alternative, to let them go their fuzzy way, is overly indulgent. All this is by way of explaining why, for a study of Renaissance or baroque literature, a preliminary discourse on term and concept is no longer obligatory, whereas in the case of mannerism the following discussion is still essential.

Vasari's Language and Thought in the Lives

In contrast to a term like *Renaissance,* which in and of itself connotes the large idea of rebirth or renewal, words like *mannerism* and *baroque* begin their journey to concept status with pitifully little connotative luggage. True, the term *baroque* probably owes its origin to a Portuguese word for pearl; but it meant an imperfect pearl, a distorted and flawed specimen of its ideal kind, otherwise priceless.[2] Hence it seemed an appropriate designation to those classicists who despised the style of buildings, paintings, and poems of the seventeenth century. *Mannerism* began *its* journey to concepthood even more ignominiously, since it is a stretching out of the word *maniera*—or manner—an ordinary household word then as now, used in a hundred different ways just as our modern English *manner* still is. And, like our *manner* (and the plural *manners),* it meant, and still means, the particular way in which something is said or done, a mode of speaking or acting. As such it occurred, in late Medieval and Renaissance literature of manners (as *manière* and *maniera),* to designate an absolute quality of refined behavior; then, thanks to a peculiar set of circumstances obtaining in the social and verbal complex of sixteenth-century Italy, as we shall see, it began a parallel existence as an aesthetic denominator in the visual arts. By the time it reached us in our own time, it had been largely replaced in art criticism by *style* and had accumulated negative meanings, like battle scars, testifying to the impact on it of the revolutions of taste that followed upon its sixteenth-century origins.[3]

An early example of the juxtaposition of the two terms occurs in the quintessential Renaissance book on manners:

Count Ludovico: Eccovi che nella pittura sono eccellentissimi Leonardo Vincio, il Mantegna, Rafaello, Michel Angelo, Giorgio da Castel Franco: nientedimeno, tutti son tra sé nel far dissimili, di modo che ad alcun di loro non par che manchi cosa alcuna in quella *maniera,* perché si conosce ciascun nel suo *stilo* esser perfettissimo. (Castiglione, *Il Cortegiano,* 1528, Book I; italics mine)[4]

[Count Ludovico: Note how in painting Leonardo da Vinci, Mantegna, Raphael, Michelangelo, and Giorgione are most excellent; nonetheless they differ from each other in their works, so that none of them appears to lack anything in that *manner,* yet each is known to be most perfect in his own *style.*]

The manner in which a literary work is composed is obviously its *style.* Derived from the Latin *stilus,* the Roman writing instrument, the Italian word *stile* (or Castiglione's variant *stilo)* was in use long before the sixteenth century—as early as Dante in fact—to designate the mode of composition of literary works. *Maniera* or *manière* has its roots in the Latin *manus* and *manualis,* meaning "the hand," or "of the hand," including the artist's hand or touch and thereby "finishing touch." And while its deployment as an art critical as opposed to a behavioral term before the sixteenth century is rare in contrast to that of *stile,* given the fact that writings by and about artists were far less numerous than literary works themselves, it is clear that although earlier a man of letters like Castiglione might use both, by the time of Vasari and for at least a century thereafter artists writing on art preferred *maniera* to *stile* as the word to designate *style* and associated ideas in the visual arts. And therein lies an important sociological tale; for, as we know, the sixteenth century marked the high point in a long struggle of painters and sculptors to achieve the status of *artists* rather than guild-bound craftsmen, which meant, among other things, that theirs was an activity involving the *head* as well as the *hand,* the liberal as well as the mechanical arts, learning as well as workshop techniques.[5]

Interestingly enough, the new status was achieved but the old word was retained as the visual counterpart of verbal *stile,* but also with an obvious attempt by Vasari and other sixteenth-century theorists to upgrade it, to make *maniera* signify, as subtly and richly as *stile* did, the essential features of high art. Similarly, Vasari's usual word for the eminent painters, sculptors, and architects he extolls is not the literary alternative, *artista,* but *artefice* (artificer). But unlike *maniera, artefice* (from the Latin *artifex)* did not require upgrading because it could connote more than a mere craftsman *(artigiano)* through its use in theological description of the world as the work of God the Creator *(Deus artifex),* thereby also being imbued with the highest status.[6]

In the sixteenth century, the meanings of *maniera* and the differences between it and *stile* could be quite complex. One complication, already referred to, was the verbal link with the *maniera* of social deportment. Another was that in the visual arts the danger of having too much *maniera* or a bad manner (of being *manierato,* or mannered, as later critics would say), was always latent in the pursuit of the artistic ideal or goal of having enough *maniera*. Thus, for Vasari and other critics of his time, the visual artist had to have *maniera* or *bella maniera,* in the sense of an achieved individual and beautiful style, but not *maniera* in the sense of excessive stylization: he had to steer a perilous course between too little and too much art in search of a stylistic mean.

In the social world, one was expected to have *manière;* but in the literary world, it was expected that a writer would have *good* style (not absolute "style"). If he lacked good style (defined as skill, sophistication, and above all freshly creative or inventive treatment of conventional themes and normative language), he was accused of merely manipulating words or aping another's manner. Hence the poet Francesco Berni's accusation, flung at the Petrarchists of his day, that whereas a Michelangelo utters "things," they utter "words"; and Sir Philip Sidney's characterization of a mere imitator of Petrarch's "long deceased woes" as a "pick-purse of another's wit."[7] Yet both Berni and Sidney knew that creative imitation of nature and other authors—to mirror the natural but to do so with polished verbal art, to use but not abuse Petrarch—was very difficult indeed. Their very anti-Petrarchism was itself a literary convention, the essence of which was to protest vigorously against excessive artifice in one of the most self-conscious of artful lyric modes.

As Vasari and other critics make clear, the difference between *stile* and *maniera,* and the preference for the latter term, was more than a matter of borrowing its connotations of social grace, or doing obeisance to the tradition that the artist uses his hands, or accommodating different nuances in conceptions of style. *Maniera,* unlike *stile,* poses a problem unique to the visual arts, that of both reproducing nature and imitating other artists in the creation of stylish images of reality. In literature, imitation of nature was considered more a matter of language than of total formal expression. And because so many great literary artists had flourished already, imitation of their works or style guaranteed access to nature *and* good style.[8]

According to one powerful tradition stemming from classical sources, an essential standard for the visual artist was considered to be *natura* and the *naturale,* with much less emphasis upon the recognizable imitation of other artists. Unlike literary critics, who stressed the imitation of great predecessors such as Vergil and Petrarch not easily surpassed, Vasari writes from a curiously combined cyclic and evolutionary view of modern cultural history that assumes the rebirth and growth of art to perfection, reached in his own time with Michelangelo and destined perhaps to decline again in the future.[9] But Michelangelo and other modern artists are frequently praised for having surpassed the ancients. For after the achievement of the classical era, from which only a few statues and reliefs, some buildings, and virtually no painting survive, there was a dark Gothic age, followed by a rebirth and greater perfection of the *maniera antica*. The modern world is thus experiencing not just a cyclical repetition of the ancient growth pattern from crude to *bella e buona maniera* but also an evolution within the modern period to a perfection never yet seen.

Hence, while poets hope to emulate the ancients and are praised as second Vergils or Ciceros reborn, recent painters or sculptors or architects are extolled as the very best ever in their *maniere*. Since many of these prodigious talents are painters, one can assume that Vasari was in part influenced by the dearth of surviving classical painting to claim superiority for contemporary artists as a group. In doing so, in any event, he gave them a stirring incentive and a distinct advantage over writers, whose achievements had to brave the adulatory attitude of Petrarch and his humanist followers toward antiquity and its unsurpassable literary accomplishments. For similar reasons, innovation (new techniques, formal inventiveness) is lauded and encouraged by Vasari, whereas in the literary world, as we know, departures from classical models or the creation of new or mixed literary types (romance-epic, tragicomedy), aroused noisy critical controversy. In this sense, *maniera* suggests greater leeway for individual artistic expression than does *stile*. Thus a modern translator of *maniera* might use *manner* instead of *style* whenever such individual creation or its influence is at stake, or, as noted below, whenever excessive stylization is meant.[10]

When the visual artist is extolled by Vasari for imitating and surpassing a predecessor, it is theoretically and paradoxically understood that the achievement of art, of having attained greater *maniera,* involves even greater fidelity to nature than the former accomplished. This fidelity to nature, unfortunately, can be interpreted in several contradictory ways, though all have classical sanction. First, it could mean a triumph of illusionistic realism, at the furthest remove from literary mimesis or imitation. This kind of realism occurs as a staple of praise in anecdotal legends of ancient artists reported by Pliny and other classical sources that the Renaissance tended to take far too seriously.[11] According to these legends, ancient artists like Zeuxis were valued because their works were deceptively real:

they created images that seemed to live and breathe. They not only num-
bered every streak of Doctor Johnson's tulip, they deceived the eye into
accepting the presence of a real flower!

But fidelity to nature might also mean a learned naturalism, the rational
representation of optical experience through the use of geometry and math-
ematics; devices of perspective, foreshortening, and chiaroscuro; knowledge
of anatomy; and other means to depict human figures and objects in their
material and spiritual fullness, and to locate them in space convincingly and
harmoniously, pleasing both the eye and the mind.[12] (As we shall see,
however, Vasari has some doubts about excessive reliance on "rules" rather
than on an instinctive artistic sense; he prefers the artist to trust at times
"the eye.") Also involved here, and equally sanctioned by classical prece-
dent, is the goal of improving upon or surpassing imperfect *natura* by
means of idealization: working with canons or systems of proportion, gener-
alizing human features, or selecting from various partly perfect objects or
figures individual flawless elements to make a composite type, an un-
blemished whole (as in the familiar Zeuxis legend). In doing so, the artist
may be improving upon an only apparently imperfect nature by revealing
its underlying ideal forms or laws. In addition, fidelity to nature may mean
effective representation of human psychological and emotional states
through facial expression, attitudes, stances, and gestures, though styliza-
tion may also modify starkly realistic representation in the interest of
achieving graceful beauty.

Finally, one also can be faithful to nature by rendering it in the light of
the individual artist's intuitive vision—according, that is, to an inner idea.
This idea (one thinks of Sidney's "*Idea* or fore-conceit") is said to be derived
from previous study of nature and art.[13] Conveying this "inner design" may
well require and justify deviation from strict mimetic, stylistic, or struc-
tural and compositional norms. But the greater beauty or style of an indi-
vidual kind thus obtained may better express the unique talent of the artist,
and ultimately the nature of art itself, than could stringent adherence to
rules or norms.[14]

These inconsistent criteria applied by Vasari are due to the mixed origins
and purposes of his enterprise. From his predecessors who had written about
ancient and modern art and artists (including Vitruvius, Pliny, Lucian,
Philostratus, Cennini, Ghiberti, Alberti, Leonardo), Vasari inherited a
jumble of theory and practice, lofty aesthetic ideas along with detailed
descriptions of materials and techniques, lists and histories of actual works
along with legendary biographies and autobiographical commentaries of
uncertain veracity.[15] These he leavened with critical terms borrowed from
the abundant and modish contemporary theory produced by critics of litera-

ture and rhetoric.[16] Unfortunately, much of that theory itself was vague or contradictory, being an amalgam of precepts—not always correctly understood—from Aristotle, Plato, Horace, and Cicero, among others. And an individual idea, like Aristotle's *mimēsis*, best grasped in relation to the formal structure of performed or narrated plot but often interpreted as imitation of human action in simplistic ways, did not flourish in the visual realm, where it tended to blend with and reinforce the venerable notion of imitating nature in an illusionistically accurate way.[17]

The bulky collections of vitae of the illustrious, a favorite literary production of Renaissance humanists, were also transferred awkwardly into the realm of artistic biography, especially since Vasari seemed bent on praising too many of his fellow *artefici del disegno* too much. In his zeal to promote the arts and their practitioners, Vasari hardly left anyone out. And in lieu of offering the kind of moral emphasis usually found in collections *de viris illustribus,* he was compelled to extol his numerous subjects, monotonously, not for their exemplary lives but for the same handful of artistic merits endlessly repeated in a limited vocabulary of praise, as we shall see.

An important feature of the *Lives* is that, in view of the influence on Vasari of ancient and contemporary literary and rhetorical theory, with its focus on the need for literature to be useful and moving as well as pleasing, he does *not* present a moral, social, or emotional justification for artistic activity. Granted that many of the works he mentions have obvious religious subjects, along with ecclesiastical settings or purposes, and are therefore assumed to serve and stir piety. Granted, too, that the full impact of the Counter-Reformation's program for sacred art had not yet been felt when Vasari began his work, hence he could say over and over again that a painting or a statue of a sacred subject was "bellissimo," as though that were its raison d'être. Perhaps, as Erwin Panofsky argued in his *Idea,* there is a continuation in Vasari of the Early Renaissance sense of the de facto autonomy of the aesthetic experience, brought about by Alberti and others who interpreted artistic beauty, in a phenomenal rather than a metaphysical fashion, as a harmony of proportional parts rather than a reflection of eternal Beauty and Truth, thereby separating the beautiful and the good (pp. 54–55). In any case, a working assumption of autonomy does free Vasari to dwell on the decorative values of a courtly, aristocratic art, on purely technical and aesthetic matters, and to recite a litany of praise and promote patronage for his famous fellow *artefici,* honored in life and remembered by posterity (thanks partly to Vasari's biographies), simply for their great artistic achievements.

If one does not find philosophical speculation, one does find moralizing in Vasari's proems to the individual lives, where he sometimes utters banal moral truths or proposes general artistic principles (without connecting them) that relate in some obvious way to the life and fortunes of his subject and serve to introduce it in an impressively serious manner. In fact, these proems are an invaluable source for any analysis of Vasari's thinking about the nature and goal of artistic creation, whether or not they have philosophical underpinnings. Despite their occasional moral tone, too, the proems tend to confirm the sense one has that Vasari was rather exclusively preoccupied with the world of art production as a self-enclosed universe. Like his contemporary Benvenuto Cellini, he avoids dealing with the turbulent politics and religious controversy of his time simply by skirting them. By his most recent translator into English this has been called typical of Vasari's penchant for playing it safe; but whatever his motives and however ignoble they might have been, Vasari's approach did allow for a concentration on the works and their creators, laboriously researched and studied, that resulted in valuable information and aesthetic speculation.[18] It may well be, too, that his preoccupation with art production as its own self-contained world is an index to the mentality of other artists and therefore a possible key to the underlying artistic motives of the creations of his time, so many of which have been involved in the discussion of mannerism.

With these general characteristics of the *Lives* in mind, we can now turn to scan Vasari's text, where the term *maniera* effectively begins its art critical history. There, too, we shall find the traces of a budding concept, mannerism *(maniera*-ism, or *manierismo), seeded by the connotations of the term and asserting itself, by implication, in contrast to a stated, official aesthetic line from which it is manifestly divergent or out of which it has grown as a set of more advanced and therefore superior insights.

Soundings of Vasari's Text

The word *maniera* occurs on virtually every page of Vasari's lengthy text. Of its various meanings, two do not present difficulties: *maniera* as the style of an era in Vasari's historical scheme, and *maniera* as the manner of an individual and widely influential artist:

> Così se vede che la maniera greca, prima col principio di Cimabue, poi con l'aiuto di Giotto, si spense in tutto e ne nacque una nuova la quale io volentieri chiamo maniera di Giotto, perché fu trovata da lui e da' suoi discepoli, e poi universalmente da tutti venerata et imitata. (1:667)

[Thus one sees that the Greek (i.e., Byzantine) style, first with the initiative of Cimabue and then with the help of Giotto, was completely extinguished, and there was born a new style that I like to call the manner of Giotto since it was discovered by him and his disciples and then universally venerated and imitated by all.]

But Vasari also uses the word *maniera* to mean an excess of art that may upset the balance with nature, an artfulness that, however necessary, can spill over into the stylized or mannered. For example, in discussing the sculptor's customary treatment of hair, he uses the phrase "più di maniera che di immitazione naturale" (Proemio, 1:154: "more manner than imitation of nature"). A few paragraphs later, referring to the employment by sculptors of a canon of proportions for the human figure, he cautions, "Ma non si debbe usare altra miglior misura che il giudicio dello occhio" (p. 155: "But one ought not to use a better measure than the judgment of the eye"), for "measure" may not suffice to give the figure graceful beauty.[19] Here another delicate balance or mean is being proposed between rational norms or rules and the artist's sophisticated instinct, as though Vasari were concerned that the artist's creativity not be cramped yet is anxious to preserve respect for artistic activity by not denying its basis in scientific and philosophical principles. As in the case of *maniera* and *natura,* a judicious and typically Renaissance harmonization of conflicting or opposing elements is officially espoused, though one suspects that Vasari, if he were compelled to choose, would tip the scales or locate a mean closer to *maniera* and the *giudicio dello occhio* than to *natura*.

Immitazione, as Vasari uses the term, has at least four different meanings. Throughout the *Lives,* whenever he refers to a painting or sculpture that is a genuine likeness of the subject, he says it is made *di naturale*. Elsewhere, he departs from this strict realism and invokes the literary ideal of mimesis— that is, realism modified by generalization and idealization in order to convey a meaningful, universal type or theme in the most aesthetically satisfying fashion. There is a third kind of imitation, according to a previous idea in the artist's mind of the experienced forms of nature. Clearly these notions of imitation relate to the meanings of *natura* listed earlier: the artist either imitates as exactly as possible the physical world, or modifies and generalizes that world according to rules and norms abstracted from it or believed to underlie it, or, finally, imitates an "idea" of that world existing in his own mind.[20]

Speaking of Masaccio, Vasari says, "invero le cose fatte inanzi a lui si

possono chiamar dipinte, e le sue vive, veraci e naturali, allato a quelle state
fatte dagli altri" (1: 792: "in truth the works made before him can be called
painted, and his, alive, truthful and natural, compared to those done by
others"). Obviously this first kind of imitation, with its classical creden-
tials, is praiseworthy and will be commended again and again as a merit in
other and later artists; but Vasari knows that it is not a skill or an ac-
complishment that can evolve significantly. Similarly, rules and norms can
be learned and mastered but cannot in and of themselves be the final goal of
art or provide standards for distinguishing between skilled artists. And so
when he contrasts Masaccio's era to his own and talks about the third
modern wave of artistic activity—namely, that of his own sixteenth
century—Vasari invokes the second and third meanings of *imitation* we
have noted, preferring the latter:

> Nella seconda poi si veggono manifesto esser le cose migliorate assai e
> nell'invenzioni e nel condurle con più disegno e con miglior maniera
> e con maggior diligenza, e così tolto via quella ruggine della vecchiaia e
> quella goffezza e sproporzione che la grossezza di quel tempo le aveva
> recato adosso. Ma chi ardirà dire, in quel tempo essersi trovato uno in
> ogni cosa perfetto? . . . Questa lode certo è tócca alla terza età; nella
> quale mi par potere dir sicuramente che l'arte abbia fatto quello che ad
> una imitatrice della natura è lecito poter fare, e che ella sia salita tanto
> alto, che più presto si abbia a temere del calare a basso, che sperare
> oggimai più augumento. (1:663)

> [In the second era, then, matters manifestly improved a great deal, in
> inventive ideas, in carrying them out with more sense of design and
> better style and greater diligence; and thus was removed the rust of the
> old style and that clumsiness and disproportion with which the gross-
> ness of that time had burdened them (i.e., artists). But who would
> dare to say that there could be found in that time even one (artist)
> perfect in everything? . . . Such praise certainly belongs to the third
> era, in which it is possible to say that art has accomplished all that is
> possible for imitation of nature to accomplish, and that she has
> climbed so high that now one has more fear that she will tumble down
> than hope that henceforth she can rise any higher.]

And in the proem to the third part of the *Lives*:

> Veramente grande augumento fecero alle arti della architettura, pit-
> tura e scultura quelli eccellenti Maestri che noi abbiamo descritti sin
> qui, nella Seconda Parte di queste Vite; aggiugnendo alle cose de'

primi regola, ordine, misura, disegno e maniera se non in tutto perfet-
tamente, tanto almanco vicino al vero, che i terzi, di chi noi
ragioneremo da qui avanti, potereno mediante quel lume sollevarsi e
condursi alla somma perfezione, dove abbiamo le cose moderne di
maggior pregio e più celebrate. (2:585)[21]

[Truly those excellent Masters we have described up to this point in
the Second Part of these *Lives* made great strides in the arts of architec-
ture, painting, and sculpture; for they added to the achievements of
the first era the qualities of rule, order, measure, design, and manner.
And if they did not reach perfection, they came close enough so that
the artists of the third era, of whom I speak from now on, could use
their achievement to raise themselves up to the highest perfection,
evident in the most valued and celebrated modern works.]

The five added elements cited by Vasari as accounting for the success of the
third era—*regola, ordine, misura, disegno, maniera*—are also defined by him
in the same place. *Regola,* or rule, and *ordine,* or order, have to do with
correct architectural plans and styles; *misura,* or measure, refers to accurate
proportions in all three arts; *disegno* and *maniera* are more complex:

Il disegno fu lo imitare il più bello della natura in tutte le figure così
scolpite come dipinte, la qual parte viene dallo aver la mano e l'in-
gegno che raporti tutto quello che vede l'occhio in sul piano, o disegni
o in su fogli o tavola o altro piano, giustissimo et a punto; e così di
rilievo nella scultura; la maniera venne poi la più bella, dall'avere
messo in uso il frequente ritrarre le cose più belle; e da quel più bello,
o mani o teste o corpi o gambe aggiugnerle insieme a fare una figura di
tutte quelle bellezze che più si poteva; e metterla in uso in ogni opera
per tutte le figure, che per questo si dice esser bella maniera. (2:586)

[Design (i.e., drawing or draughtsmanship) is the imitation of the
most beautiful in nature, in all sculpted as well as painted figures; this
results from the hand and the mind being able to represent all that the
eye sees, accurately and precisely, on plans, in designs, or on paper or
panel, or other planes. And also with relief in sculpture. Manner is,
then, the attainment of the highest beauty through having frequently
practiced copying the most beautiful things in nature, and from the
most beautiful to join together hands, heads, torsos, legs to make a
model of as many of those beauties as possible, and then to use it in
every work for all figures. For this is what gives his work beautiful
manner (i.e., style).]

Earlier, Vasari had defined *design* more philosophically[22] in relation to the third type of *imitation* we have noted:

Perchè il disegno, padre delle tre arti nostre, architettura, scultura e pittura, procedendo dall'intelletto, cava di molte cose un giudizio universale, simile a una forma or vero idea di tutte le cose della natura, la quale è singolarissima nelle sue misure, di qui è che non solo nei corpi umani e degl'animali, ma nelle piante ancora, e nelle fabriche e sculture e pitture cognosce la proporzione che ha il tutto con le parti e che hanno le parti fra loro e col tutto insieme. E perchè da questa cognizione nasce un certo concetto e giudizio che se forma nella mente quella tal cosa, che poi espressa con le mani se chiama disegno, si puó conchiudere che esso disegno altro non sia che una apparente espressione e dichiarazione del concetto che si ha nell'animo, ed di quello che altri si è nella mente imaginato e fabricato nell'idea. (1:178)[23]

[Because design, father of our three arts—architecture, sculpture, and painting—proceeding from the intellect, draws from many things a universal judgment, similar to a form or true idea of everything in nature, which is most singular in its measurements, there comes about a recognition of the proportion that obtains between the whole and its parts and between the parts among themselves and the whole, not only in human and animal bodies but in plants, buildings, statues, and paintings. And since from this recognition there is born a certain concept and judgment of things that when later expressed by the hands is called design, we can conclude that this design is no other than an outward expression and declaration of the concept in the intellect, and of that which others have imagined in the mind and fabricated in the idea.]

Without explicitly identifying this "inner design" or idea as its source, Vasari points to several instinctive deviations from the rational norm as ingredients of the perfection of the third era: "una licenzia . . . senza fare confusione o guastare l'ordine" (a license . . . without confusion or spoiling order, p. 586); "una grazia che eccedesse la misura" (a grace that exceeds measure, p. 587);[24] "uno spirito di prontezza" (a spirited boldness, p. 587). The implication is there: the artists of the third *maniera moderna,* thoroughly in possession of the highest skills and adhering to the *idea* of nature within them, have gone beyond the rational, learned naturalism of the second era (largely the fifteenth century) to attain greater beauty and artistic perfection of style, or *bella maniera,* defined as the modification of nature by skillful abstraction and inner idea.

This is confirmed also by Vasari's ambivalent attitude toward the fourth
type of imitation, that of one's classical predecessors and contemporaries.[25]
In his introduction to the life of Mino da Fiesole, he takes up several threads
we have analyzed thus far and can be seen struggling to keep *natura* and
maniera in precarious balance:

> . . . perché la imitazione della natura è ferma nella maniera di quello
> artefice che ha fatto lunga pratica diventare maniera. Conciò sia che
> l'imitazione è una ferma arte di fare apunto quel che tu fai, come sta il
> più bello delle cose della natura, pigliandola schietta senza la maniera
> del tuo maestro o d'altri; i quali ancora eglino ridussono in maniera le
> cose che tolsono da la natura. E se ben pare che le cose degl'artefici
> eccellenti siano cose naturali o verisimili, non è che mai si possa usar
> tanta diligenza che si facci tanto simile che elle siano com'essa natura;
> nè ancora, scegliendo le migliori, si possa fare composizion di corpo
> tanto perfetto che l'arte la trapassi; e se questo è, ne segue che le cose
> tolte da lei, fa le pitture e le sculture perfette, e chi studia strettamente
> le maniere degli artefici solamente e non i corpi o le cose naturali, è
> necessario che facci l'opere sue e men buone della natura e di quelle di
> colui da cui si toglie la maniera; laonde s'è visto molti de' nostri artefici
> non avere voluto studiare altro che l'opere de' loro maestri e lasciato da
> parte la natura; de' quali n'è avenuto che non le hanno apprese del
> tutto e non passato il maestro loro, ma hanno fatto ingiuria grandis-
> sima all'ingegno ch'egli hanno avuto, ché s'eglino avessino studiato la
> maniera e le cose naturali insieme, arebbon fatto maggior frutto
> nell'opere loro che e' non feciono. (2:309– 10)[26]

[. . . since imitation of nature is secure in the manner of that artist
who through long practice has achieved style. For imitation is the
secure art of doing precisely that which you aim to do, to understand
the most beautiful of the beautiful things of nature, grasping her
directly, not through the manner of your teacher or other artists, who
have themselves converted into style the things they took from nature.
And if it is true that the works of excellent artists seem natural or
verisimilar, it is not possible ever to use such diligence that one can
create a work that is so similar to as to seem nature itself; nor yet is it
possible for an artist, choosing from the best models, to compose a
body so perfect that art surpasses nature. And if this is true, it follows
that the things taken from nature by you make your paintings and
sculptures perfect, and that he who studies strictly only the manner of
other artists and not human figures or other natural things, necessarily
produces works that are less good than nature and than the works of

the artist from whom he has derived his manner. Whence it has been seen that many of our artists, not wishing to study other works than those of their masters, and having put aside nature, as it turns out have not learned everything possible from or surpassed their master but instead have done great injury to the genius they possessed, for if they had studied manner (i.e., art) and natural things together, they would have created more successful works than they have.]

At the end of the Proemio to the third part, Vasari trumpets the achievements of his hero, the divine Michelangelo, in words that suggest not just a glorious climax to his historical scheme but also the final defeat of nature by art:

Costui supera e vince non solamente tutti costoro, ch'hanno quasi che vinto già la natura, ma quelli stessi famosissimi antichi, che sì lodatamente fuor d'ogni dubbio la superarono: et unico si trionfa di quegli, di questi ed di lei, non imaginandosi appena quella cosa alcuna sì strana e tanto difficile, ch'egli con la virtù del divinissimo ingegno suo, mediante l'industria, il disegno, l'arte, il giudizio e la grazia, di gran lunga non la trapassi. (2:591)[27]

[He surpasses and conquers not only all those who have all but conquered nature already, but those very most celebrated ancients who beyond doubt and to so much praise did so; and, uniquely, he has triumphed over both ancient and modern artists and over nature herself, who has hardly imagined anything so strange and difficult that he, with the power of his most divine genius, and through industry, design, artistry, judgment, and grace, has not by far surpassed.]

As though this were not sufficiently lavish, Vasari goes on to propose, in the opening sentences of his actual *vita* of Michelangelo, that the Supreme Artist, looking down at the world and distressed by the wretched condition of the arts, graciously decided to send a messiah among us, Buonarotti himself, to rescue art by demonstrating the perfection to which it could attain (4:12). As George Bull has noted in the preface to his Penguin translation of selected lives, Vasari here proposes that Michelangelo's extraordinary *virtù,* like that of Machiavelli's effective prince, can stave off for a time the inevitable decline that must set in when an art, or a political organism, has reached its maximum health (p. 15).

What does Vasari have to say about those other sixteenth-century artists who, like Michelangelo, have been prominent in modern discussions of mannerism? Let us focus briefly on his biographies of a few of them to determine whether his comments on their work contribute to the incipient concept or theory of mannerism we have been tracking in Vasari's text. Rosso Fiorentino (1494–1540) and Jacopo Pontormo (1494–1556) have been key figures in notions of mannerism that stress its rebellious, anticlassical stance or its troubled psychological content. Of Rosso, Vasari says little that suggests revolt. He is said to favor the extravagant, bizarre, and capricious, to be somewhat of an individualist, and eccentric. Of the famous *Deposition* at Volterra (1521), which has been an obligatory illustration and topic of discussion in so many studies of mannerism, Vasari remarks only that it was "bellissimo." Of another work he says that its "bravura" and the "abstract attitudes" of its figures were considered "extravagant" and took some time to be accepted because they were unprecedented. More important than these tame and trite comments, however, is Vasari's assertion that Rosso had fled the Sack of Rome (1527), during which he had been treated roughly by the invading armies. This information, along with the anecdote about his having kept a pet ape and the report that he ended his own life with poison, have fostered subsequent psychological interpretations of the artist and of the allegedly tense atmosphere in which he and his generation worked, as we shall see (3:237–54).

The much longer life of Pontormo (3:846–88) also offers us a portrait of an eccentric, moody and solitary, afraid of death, and obviously paranoid. Here, too, extravagance and capriciousness are emphasized, but even more so, what with Pontormo's restless experimenting in different *maniere* and his reactionary and deplorable abandonment (as in the decoration of the Certòsa near Florence) of the *bella maniera moderna* (i.e. *italiana*) under the influence of Dürer's prints, with their *maniera tedesca* (i.e., Gothic).[28] Vasari really struggles to defend Pontormo, not simply because he was conservative but, more important, because he saw his own era as the climax of a progressive movement toward perfection in the arts. Vasari did not and could not imagine or postulate a countermovement or style, an opposing or subversive current within the larger flow of art history, as already asserting itself at the moment of supreme achievement. Even less could he imagine that what he accepted as necessary deviations from the norm, rather than the norm itself, would spread elsewhere. Thus, he knows about and admires what he has heard of Rosso's decoration of the gallery at Fontainebleau, but does not, nor could we expect him to, grasp its historical role in the spread of mannerism beyond Italy.

Vasari is unhappy about Pontormo's strange anatomical disproportions, his obscurity, his emotionalism, his abandonment of due measure, accurate perspective, and "order" (p. 886). But he attributes these deviations and distortions to the artist's restless and introverted temperament, easily seduced by novelty, too pensive and introspective for his own sake, and hence prone to "sforzare la natura" (to force nature, p. 887). Thus Vasari might be puzzled, and even disturbed at times, by his work, but he did not see the shocking revolt that some modern observers find in Pontormo's *Joseph in Egypt* (1519) or the Santa Felicità *Deposition* (1525). Indeed, of the former he says that many contemporary artists thought it the best thing Pontormo had ever done (p. 861); of the *Deposition,* widely regarded today as Pontormo's masterpiece, and as a work invoked with awe in virtually every modern study of mannerism, Vasari remarks that it is proof that "quel cervello andava sempre investigando nuovi concetti e stravaganti modi di fare, non si contentando e non si fermando in alcuna" (p. 871: "that brain of his was always poking into new conceits and extravagant ways of doing things, never content with and never pausing for very long in any of them"). In sum, Pontormo's aberrations and deviations were deplorable but understandable, to be judged finally not only as a matter of temperament but also as an inevitable and necessary risk that had to be taken in the pursuit of extraordinary achievement in art. Even Michelangelo's restorative influence could not keep Pontormo on track for long; Vasari's own ideas about following other masters' *maniere* make him reluctant to recommend safe imitation, even of Michelangelo, over daring innovation (p. 877).

Francesco Parmigianino (1503−40) has been claimed both by advocates of an anxiety-ridden mannerism and by proponents of a mannerism of extraordinary aesthetic refinement, as we shall discover. For Vasari, of course, these distinctions did not exist. In his life of Parmigianino (3:299−316), he tells us that the painter was, like Rosso, caught in the Sack of Rome, though not with the same dire results. Like Rosso and Pontormo, he is said to have been quite eccentric; in his case, he was addicted to alchemy. Yet his work is lauded for its style, especially its beauty, sweetness, and loveliness, which was widely imitated by other artists, and not for any bizarre features. Most surprising is that Vasari mentions and praises briefly but expresses no particular shock at either the elongation or the erotic aura of the famous *Madonna of the Long Neck* (1535), though he notes the painter's dissatisfaction with it as the reason for its unfinished state (p. 311).

To sum up what we have learned from this analysis of Vasari's text, even granted that because his working terminology and principles are an eclectic mix, drawing rather messily upon literary, rhetorical, and philosophical sources as well as the practical experience of a working artist, Vasari is both inconsistent and contradictory in his ideas.[29] Nevertheless, it would be a mistake to discard him as a guide to either the *teorica* or the *pratica* of both visual and literary mannerism. His theory may be no more than a rationalization of what his contemporaries were actually doing, in order to put their activity in the tradition and at the center of Renaissance high culture. For the same reasons, he may give a less than reliable account of some actual works in order to preserve the theory in both its historical and evaluative application—hence his refusal to acknowledge fully the bizarre, the reactionary, the anticlassical features of some of them. However, a reader who keeps both these limitations in mind and allows for them, who realizes that Vasari does not know about "mannerism" but knows what is going on around him, can find in his *Lives* some valuable evidence for the modulation of High Renaissance standards and practice into another and different stylistic mode of expression.

First, Vasari cannot conceal the fact that his idealized account of a long historical struggle to imitate and conquer *nature,* while traditional, literary, and respectable, does not explain what he and his contemporaries were really doing—namely trying to excel in *art,* and to attain an ever *più bella maniera*. Second, while eschewing moral issues, whether out of a prudent desire to avoid political and religious matters or an exclusive preoccupation with matters of art, Vasari inevitably suggests the autonomy of the world of art and its creations. (The anecdote he tells about the dying Verrocchio's insistence on having a crucifix made by Donatello brought to him neatly encapsulates this view of art as literally a matter of life and death!)[30] Third, Vasari insists that his own era had witnessed a revival of the achievements of antiquity; but at the same time, he warns against mere *imitazione* of the *maniere* of past or contemporary masters, in fact against the danger of being *mannered*. The antidote he proposes is the priority of the artist's own interior *idea,* the fruit of constant observation of the beauties of nature to a point where it is not needed. At the same time, *imitazione* of other artists can be a valuable starting point, a valid way to hone one's skills.

One of several problems raised by this set of injunctions is that in an evolutionary situation each work will be judged by the works of others who have already been successful at reviving antique achievement and imitating nature. As a result, Vasari is compelled to call upon contemporary artists to excel in refinements of *style*—grace, inventiveness, diligence, ease and speed of execution, ever more limpid beauty of design and coloring—even to risk the abstract, extravagant, and bizarre. This theoretical bind, which may also reflect the actual creative dilemma of his fellow *artefici,* certainly indicates why Vasari has been seen as a better guide to the later, or second, "artificial" mannerist style of Bronzino, Salviati, Giambologna, and Vasari himself than to the first, anticlassical *maniera* of Pontormo, Rosso, Parmigianino, and Giulio Romano (to which modern critics add the names of

Tintoretto and El Greco). But surely the flexible and eclectic theory found in Vasari's text, and his contradictory judgments, cannot and should not be constrained to support a particular modern view or explanation of mannerism.

After Vasari: The Controversies over Mannerism

Aretino: Seppe ancora il gran Rafaello fare iscortar le figure, quando egli volle, e perfettamente; senzachè io vi ritorno a dire che in tutte le sue opere egli usò una varietà tanto mirabile, che non è figura che né d'aria né di movimento si somigli, tal che in ciò non appare ombra di quello che da' pittori oggi in mala parte è chiamata maniera, cioè cattiva pratica, ove si veggono forme e volti quasi sempre simili. E sì come Michelagnolo ha ricerco sempre in tutte le sue opere la difficoltà, così Rafaello, all'incontro, la facilità, parte, come io dissi, difficile a consequire; et halla ottenuta in modo che par che le sue cose siano fatte senza pensarvi, e non affaticate né istentate. Il che è segno di grandissima perfezzione, come anco negli scrittori, che i migliori sono i più facili: come, appresso voi dotti, Virgilio, Cicerone, et appresso noi il Petrarca e l'Ariosto.[31] (Lodovico Dolce, *L'Aretino,* 1557)

[*Aretino:* The great Raphael also knew how to foreshorten figures when he wished, and perfectly. But then, as I do not have to repeat to you, he practiced such a wondrous variety in all of his works that there is no figure of his, either in its attitude or movement, that resembles any other. Thus there is not a shadow in his work of that which painters today called with negative intent, manner—that is, bad practice—by which forms and faces are seen to be almost always the same. And just as Michelangelo has always sought difficulty in all his works, so Raphael, in contrast, has sought effortlessness, a thing, as I have said, difficult to achieve; and he has attained it in such wise that it seems his works have been made without thought, and not labored, nor forced, which is the sign of the greatest perfection, just as it is in writers, among whom the best are the most effortless—as are Vergil and Cicero for you learned men and Petrarch and Ariosto for us.]

For convenience of discussion, the controversies over mannerism may be grouped into and analyzed in three successive stages. The first, as the above quotation indicates, was the so-called mannerist period itself, when *maniera* was in the ascendancy but was by no means the only, or even the dominant, uncontested stylistic mode in the visual arts. This stage may be said to extend from the third decade of the sixteenth century, when the first generation of mannerists began to attract attention, to the fin de siècle in Italy and, especially in other European countries, well into the baroque era. During the second stage, from the seventeenth to the end of the nineteenth centuries, the occasional reaction and hostility of the earlier period evolved into outright rejection. The third stage began after World War I against the background of European expressionism and surrealism; after a pause between wars, interest in our subject crested again after World War II, in both America and Europe, in the context of abstract and other modes of modern and postmodern art. This stage was characterized by the revaluation and rehabilitation of what had come to be called mannerism, but also by confusion and disagreement, especially regarding the hypothesis of a recurring and universal, as opposed to a historically delimited, form of expression. Controversy raged around the questions of the extent or limits of the application of mannerism to visual art and late Renaissance culture generally, its connection with the baroque, its possible meaning in the other Renaissance arts (most notably literature, but also music) and finally, its alleged anticipation of modern art.

In the first stage, there was, of course, no consciousness of "mannerism" but only an awareness of some serious issues that had arisen in the practice and theoretical discussion of contemporary art as it had evolved from the work of an earlier generation of artists. Similarly, when the influence of Italian Renaissance art reached other countries, often, as we now recognize, in its latest (i.e., mannerist) rather than its earlier stage of development, there was little consciousness of other than a single "modern" style.[32] These simple truths need not and should not restrain our own historical analyses and arrangements of events in the interest of comprehending the past; but they do serve to keep in check our tendency to force the evidence into conceptual molds. And so if, for example, we recognize that mannerism was not the exclusive style of its time in the visual arts, we may appropriately hesitate to make large claims for it as an index to an entire period or culture, or even to the multifaceted and widespread literary and musical production of the late Renaissance. A powerful rationale for treating the whole period in such large terms has always been the fact that the Renaissance knew it was experiencing a cultural revolution—in sum, having a renaissance. There was *not* at the time the same kind or degree of self-consciousness about its mannerism.

When Vasari completed and published the first version of his *Lives* (1550), the first generation of artists then associated with mannerism, including Michelangelo, had made their presence felt. Now his own generation was both creating and theorizing about art, looking back to the High Renaissance works of Leonardo and Raphael, and including in their overview not only the first mannerists (Pontormo, Rosso, Parmigianino, Beccafumi, Giulio Romano) but also the still active and awesome Michelangelo and his rival Titian. This perspective is embodied in the conversation of Dolce's dialogue. But in the interval between the publication of the first and second versions of Vasari's *Lives* (1568), several developments occurred that sharpened the issues debated by Dolce's interlocutors. In 1562, Vasari himself founded the Florentine Accademia del Disegno under ducal patronage, the first of several to be established in Italy and eventually elsewhere, and a sure sign that artists had "arrived." Like their literary counterparts of earlier vintage, the art academies would provide a locale and a stimulus for sometimes abstruse theorizing and criticism. But as replacements for the repressive guilds, they differed from the literary academies in including the direct teaching of both the theory and practice of the arts in their purview. An inevitable result of such institutionalization of art activity was, of course, official patronage, prestige, mutual support, and a guarantee of a minimum competence; but it also brought with it all of the dreary uniformity and pedantry that the term *academic art* still conjures up.[33]

By the time of Vasari's second version of the *Lives,* too, the Council of Trent had completed and published its deliberations on the standards for sacred art (1563). Already the nudes of Michelangelo's *Last Judgment* had been partially painted over by papal decree. And in July of 1573 Veronese appeared before the Inquisition to defend his *Feast in the House of Levi* against the charge that he had inserted inappropriate secular details into the biblical story.[34] Against these well-known incidents of Counter-Reformation concern with the orthodoxy, decency, and decorum of religious art should be placed these facts: first, that the value and efficacy of sacred images was affirmed at Trent, hence the production of such works continued to be encouraged; and, second, that because greater license was granted to works of fantasy, the objects of reformist zeal in purely secular or nondoctrinal art (i.e., idealized portraits, landscapes, mythologies, allegories, genre, decorative cycles) were limited mostly to erotic portrayals of the nude or other allegedly lascivious subjects.[35] Here, too, the classic instance often referred to is the suppression of the engravings of Giulio Romano's illustrations of Aretino's sonnets on the various sexual positions (Roskill, pp. 304–06). Granted, this episode occurred much earlier in the century, after the Lutheran revolt but before the Council and during the papacy of Clement VII; but if it is true, as Aretino claimed, that he obtained from the pope the release of the imprisoned engraver Marcantonio Raimondi, the incident is more typical of the comparatively relaxed attitude toward such jeux d'esprit still possible at the time than of later responses to them. Yet the persistent notoriety of the case compelled Dolce in 1557 to have Aretino still defend the illustrations, on the ground that they were circulated privately rather than being publicly displayed like Michelangelo's nudes in *The Last Judgment*. In this later period of increasingly intense and militant piety, the illustrations had to be acknowledged as an example of impropriety, even if Aretino excuses them as comparatively harmless.

On the whole, then, despite unpromising external conditions, art was flourishing. Indeed, like the literary world of the late Italian Renaissance, which was characterized by an abundance of both creative works and literary criticism—poems, plays, and treatises gushed from the presses—the art world did not lack either bustling artistic activity or fulsome theorizing, despite the political, economic, social, and religious pressures on Italian life. If, as the traditional historiography of the late Renaissance would have it, this was a decadent period and its art subservient and formalistic, one would still have to admit that art was certainly not exhausted. And as long as it could boast individual creators like Tasso, Tintoretto, and Gesualdo, it was far from sterile.[36]

As the excerpt quoted above from Dolce's dialogue suggests, already abroad in 1557 was the fear that art, particularly painting, was liable to *maniera* in the sense of "cattiva pratica"; here the term is identified with stylization, and indirectly with possible imitation of Michelangelo rather than Raphael, though both have been implicated in the genesis of mannerism by modern critics. Note also the other issues raised, not about fidelity to nature, which is taken for granted, but about foreshortening, difficulty, effortlessness—especially the last as a quality in both literature and art—Dolce's *facile* evoking the venerable Latin tag *Ars est celare artem*, the idea that the best art (and the best artist) conceals art. This assertion raises the question of how much art in general can strive to conceal itself and follow canonical models like Raphael or Petrarch without revealing itself even more; and, for the visual arts, the problem of *maniera* as the result of imitating either Raphael's gracefulness or Michelangelo's difficulty, or both.

During this period, there appeared other dialogues, treatises, and miscellaneous writings about art by learned churchmen or laymen like Dolce, as well as by practicing artists and academicians like Vasari. Specimens of this theoretical activity which have been studied particularly for their relationship to mannerism include: the letters of Aretino; Paolo Pino's *Dialogo di pittura* (1548: Dialogue on Painting); Vincenzo Danti's *Il primo libro del trattato delle perfette proporzioni* (1567: The First Book of a Treatise on Perfect Proportions); Raffaello Borghini's *Il Riposo* (1584: named for the villa of one of the interlocutors, where the dialogue occurs); G. B. Armenini's *Dei veri precetti della pittura* (1586: On the True Precepts of Painting); G. P.

Lomazzo, *Trattato dell'arte della pittura, scultura, et archittetura* (1584: Treatise on the Arts of Painting, Sculpture, and Architecture); and *Idea del Tempio della Pittura* (1590: The Idea of the Temple of Painting); Gregorio Comanini, *Il figino* (1591: named for the painter who is one of the interlocutors), Federico Zuccaro's *Idea de'pittori, scultori e architetti* (1607) and *Lamento della pittura* (1605: Lament of Painting); and several others that deal exclusively with sacred art.[37] Though we cannot treat these writings in detail here, we should be aware of several topics, speculative themes, and critical notions that appear in them and are relevant to the concept of *maniera*.

Of particular interest is the attention given in these writings not just to the works but to the utterances of Michelangelo—"come diceva Michelangelo"—drawn from his letters, his poetry, and various biographies and memoirs of the artist.[38] The Michelangelo remarks quoted tend to support, among other preoccupations of these theorists, the notions that the "rules" (the proportions of geometry and mathematics, constructed perspective and foreshortening) should be intuitive, in the eye rather than the hand; that *disegno* is the basis of all the arts and crafts; that the artist does not imitate actual nature but an idea, or form, of divine origin, said to be within the artist's mind as well as within the uncarved block. His preference for the *figura serpentinata* and his defense of execution both speedy and effortless are also mentioned in support of an emerging mannerist aesthetic.

In addition to these strictures against "rules" and bondage to natural appearances, the theorists, especially Lomazzo and Zuccaro, also pondered and expounded upon Vasari's "idea" (what Zuccaro calls *disegno interno* as opposed to *disegno esterno*, the latter being defined as the realization of the former through line, hence the external, visible manifestation of the inner idea). Whereas Vasari, as we have seen, thinks of the "idea" as derived from previous experience of and therefore as dependent upon actual nature, Lomazzo, echoing Ficino, Platonizes it into an inner sense of eternal beauty, of the divine archetypes imprinted on the soul; hence the artist renders not the external appearance of nature but an intuition of its intended perfection, its divine *grazia*, infused in matter. Zuccaro, working with Aristotelian-Scholastic principles, draws a parallel between the activity of the artist and the activity of nature herself in creating her works. The *disegno interno*, or idea, of Zuccaro is an intellective principle like that which guides nature to its appropriate goals and operations, hence sensory experience does not precede it, and in fact is subordinate to and is clarified by it. But, as Erwin Panofsky, who studied these treatises in his *Idea* (1924), points out, "Both the Peripatetic and the Scholastic view and the Neoplatonic view agreed in that which most clearly distinguishes the Mannerist from the real Renaissance attitude towards art—in the conviction that the visible world is only a 'likeness' of invisible, 'spiritual' entities and that the contradiction between 'subject' and 'object' which had now become apparent to the intellect could be solved only by an appeal to God" (p. 98). He goes on to argue that "the Mannerist transformations of the compositional principles accepted by the Renaissance operated as a 'spiritualization' of the representations themselves" and attained what he referred to earlier as "a more intense expressivity" (pp. 98, 73).

Lest the reader think that Panofsky overstressed the link between this metaphysical strain in late Renaissance art theory and the actual works produced at the time, it should be realized that it was very much the fashion when he wrote *Idea* to see "spiritualization" and "intense expressivity" in mannerism. As for the high marks he gives the previously ignored or, if noticed, much maligned theorists, noting their attempts to provide theoretical legitimacy for art and the activity of artists, his rehabilitation of them does not overlook their less interesting tendencies: their habit of including and accommodating earlier notions that had become standard; their attempts to account for but not successfully synthesize the divergent trends in the art of their time; their incorporation of contradictory advice about, for example, imitating nature and other artists, using detailed proportions, or working speedily to attain a fresh execution. Once again we are reminded that not only was there *not* a mannerist monopoly of artistic production but also that there was no "purely" mannerist theory to support or explain it. And that the theory, like much of the art, represents neither decadence nor a degeneration of the theory and practice of the earlier Renaissance, nor yet a sufficiently novel or revolutionary trend that signals a break with the past and a fresh start. Mannerist theory is perhaps best explained as the product of a ripe Renaissance culture turning in on and exhaustively exploiting itself.

Thus, like the literary theorists who were penning similar treatises in what has been called an age of criticism, the art theorists in practice loyally follow the Renaissance penchant for incorporating or assimilating previous thought into a cumulative pattern.[39] Indeed, it is usually the case that both the literary and art theorists' distinctive approach, if they have one at all, is due more to a particular combination of familiar matter than to the presentation of totally new ideas. Whereas in Montaigne this kind of composition in "layers" does not offend because it reflects and dramatizes the mental process of such composition itself, which is his subject, in the critics the result is often an irritating pastiche. In this respect, Armenini, Lomazzo, and Zuccaro are very much in the same critical mold as their literary counterparts (Castelvetro, Mazzoni, Tasso), who were engaged in what Joel

Spingarn once described as the fundamental task of Renaissance literary criticism: the justification of imaginative literature.[40]

The second stage of controversy over mannerism begins in the closing decade of the sixteenth century, without any theoretical fanfare but with the rejection of *maniera* as it had been practiced by the second generation of Italian mannerists (from Vasari and Bronzino to Allori and the Cavaliere d'Arpino). The change in taste is evident in, on the one hand, the return to High Renaissance principles in the works of the Carracci, and on the other, in the uncompromising naturalism of Caravaggio. Both of these developments served not only to undermine mannerism but also to usher in the baroque style of the seventeenth century. Henceforth the fate of mannerism would be entwined with that of the baroque, for it was in the writings of classicists from the late seventeenth century on that *maniera* was condemned not only for itself but as the first phase of what were regarded as the anticlassical, or decadent, features of post-Renaissance or baroque art. This failure to distinguish between the two condemned styles, and to see mannerism as more than a mere transition between Renaissance and baroque when it *was* noticed separately, persisted into the nineteenth century, even when the baroque began to be rehabilitated. Witness, for example, Heinrich Wölfflin's *Renaissance and Baroque* (first published in 1888), in which the first stage of the baroque, what is now called mannerism, is taken up as "the style into which the Renaissance resolved itself or, as it is more commonly expressed, into which the Renaissance degenerated" (p. 15). And Arturo Graf, writing just a few years later (1905) and asking what mannerism is, concludes that part of its seventeenth-century manifestation is to be identified with the gaudy baroque.[41]

It is in the various writings (essays, letters, dictionaries, treatises, collections of biographies) of the Italian and French classicists of the seventeenth and eighteenth centuries that the abuse of *maniera* comes into its own both as a critical weapon and as a way of characterizing a particular historical moment. Preeminent among these critics are Giovanni Pietro Bellori, Fréart de Chambray, and Luigi Lanzi, but also contributing to the assault are Malvasia, Giustiniani, and Baldinucci. Henceforth, thanks to the efforts of these detractors, *di maniera, maniériste, manierato,* and *manierismo* would designate a style condemned for its departure from nature and truth, for its exclusive reliance on the works of one's masters or one's own fantasy, and on mere technique rather than on the fresh observation of both nature and good antique models. What might earlier have been approvingly designated as *manieroso* was now scornfully called *manierato*. As Panofsky noted in *Idea* (p. 240, n. 5), the new attitude was connected with the gradual disappearance of *maniera* from the vocabulary of art history and criticism, and its permanent replacement by *stile,* borrowed from literature and rhetoric. Since to Bellori *maniera* meant "ugliness and errors" and was not redeemed by "disegno interno," which he dismissed as "fantastica idea," it is clear that even the word itself was contaminated.[42]

There was not much more sympathy than this to be found among art and literature scholars of the nineteenth century. Francesco De Sanctis, for example, is pleased to note that Ariosto has no *maniera,* because his genius responds to the varied nature of things rather than to a subjective vision, the latter being associated with Petrarch, Tasso, and Marino.[43] Indeed, for mannerism to be rehabilitated, it was not only necessary that the hostility of the previous centuries be overcome, but also essential that certain nine-teenth-century attitudes and beliefs either wane or disappear, including the century's hostility to aristocratic court art and the pious products associated with oppressive institutional religion. And while some late romantics might find both mannerist and baroque works fascinating for their "purely" aesthetic traits, others would dismiss them for their lack of significant content, their aloofness from political or social reality, De Sanctis's "natura delle cose." Thus, while some mannerist works might attract attention as part of a renewed interest in the baroque, it was largely left to the next century to begin a fresh reexamination and eventual rehabilitation of the style, though not without new and different kinds of controversy.

The third stage of controversy over mannerism, then, belongs to our own century and began in its early decades with the renewed interest in and partial rehabilitation of mannerism in art, with some attention given also to literary analogues such as Rabelais, Shakespeare, and Cervantes. There are several possible reasons, in addition to those mentioned above as waning nineteenth-century prejudices, why a group of art historians—first Walter Friedlaender, Max Dvořák, and Werner Weisbach, then Nikolaus Pevsner and Erwin Panofsky—undertook the revaluation. For one, there was the prior experience of the curiosity that arose during the romantic and dec-adent periods about the baroque—another condemned style, as I have indicated—and the influence which *its* revival had exerted on the arts and literature. What is more, that revival was still an ongoing and compelling enterprise in the early decades of the twentieth century—witness, for one example, the revival of English and French metaphysical and baroque poetry. Another reason perhaps is that, as suggested above, the notion of baroque that especially attracted late romantic taste—its alleged anticlassi-cal, grotesque, and bizarre features—had also been attached to mannerism when considered either as a transitional style or as a first wave. And these

qualities, along with what were felt to be the mannerists' expressive con-
tent, spiritualization, subjectivity, and willful rejection of both material
nature and established artistic norms, must have made the style appealing
to the period of expressionism, dadaism, and nascent surrealism. The man-
nerists of the sixteenth century, like the poets of the seventeenth century,
suddenly seemed modern.[44]

During this early period of rediscovery and reexamination, though it
tended to stress the first generation of radical mannerists along with El
Greco (Friedlaender, Dvorák), or the aesthetic theories of the late
sixteenth-century critics (Panofsky), criticism also took up larger questions
of mannerism as a period (Dvorák), the relations of visual to literary man-
nerism (Dvorák, Weisbach) and to the Counter-Reformation and the
baroque (Weisbach, Pevsner). There was no agreement about the ultimate
worth of the style, but by contributing both formal analyses and inter-
pretations of the mannerists and their milieu, the first modern historians
and critics of mannerism initiated a potentially full-scale, multidisciplinary
inquiry that flourished soon after and is still going on today. And that
inquiry still deals with some of the questions they raised, though others
have been added to constitute the "problem of mannerism." It may be
helpful to list these questions and then use them as topics for summarizing
and discussing briefly the main threads of the modern discussion of the
meaning of mannerism.

First, there is the art historical question of whether the concept of man-
nerism can be applied to the several generations of artists who worked from
about 1520 to the end of the century in Italy, and how it may be applied to
the European diffusion of the style. Second, there is the matter of how to
interpret the formal qualities of mannerist works, in and of themselves and
in relation to their times. Third, there is the place of mannerism within the
larger cultural movement of the Renaissance and in relation to the baroque,
a related issue being its recapitulation of early Renaissance or late gothic
elements. Fourth, there is the specific relationship to literature and music,
although both are also involved in answers to the first three questions.
Fifth, there is the awesome, unmanageable, and probably unanswerable
question of whether mannerism is a universal, recurring form of expression
of the human spirit. Finally, there is for us the especially intriguing ques-
tion: to what extent does mannerism anticipate modern art? And, whether
it does or not, does the whole problem of mannerism have any value or
interest for us other than its having been an issue that has preoccupied and
continues to engage an international community of scholars and critics
working in different disciplines?

In a lecture given in 1914, then published in 1925 and later in English, as part of his now classic *Mannerism and Anti-Mannerism in Italian Painting* (1957), Walter Friedlaender did not overly stress interpretations of a psychological or cultural kind, nor did he venture literary analogies, as Dvořák and Weisbach were to do. He focused instead on the formal qualities of the first generation of mannerists; hence he can help us to understand the stylistic elements involved and to grasp the issues of the first question raised above. He begins his acute analysis with Vasari's reaction to Pontormo's Certosa frescoes, which he interprets as fear that the imitation of Dürer portended "a change of style which threatened the whole structure of Renaissance painting" (p. 4). According to Friedlaender, however, it was not the influence of Dürer, but a psychological dissatisfaction felt by Pontormo himself with the "classic" art of the High Renaissance that led him to turn to the German artist in reaction against its ideals. The harmony, symmetry, balance, and normativeness of High Renaissance style, as embodied in the works of Raphael's mature period, were rejected, the delicate balance of naturalism and idealism upset. As Friedlaender puts it, "just as one sees it" or "just as one ought to see it" yield to "as one does not see it" or as "from purely autonomous artistic motives, one would have it seen" (p. 6). Rationally constructed space, perspective, and proportion are sacrificed; in what the critic thinks is a thirst for spiritualization, the human figure, while still retaining a certain plasticity, is elongated "unnaturally and more or less capriciously" out of a "particular rhythmic feeling of beauty" (p. 7); heads are made smaller, limbs twist and twine, so that there arises "a new beauty, no longer measurable by the model or on forms idealized on this basis, but rather on an inner artistic reworking on the basis of harmonic or rhythmical requirements" (p. 8).

Later, in discussing the works of Pontormo along with those of Rosso and Parmigianino, Friedlaender adds to the list of mannerist or anticlassical features: the tendency toward the abstract; the recollection of late gothic verticalism; the crowding of the picture space with figures in layers that overlap or shuttle back and forth; the use of *repoussoir* figures; limbs and garments that spill out of the picture frame, "contrary to every Renaissance feeling" (p. 29); "an astonishing, soulful expressiveness" (in Rosso, p. 31); cold, unreal colors, and, in Parmigianino especially, grace, elegance, "preciosity of movement and turn in the body" (p. 41). He also finds in Parmigianino "narrow, exaggeratedly long-fingered hands"; by contrast, in Rosso and Michelangelo there is an anatomical emphasis with drastic foreshortening and *contrapposto* in nude and clothed figures. (Michelangelo's *Victory* is seen as "the Mannerist figure par excellence" [p. 13], and is frequently invoked by other critics, along with the Libyan Sibyl of the Sistine ceiling, as an example of the twisting, serpentine, double-*contrapposto* pose which he advocated and his followers endlessly imitated.)

In his second essay, dealing with the reaction to *maniera* beginning in the closing decades of the sixteenth century, Friedlaender acknowledges that he calls the first generation he had discussed earlier "anticlassical" for want of a better label; that is, he knows the term *mannerism* should be applied only to the "real enemy" of the classicists, the "mannered mannerism" of the second phase or generation, the artists of the *maniera* proper. But he is also aware that the term *mannerism* is being applied to the first generation as well as the second that arose "by a process of reverse derivation from its offshoot" (p. 48). He characterizes the mannered mannerism of the later sixteenth century as overbred, merely ornamental and decorative, repetitive, and playfully exaggerated, though he exempts El Greco, "in whom the original, true, and spiritual Mannerism again bursts into life" (p. 52n.).

Much of what will be said by subsequent critics will only add to the impressive analysis Friedlaender presented at that early date. Later critics will of course be motivated by such typical twentieth-century concerns as Freudian psychology, existentialism, the autonomy of art, the history of ideas, the social sciences, cultural history, and more recently, linguistic theory and semiology. On the one hand, they will deploy many of the analytical tools our century has available to explore a single subject; on the other, they may use one such tool to explain a whole culture.

Some critics will point to the obscure and learned allegories, frigid sexuality, and minute naturalism of detail that often combine in second or high mannerism, as in the erotic allegories and portraits of Bronzino, Clouet, and Spranger, and the fresco cycles of a Vasari. Other critics will emphasize the witty, bizarre, grotesque aspects of mannerism, as in the anthropomorphic still lifes of Arcimboldo (that favorite of the court of Rudolf II at Prague and later of the surrealists), or the witty sculpture-gardens of Bomarzo. The individualism, eccentricity, and neurotic anxieties and ambivalences of mannerist artists will be interpreted along with their allegedly ambiguous and dissonant works. Those especially concerned with anxiety, tension, and strain in architecture and sculpture will instance Michelangelo's statues and the Laurentian Library, Giulio Romano's perversely anticlassical treatment of the façade of the Palazzo del Tè at Mantua (including, within, his bizarre "Fall of the Giants" fresco); for those who seek a mannerism that is all elegance and exquisite poise, there are the etchings of Bellange, Giambologna's *Venus* and *Mercury* statues and Cellini's *Saltcellar,* the latter representative of the prolific activity of goldsmiths, jewelers, and other minor artists who turned out many such dazzling objects for palace and church. Thus, when Friedlaender and his colleagues both opened the debate over mannerism and provided their successors with several of its principal lines of inquiry, they could hardly have anticipated that they were launching a revaluation of an entire culture.

A slackening of the pace of the debate then occurred, due no doubt to the onset of another world war with its attendant upheavals. Between 1928 and 1938, for example, there are only a few noteworthy studies, by Enrico Carrara (1928, on Cellini), and by Margarete Hoerner (1928), Wilhelm Pinder (1932), and Hans Hoffman (1938) on the concept of mannerism, that at least kept the question alive and, in the case of the latter two scholars, who were to be cited by Wylie Sypher and others, exerted some small influence on the debate that resumed full-scale in the period from 1940 to 1960. At this time all of the visual arts became fully involved in the discussion, and literature as well as music was fulsomely invoked by the controversialists. Inevitably, as individual scholars reached out to enfold a multitude of works within their conceptual embraces, confusion spread among the believers and a wave of skepticism engulfed the nonbelievers.

Typical of this period and especially important because of the large issues they raised were the works of Pevsner, Curtius, Hauser, and Sypher. Though anticipated in part by Wittkower's 1934 study of Michelangelo's Laurentian Library, Pevsner's pioneering survey, "The Architecture of Mannerism," appearing in *The Mint* (vol. 1, 1946), was notable for its delineation of the specific features of several sixteenth-century buildings that he characterized as asymmetrical, dissonant, incongruous, and unstable in abandonment of High Renaissance harmonies.[45] But he also emphasized that preciosity and self-consciousness go hand in hand with troubled spirituality in mannerism. Thus, in an attempt to explain the style, he asserts that "Mannerism has no faith in mankind and no faith in matter" (p. 146), and that "Mannerist art is full of contradictions: rigid formality and deliberate disturbance, bareness and over-decoration, Greco and Parmigianino, return to medieval mysticism and the appearance of pornography (Giulio Romano and Aretino). For pornography is a sign of sensuousness with a bad conscience, and Mannerism is the first Western style of the troubled conscience" (p. 147). Pevsner here recapitulates some of the ideas and interpretations of his colleagues among the early modern historians of mannerism, but with his own intense emphasis on the Reformation as initiating a "split world" (p. 146) in which "tormenting doubt" and "rigorous enforcement of dogma," along with "an uneasy neutrality rife with potential disturbance everywhere," witnessed the end of the innocence of the Middle Ages. Pevsner was to remind the reader that his essay "is a gross oversimplification" (. 147), with much unaccounted for, but what was remembered was his powerful sketch of an anxiety-ridden, if not neurotic, art.

Ernst Robert Curtius's *European Literature and the Latin Middle Ages,* first published in German in 1948, then in English in 1953, an enormously impressive work that is a classic of its kind, proposed in its brief chapter on mannerism a radically different approach to the problem. According to Curtius, who would have no truck with art history or *geistesgeschichte,* preferring to concentrate instead on *stilgeschichte,* literary mannerism was to be identified with formal eccentricity, verbal ornamentation, and pointed thought. A recurring phenomenon in the history of style, and typified by rhetorical excess, it breaks out like a rash after, and even during, periods when ideal classical values are prized. It is evidence of a perennial human inclination to respond to order, symmetry, balance, clarity, and restraint (in sum, the so-called classical values) by reveling in excessive verbal artifice and complex meaning. What is more, since verbal artifice, rhetorical ornaments, and Asiatic style can be found in antiquity, they have a classical pedigree, too. Examples are drawn from Rabelais, Marino, Góngora, and Joyce, among others. Finally, Curtius proposed that *mannerism* as he defined it be substituted for *baroque* henceforth as the more appropriate term for a recurring literary phenomenon not tied to any particular century. And several of his followers, especially in Germany, have done just that.[46] One of them, Gustav René Hocke, also published two studies (1957, 1959) ranging widely through the arts and across the centuries in search of a universal fantastic mannerism that includes various expressions of the beautifully aberrant, the esoteric, and the grotesque, from the Alexandrian to the modern age, and from Asiatic prose to Rimbaud.[47]

Curtius's stylistic approach, also the general approach of Helmut Hatzfeld and Georg Weise, has had great value for literary study, but it is doubtful whether *mannerism* can be used by literary scholars in one sense while it is being used differently in other disciplines, especially when we have terms like *mannered, witty, rhetorical,* and *conceited* that serve us just as well, or better. And while Curtius's banishment of art history is attractive at first glance to literary historians impatient with indiscriminate juggling of poems and paintings, ultimately we do not need to bother with mannerism at all, as label or concept, if we do not wish to profit from a comprehensive vision of late Renaissance culture. As for the idea of a universal or perennial mannerism, even if such a thing could be proven to exist, we would still have to define the sixteenth-century variety, and to do so without some reference to the other arts would be inconceivable.

In 1951, Arnold Hauser published the two-volume version in English of his *The Social History of Art,* which was followed in 1957 by a popular paperback version in four volumes (no one has done so, but the discussion of mannerism at this stage might well have been called "the polemics of the paperbacks"). Written from a sociopsychological point of view, his brief treatment of the concept of mannerism in volume 2 (1957, pp. 97–106), starts from a notion that "the predominant mood in Italy is one of impending doom" (p. 99). Since the "tension-free" formulae of classical art will not do, they are either desperately adhered to or distorted by the young artists responding to the High Renaissance. In language that adumbrates Harold Bloom's "anxiety of influence" among poets, Hauser stresses the insecurity, ambivalence, alienation, and rebelliousness of these artists, bent on replacing the "supernormativity" of their models by "more subjective and more suggestive features" (p. 100). Hence their deepening and spiritualizing of religious experience, as well as their "exaggerated intellectualism" and, at other times, "fastidious and affected epicureanism, translating everything into subtlety and elegance" (ibid.). What is more, mannerism is held to be "the first modern style, the first which is concerned with a cultural problem and which regards the relationship between tradition and innovation as a problem to be solved by rational means" (pp. 100–01). We cannot understand mannerism, says Hauser, unless we grasp the fact that "its imitation of classical models is an escape from the threatening chaos, and that the subjective overstraining of its forms is the expression of the fear that form might fail in the struggle with life and art fade into soulless beauty" (p. 101). That mannerism should interest our age is symptomatic of our own century's tension-ridden intellectual climate (ibid.), and its awareness of the world of "mingled reality" that is the dream (p. 103); it is significant for us moderns because it is reminiscent of surrealist painting, Franz Kafka's dream world, the montage technique of Joyce's novels, "the autocratic treatment of space in the film" (p. 103). As we shall see, Hauser will later expand upon his suggestions here of a literary mannerism, but as I hope my deliberately fulsome quotations from his text have shown, what Hauser did say in summary in those brief pages of his book must be characterized as easily the most provocative, wide-ranging, and potentially contentious remarks made up to that time about mannerism as a Renaissance phenomenon *and* as a modern preoccupation.[48]

With Sypher's *Four Stages of Renaissance Style* (1955), originally published in paperback, we have the first American attempt to deal with our subject as a cultural panorama. As such, and for the stimulation it provided young scholars and critics (as well as veterans) caught up in a fashionable wave of interdisciplinary study, it was a tour de force, initially much misunderstood as a culminating assessment when in fact its purpose was to introduce and explore as a hypothesis the European concept of mannerism, in all of its facets, for the benefit of its American readers. In the event, its bold multidisciplinary range and risky interdisciplinary generalizations managed to stir up objections from all quarters. Yet, although Sypher relied as heavily on the pioneer German and other art historians as he did on literary critics, his interpretative synthesis, with its postulate of successive stages of stylistic development, retains a definite literary flavor.

If the mannerism of Curtius is a matter of rhetorical excess, the mannerisms of Pevsner, Hauser, and Sypher are dominated by the motif of "unresolved tension"—what, in a moment of weak-wittedness, I once called "Angst-Mannerism."[49] For Sypher, mannerism, "an intervening form of vision" between Renaissance and baroque (p. 4), is also the perennial mannerism of Curtius, because styles have a life of their own (p. 9) and can recur when needed. It was needed in the late Renaissance because "all western Europe was inwardly shaken by some tremor of malaise and distrust" (p. 100). Then, as now, there was "a crisis of history and consciousness" (p. 102).[50] As a result, Renaissance optimism faded, and "approximation, equivocation, and accommodation are accepted as working principles" (ibid.). Mannerism as analyzed by art historians could now offer literary critics "a chance to look again at the 'dissociations' in metaphysical poetry and Jacobean drama, the uneasy license in Donne's wit, the dubious motives in Ford's plays, and the sordid but dazzling world of Bosola in Webster's *Duchess of Malfi,* or the perilous world of Middleton and Rowley's *The Changeling,* where De Flores feeds strangely upon the impure virginity of Beatrice-Joanna" (p. 103). There are other literary inhabitants of "the unhealthful mannerist climate" (ibid.), including Hamlet and Don Quixote, and its dissonances are still audible in "Lycidas," "To His Coy Mistress," and the lyrics of the Cavalier poets addressed to an "exquisite neurotic society" (p. 110). Of some of the celebrated mannerist art works Sypher says many things that have proved frustrating in their evocative but vague phrasing: thus, Cellini's Perseus statue "stands cruelly and gracefully under the troubled sky of the later sixteenth century" (p. 104), and Parmigianino's *Self-Portrait in a Convex Mirror* is "preposterously contrived, like some of Donne's poems" (p. 112).

After his introductory pages, Sypher goes on to take up six categories of a formal and psychological character that he finds useful in associating mannerist works in different media: disturbed balance, techniques of accommodation, dramatic artifice, the revolving view, unresolved tensions, and shifting planes of reality. To illustrate these categories he makes some startling juxtapositions: Donne's dissonant stress is said to make "the ear jump just as the eye jumps across a mannerist façade" (p. 128); the *figura serpentinata* and the revolving view required by some mannerist statues are likened to the multifaceted personality of Hamlet (p. 156); the unresolved conflict between flesh and spirit is instanced by both the Council of Trent's contradictory doctrine on images and the "torments" of Saint Teresa and George Herbert (pp. 165– 69). That Sypher elsewhere in his chapter on mannerism also discusses Thomas Browne, Caravaggio, Velásquez, and Milton—the *Maids of Honor* is a "belated mannerist composition" (p. 171) and "Lycidas" is "perhaps the greatest mannerist poem" (p. 174)—reminds us that figures and works regarded by others as baroque are here treated as mannerist because they are tension-ridden. Like Pevsner, Hauser, and some of his other European predecessors, Sypher sees mannerism as a sick patient languishing after the good health of the Renaissance has deteriorated, with the baroque marking a robust return to resolution of conflicts. And when he says that "mannerist art has discovered the existential" (p. 172), we recall Hauser's argument for the modernity of the style and the modernist bias of Sypher's analysis.

Also undertaken during the decades of the 1940s and 1950s, though not earning the clamorous attention given to Sypher's book, was a series of essays in the historiography of mannerism, studies of how the word itself originated and was used, and how the concept developed to the present day. These were articles printed in journals or as prefatory chapters like this one, in books that dealt with mannerism or Renaissance literature, or art generally. On the ground that we might better understand what mannerism means *now* by inquiring into what it meant *then,* scholars such as Mario Treves (1941), Giuliano Briganti (1945), Luigi Coletti (1948), Georg Weise (1952), Luisa Becherucci (1954), and G. N. Fasola (1956) steadily accumulated a wealth of historical allusion and critical opinion. Though more than occasionally partisan, this activity has been and remains a valuable and necessary prolegomenon to the current debate. And as we shall see, it has continued in the past three decades at so vigorous a pace that it has earned a separate heading in my bibliography ("Term and Concept") to which I am forced to refer the reader for details. Suffice to say that the energy.and output of the mannerism "industry" has been such that to survey and analyze even this part of it would require a chapter of its own.

As the fifties came to an end, and in 1959 precisely, Riccardo Scrivano published one of the first attempts to deal with cinquecento Italian literary mannerism as a separate theme. His brief *Il manierismo nella letteratura del cinquecento* focused on Italian literature of the sixteenth century (and more particularly on thematic and stylistic trends, especially anti-Aristotelian literary theory and the time-haunted lyric poetry of the "secondo cinquecento"), between Vasari and Tasso, and in relation to the culture and sensibility of the time. In that same year, another direction was indicated for mannerism, this time toward popular awareness and pedagogical use. In America that year appeared an anthology edited by Donald J. McGinn and George Howerton, *Literature as a Fine Art,* with a section devoted to mannerism (including poems by Ralegh, Donne, Shakespeare, Saint John of the Cross, etc., along with suggested "parallel examples in the fine arts" drawn from the repertoire of Friedlaender, Pevsner, and Hauser). Needless to say, it did not threaten the monopoly of more conservative and purely literature-oriented anthologies of the time. Much greater attention and wider acclaim was given to Mary McCarthy's *Stones of Florence* published the same year, an exalted travel guide that included some delightful pages on Pontormo's *Deposition* (pp. 108– 14).

The fifties and early sixties were not without murmurs of discontent in reaction to this burgeoning interest in literary mannerism, which seemed to some a dangerous contemporary intellectual hobby that threatened to blur hopelessly the received and solidly established configurations of Renaissance literature. Particularly irksome was the practice of affixing labels— mannerist or baroque or both—to sixteenth- and seventeenth-century authors and works, on the basis of tendentious interpretations resting on very shaky historical or critical criteria. Thus E. B. O. Borgerhoff's article "Mannerism and Baroque: A Simple Plea" (1953) and Rosemond Tuve's essay, "Baroque and Mannerist Milton" (1961), as well as A. M. Boase's "The Definition of Mannerism" (1962) were typical both in their efforts to clarify the problem and their disagreement with each other as to whether or how the terms might be profitably used—Borgerhoff opting for distinctions based on deviation from and return to Renaissance norms, Boase arguing for a variety of straining mannerisms seen as phases of a single post-Renaissance development, and Tuve probably preferring that the whole business go away! Perennial mannerism also complicated matters: a work like Giorgio Melchiori's *The Tightrope Walkers: Studies of Mannerism in Modern English Literature* (1956) appeared at the same time as Rudolph Stamm's *Die*

Kunstformen des Barockzeitalters, which proposed Renaissance Shakespeare and Donne as mannerists. Most ominous of all, the German scholars and critics who had dominated the pursuit of visual and verbal mannerism were now being joined in considerable numbers by American as well as other European and East European colleagues; and the previous focus on Italian and English literature, along with a few Spanish authors like Cervantes and Góngora, was now to broaden in scope. Although matters had not reached an utter impasse, it was evident that as the decade of the sixties began, art and literary history were in mannerism's favorite state of crisis.

In part to ease this crisis, two international congresses were held, in 1960 and 1961, one dealing primarily with literature, the other with art. The 1960 congress, sponsored by the Roman Academy of the Lincei and named "Manierismo, barocco, rococò: concetti e termini" (acts published in 1962), featured several prominent papers on mannerism and baroque, including Ezio Raimondi's survey of the notion of a literary mannerism (pp. 57–79) and Georg Weise's presentation "Sulla storia del termine *Manierismo*" (pp. 27–38). But it cannot be said that any conclusions were reached about tidying up the definition of literary mannerism; indeed, Weise's seeming to opt for the term "late Renaissance," with a neutral *mannerism* absorbed back into a concept of classical Renaissance that extends to the eighteenth century, hinted that perhaps the enterprise was nearly hopeless.

At the Twentieth International Congress of the History of Art held in New York in 1961 (acts published 1963), a more fruitful exchange occurred, with implications for literary as well as visual mannerism.[51] Ernst Gombrich, who had suggested earlier that the so-called sixteenth-century crisis of mannerism was less the spirit of the age than a result of the conception of art held during it, reiterated that view. He went on to emphasize how the concept—though meeting the need of those in the succeeding period, and in our own time, to separate out the "unclassical"—had also created the dilemma of seeing mannerism as symptomatic either of decline or rebellion. In concluding, Gombrich made clear his preference for "looking at the works produced in the period as efforts in their own right, created in a given situation" and endorsed those notions of mannerism that allowed such an investigation.[52] It was to this kind of reading of the "texts of the period" (Zerner, p. 113) that Craig H. Smyth and Sidney J. Freedberg contributed their impressive papers on how mannerist works are composed with regard to nature, previous works, and formal structure. But it was undoubtedly John Shearman's paper on "Maniera as an Aesthetic Ideal" that proved the most contentious of the presentations.[53] And since he followed this polemical foray with a full-scale multidisciplinary assault on anguished mannerism in his 1967 paperback, *Mannerism* (Penguin Books' Style and Civilization series), we can consider both his 1961 paper and his later book together.

Almost single-handedly, Shearman attempted nothing less than a thorough revision of the whole concept of mannerism, with the result that a third view of our subject now contended with those of Curtius and the proponents of anguished mannerism. In 1961, following a similar proposal of Luisa Becherucci in 1955, Shearman argued that *maniera* really has little to do with the "shock, tension, and violent expression" so often associated with it and the early or first generation of Florentine mannerists. Since *maniera* first appeared in Rome, denoted elegant refinement, and was used by and with reference to the later sixteenth-century practitioners of the style, *mannerism* ought to be used only of works that have *maniera* so defined. If subsequent critics rejected *maniera*, we are not bound to their prejudices and can again enjoy the style on its own terms of sophisticated and exquisite beauty. In his 1967 study, having laid the polemical ground, Shearman proceeded to define and defend the "stylish style" and what were regarded as its virtues in its own time—artifice, difficulties overcome, facility, dexterity, *sprezzatura,* grace, complexity, copiousness, and caprice (pp. 21—22). He states further that "Mannerist art should not be identified with mannered art, for while the first is always to some extent mannered, the second is not always Mannerist, since it may be anything but graceful and accomplished" (p. 22). Here we have one of the several stubborn difficulties raised by Shearman's narrowly historical approach: how *can* we tell the difference between mannered and mannerist, *for us?* If we refuse to be bound by Vasari's verdicts and the judgment of his time as to what is enduringly beautiful, this implies that we lack historical imagination. Though I would agree that we ought not to read twentieth-century anxiety into sixteenth-century works that may express other feelings or ideas, we did not invent anxiety, tension, and neurotic despair; and we can legitimately look for them and other qualities in earlier art if that is meaningful and keeps it alive for us, provided we do not distort or otherwise abuse it. Shearman insists, however, that such qualities are not there.

What is more, although he asserts that *maniera* is not the exclusive ideal of the time, Shearman goes on to find it not only in art and music but also in much of the literature of the sixteenth century. His range of reference is from Serafino to Guarini in Italy, and includes Desportes in France, and Lyly and Spenser in England; pastoral plays, intermezzi, and ornamental rhetorical style are also invoked, along with such general features as variety, abundance, obscurity, formalism, lack of decorum. And like Sypher and Hauser, he uses Curtius's literary mannerisms in a limited chronological frame to illustrate shared stylistic vocabulary: thus, the *contrapposti* of the *figura serpentinata* are juxtaposed to the verbal *contrapposti,* or antitheses, of Guarini's rhetoric in the *Pastor Fido,* since they aim at the common aesthetic goal of delightful artificiality and difficulty overcome with *grazia* (pp. 91−96). In sum, having outlined what is in effect a literary age of mannerism, Shearman asks us to take it or leave it on its own exquisite terms.

Obviously so drastic a revision of the terms of the debate over mannerism was bound to send out some shock waves. Unlike Hauser, Sypher, and others he opposes, Shearman argues that mannerism is not merely a convenient hypothesis or useful instrument of investigation but something that really happened, buttressed by evidence that the word and the aesthetic ideal it connotes were actually current at the time, hence not to be distorted by a modern superimposed meaning or construct. But while it may seem wonderfully refreshing, at first, to look at what actually happened rather than to ponder different opinions of what happened, conclusions as to what really occurred may themselves be complex and rest on underlying interpretations. Thus, tempting as it might be to have the debate I have been tracking in these pages settled at last on the basis of Shearman's attractive proposal of a historically limited and guaranteed stylish style, we might well have such a truce at the cost of a limited view of mannerist art that short-changes both it and us.

Finally, there are two specific literary phenomena, euphuism and Petrarchism, to which Shearman's theory of mannerist and mannered is singularly appropriate and may therefore serve as a crucial test of its validity. If, prodded by Shearman into subduing our suspicions that it is a mannered style, we take another look at euphuism, we may decide that it *is* beautiful in its own way—but still superficial and lacking in enduring worth as we understand such criteria. Whatever his contemporaries thought about it, we need our own reasons for finding Lyly's packaged prose interesting. It must be more mannerist than mannered for us. In the case of a Petrarchan sonnet that Shearman would treat as mannerist because it is graceful and accomplished, it may well seem that he has elevated it, or at least rescued it from our prejudices. But it may also be that by not risking our looking at it for other values and meanings, he may be depriving it of a richer aesthetic life and a fuller appeal to its modern readers. By limiting it to the status of an elegant verbal display of style, he may also be condemning it to the ultimate judgment that it is after all simply another exercise in the *maniera* of Petrarch, and therefore, as Vasari himself might have put it, *di maniera* or mannered. The idea of the mannered cannot be limited to what is *not* graceful or accomplished, for then it could not be even a part of the purely mannerist work that Shearman postulates. The mannered does lurk in the mannerist, but not as slippage of poise or control; rather, it is Hauser's "soulless beauty," what I would prefer to call with Boase "a sometimes misplaced elegance" (p. 143). And this is why we may feel perplexed about using the term *mannerist* in Shearman's sense for both euphuism and a love lyric by Donne.

Shearman's provocative argument so dominates the decade of the sixties we are surveying that one may easily overlook some important trends that also belong to those years. They include a continuing and increasingly sophisticated inquiry into the historiography and controversy of mannerism, keeping pace with the progress of studies in various disciplines. If Catherine Dumont's "Le Maniérisme: Etat de la question" (1966) concentrated on art and concluded that "le tableau de l'art et de la culture du XVIe siècle est toujours à refaire" (p. 457), other essays and review articles by Battisti (1960), Della Terza (1960), Hatzfeld (1966), Scrivano (1966), and Ulivi (1967) included or dealt entirely with literary issues. At the same time, the gradual infiltration of popular media by the mania for mannerism revealed itself strikingly in Pier Paolo Pasolini's scene from the episodic film *Ragopag* (1962), a visual parody of Rosso's famous *Deposition*.

In that same year, Giuliano Briganti's *Italian Mannerism* (an English translation of his *La maniera italiana*) renewed the spirit of protest by opting for *maniera* but not mannerism. This critic, who along with Luisa Becherucci had published pioneering studies of Italian mannerist art in the 1940s, now echoed her reservations, and those of Shearman and Roberto Longhi, with polemical force. The persistence of German scholars in positing a mannerism that is anticlassical and anti-Renaissance, he argues, promotes an "eternal Gothic spirit" and barely conceals "that chauvinistic complacency from which German criticism has always had difficulty in abstaining" (p. 9). In a similar revisionist mood, Sir Kenneth Clark's Bickley Lecture, *A Failure of Nerve, Italian Painting 1520–1535* (1967), pointed out that examples of "disquiet, melancholy, and neurasthenia" were already perceptible in Italian art by 1512, before the Sack of Rome (p. 10). Clark, who did not bother to conceal his lack of sympathy for mannerism, inadvertently explained why, when he associated a rejection of Renaissance humanism with the "failure of nerve" of his title. Meanwhile, in the literary camp, Robert M. Burgess was able to compile as part of his 1966 essay on "Mannerism in Philippe Desportes" a list of no fewer than forty-five different terms and phrases used to date in discussions of our subject!

In 1964 Jacques Bousquet's sumptuously illustrated, lavishly produced, and extravagantly argued *Mannerism: The Painting and Style of the Late Renaissance* appeared. No previous exponent of a universal mannerism in which both the Renaissance and modern art are implicated, and none since, has come close to matching Bousquet's exuberant claims, backed by familiar and unfamiliar visual evidence interspersed and juxtaposed with verse and prose excerpts from Renaissance and baroque authors. For Bousquet, mannerism is both "the artistic expression of an epoch" (p. 23) and "the artistic epoch of the past most akin to our own" (p. 25). All is not generalization, however, since this critic can be usefully precise in, for example, proposing a typology of stylistic and thematic features for mannerist art: extreme clarity of contours, lustrous forms, sculptural painting, tendency toward cubism, use of geometric forms, deformation/elongation of figures, plays of perspective, acromegaly, serpentine line, exaggerated gestures, harsh metallic colors, evocative atmospheres such as stormy twilights, painted frames, juxtaposition of distinct spaces, multiple viewpoint, shallow space crammed and deep space left empty, perverse sensuality and voyeurism, and so on. This welcome specificity is offset, however, by statements such as the following: "all the elements of Romantic art and of Contemporary art are already embodied in Mannerism," which is also said to be "far richer, broader and more stable than either the Baroque or the classicism of the High Renaissance and in addition a phenomenon which is far more clearly defined than either of these" (p. 31).

In the following year (1965), Morse Peckham's *Man's Rage for Chaos: Biology, Behavior, and the Arts,* taking up the problem of mannerism in the context of the author's aesthetic theory, devoted its first section (pp. 3—40) to a sharp critique of the books by Daniells (see below) and Sypher that had appeared earlier. In 1965 also Hauser published his two-volume study of *Mannerism: The Crisis of the Renaissance and the Origin of Modern Art,* in which anguished mannerism received its definitive statement. In addition to expanding considerably upon his earlier treatments of the Marxist and Freudian themes of alienation and narcissim (pp. 94–130), Hauser took up literary mannerism in a chapter entitled "The Principal Representatives of Mannerism in Western Literature" (pp. 302—54) and a section devoted to the moderns (pp. 355—94). Here the familiar Renaissance and baroque names are joined by those of Baudelaire, Mallarmé, Proust, and Kafka.

Eugenio Battisti's 1967 article on the concept of mannerism in architecture reminds us that although painting and sculpture have preempted the foreground of many discussions of visual mannerism, the issues raised by Pevsner and others concerned with mannerist buildings have remained in contention. We are also reminded that Battisti himself has occupied a significant place in the controversies of the sixties with his various essays and two books: *Rinascimento e barocco* (1960) and *L'antirinascimento* (1962). The former includes his important studies of imitation in Italian sixteenth-century literature and art and his historiographical essay on the "misfortunes" of mannerism. The latter echoes the title of Hiram Haydn's *The Counter-Renaissance* (1951), but is not concerned with intellectual crosscurrents so much as with the nonrational undercurrents of Renaissance culture as they reveal themselves in images of fairies, witches, and automata, and in the pervasive influence of magic and astrology. As his opening essay on "Mannerism and Anti-Renaissance" suggests, Battisti associates these undercurrents with the mannerist sensibility.

The attempt to distinguish sickly mannerist from robust baroque also continued to preoccupy scholars and critics.[54] In 1962, F. B. Artz published one of the rare attempts up to and since then to take up mannerism and baroque within a panoramic cultural survey, in his *From Renaissance to Romanticism: Trends in Style in Art, Literature, and Music, 1300–1830*. Like Sypher, who greatly influenced him, Artz tended to include as mannerists authors whom others claimed as plain Renaissance or baroque (Montaigne, d'Aubigné, Marino, Góngora, Cervantes, Lope de Vega, Lyly, Shakespeare, Donne). In an article published in 1966, Helmut Hatzfeld complained that "Mannerism is not Baroque," but of course he had his own notion of mannerism as a multiplicity of *maniere* resulting from the disintegration of Renaissance humanistic ideals, and consequently his own list of mannerists (including Michelangelo and Góngora though *not* "baroque" Lope de Vega and Cervantes). At the same time, other Hispanists, like Manuel Durán, were discussing mannerism in precisely these "baroque" figures, as well as Saint Teresa, Quevedo, and Gracián. In an article published in 1962, Durán takes up the "re-clasificación manierista" of authors hitherto thought to be baroque, and proceeds to probe Lope de Vega's works as a test case. While finding the plays unpromising, he discerns in the romance *La Dorotea*, the prose *Soliloquios,* and certain lyrics evidence of Sypher's "tensiones no resueltas" (p. 80). Five years later, writing on Quevedo and, as he did with Lope, invoking paintings by Tintoretto and El Greco, Durán concluded that there were two strains in the poet, a grotesque and a mannerist mode that are distinguishable (p. 307). In 1967, the first issue of *Colloquia Germanica* featured articles by A. G. De Capua ("Baroque and Mannerism: Reassessment") and B. L. Spahr ("Baroque and Mannerism: Epoch and Style") that continued attempts to explore and distinguish between the concepts, and Davy A. Carozza's "For a Definition of Mannerism: The Hatzfeldian Thesis." A few years later (1969), it was time for Gregor Sebba's "Baroque and Mannerism: A Retrospect," which viewed both "crisis Mannerism" and "aesthetic convention Mannerism" as reflecting a "new mood," whereas baroque, especially architecture, represented a "new symbolic function" (p. 158).

As Hatzfeld and Durán demonstrated in Hispanic studies, the close study of particular themes and texts was essential to ballast theoretical speculation. Other examples from the decade under review are an article by R. O. Jones, "Renaissance Butterfly, Mannerist Flea" (1965) and Daniel B. Rowland's prize-winning undergraduate essay published as *Mannerism—Style and Mood* (1964). Though perhaps unduly influenced by crisis mannerism, Rowland focused on specific works: Depositions by Rosso and Pontormo, Gesualdo's madrigals, Donne's *The First Anniversary*. Another welcome trend of the sixties was close study of single authors, as in Roy Daniells's *Milton, Mannerism and Baroque* (1963) and Ferruccio Ulivi's study of anguished mannerism in Tasso (1966). At the end of the decade, too, Louis Martz's *The Wit of Love* (1969) took up Donne, Carew, Crashaw, and Marvell, with some particularly acute interdisciplinary comments on Carew and Marvell as mannerists that utilize Shearman's stylish mannerism and propose a solution to the dilemma of distinguishing mannered from mannerist:

> A Mannerist painter has learned all that can be learned from the earlier great masters and he now proceeds to turn their art and craft toward other ends, creating a different kind of art in which the high style stands at the front, taking the eye with its elegance and its sophistication. Such art can, of course, be mere imitation in the bad sense of that word, but it may also be creative imitation—that is, imitation of the manner of the great masters which moves into a different era of sensibility and creates a new world of art. Now transferring cautiously this term into the poetic realm, perhaps we might say that Carew is a Mannerist because he imitates so skillfully the works of the great masters who preceded him and yet brings their art into a different dimension, celebrating values different from those presented by Donne and Jonson and other poets to whom Carew is obviously indebted. (p. 94)

Another development of the late 1960s was the intensification of a previously sporadic interest in French literary mannerism. Although Italian, Spanish, and English authors and works had seemed to dominate earlier debate, individuals like Scéve, Montaigne, and Desportes had been taken up as mannerists from time to time, as we have noted. And, of course, in the visual area the surviving art of Fontainebleau had also been studied by Panofsky (1958), Sylvie Béguin (1960), and others as the locus of diffusion of imported Italian mannerism. In an article published in 1958, Jean Adhémar had argued that the poetry of Ronsard had strong affinities with the painting of Primaticcio and other Fontainebleau artists. But much of the study of French literary models had been done by nonspecialists or comparatists. What was different at this time, therefore, was the involvement of specialists in French literature in a new look at the texts of the sixteenth century, and especially the Pléiade, Ronsard and his contemporaries, as well as Jean de Sponde. Thus an issue of *L'Esprit Créateur* (1966), for example, included essays by Hatzfeld, Burgess, Sayce, and others, that ranged from Ronsard to Malherbe. Particularly noteworthy was Sayce's juxtaposition of Ronsard's "Elegie à Janet" and a painting attributed to Clouet depicting Diana at her bath (pp. 234–37). In the same year there also appeared *Lumières de la Pléiade,* papers from a 1965 conference on humanistic studies at Tours, including Marcel Raymond's "La Pléiade et le maniérisme" (pp. 391–423). Raymond acknowledged that the concept of mannerism entailed for him, as it had for so many others, a modification of his earlier views of the baroque, but he hesitated to espouse a wholesale revision. At most, he granted, mannerism might help clarify some aspects of French sixteenth-century poetry. And as for Ronsard, "Ainsi, Ronsard n'appartient pas au maniérisme, bien que celui-ci puisse contribuer à expliquer une partie de ses oeuvres" (p. 423). In another paper given a few years later and published in 1970, Raymond returned to the disputed "frontières du maniérisme et du baroque," where he might have met Marcel Tetel attempting to assess "Mannerism in the Imagery of Sponde's 'Sonnets de la Mort,' " the subject of a 1968 essay dealing with "the general consensus now . . . that Sponde is a manneristic poet" (p. 5). Finding "intricate and conflicting patterns with no solutions anywhere" and "sterile cerebration and abstractedness" (p. 6) in the sonnets, Tetel emphasizes the poet's inability to resolve the conflict of world and spirit until his conversion to Catholicism, when "conflict ceases and he will no longer be a poet" (ibid.). In the following year (1969), Claude-Gilbert Dubois devoted the first of two volumes of baroque poetry to the period 1560–1600, with the title *Du maniérisme au baroque.*

In the other arts, a similar trend toward focusing on individual artists and relevant "texts" was also evident in the sixties. And in the visual arts expecially, what with Freedberg, Smyth, Zerner, and other art historians engaged in precisely such an enterprise, an outside observer from the literary camp senses that the debate over the meaning of mannerism has not diverted energies from the ongoing and crucial tasks of research and analysis. One exception, another border war, deserves note since it involves the crucial question of Northern mannerism, which in turn stirs up the larger and much disputed issue of the impact of Italian Renaissance styles beyond the Alps. The problem of mannerism in the Netherlands had been raised earlier in, for instance, Antal's 1928 essay, and in the meantime the inquiry had broadened to embrace central and eastern Europe. Because a connection had been posited between mannerism and international gothic at an equally early stage of the debate, this too remained an unresolved question. In the decade of the sixties the continuation of these speculations is evident in, for example, articles by Anna Maria Göransson and Jan Białostocki, she arguing in her "Studies in Mannerism" (1969) the "double nature" of mannerist works "taken from both Gothic and Antique art" (p. 134), and he positing "Two Types of International Mannerism: Italian and Northern" (1970). In his essay and his later book, *The Art of the Renaissance in Eastern Europe* (1976), Białostocki elaborated on a thesis, first proposed in his contribution to the Friedlaender festschrift (1965), that one can distinguish an international mannerism of Italian vintage and a decorative style with native roots, and both of these in turn contrast to a "vernacular" style that is noncourtly and nonclassical.

Perhaps in response to the cavalier manner with which some nonspecialists were tossing off musical examples, usually dissonant madrigals, in surveys of mannerism, musicologists now began to quicken the pace of their previously limited discussion of mannerism in music of the Renaissance.[55] Under the influence of the art historians, European scholars had made some attempts earlier to join the debate on behalf of music—for example, Hilmar Trede wrote his dissertation on mannerism in the madrigal in 1928 and Leo Schrade had published an article in 1934 on *maniera* in sixteenth-century composition. In America, Paul Henry Lang's *Music in Western Civilization,* published in 1941, spoke of Palestrina's spiritualism and related it to "the new idiom which the historians of art call 'manneristic' . . . and the spirit of the Counter-Reformation" (p. 34). But in the sixties, as articles by Helmut Hucke (1961), Maria R. Maniates (1966), and Don Harran (1969) suggest, there was a trend building that would reach a peak in the decade to come.

As a happy symmetry would have it, the decade of the seventies, like its predecessor, began with a scholarly gathering, in this instance a multidisciplinary symposium on "The Meaning of Mannerism" held in the fall of 1970 at Dartmouth College (papers published 1972). Two of the papers presented, Henri Zerner's and my own, dealt with the present status of the discussion of mannerism in art and literature. Though both papers expressed some dismay at the confusion created by contending views of mannerism, they both also sought, as Martz pointed out in an acute review of the published proceedings, to find some middle ground between anguished and stylish mannerism.[56] My effort to deal also with the specific problem of literary mannerism, recapitulated in the final section of this chapter, was matched by Zerner's insistence on "reading the texts"; but we diverged in the degree of our negative assessments of Shearman's ideas. Indeed, Zerner reacted so strongly to the historicism of Shearman's stylish mannerism that his own conclusions finally tipped the scales to anguished mannerism: "The rhetorical exaggeration, the emptiness of expressive poses, are playful on one level but also reveal an underlying unrest, an unadmitted torment" (p. 116). On Cellini's *Saltcellar:*

> The gold and enamel are festive; the extreme elaboration for so little salt and the iconography of Neptune in such a context are playful. But at the same time there is something extremely serious about the work, in the very expression of the faces, in the heroic nudes so strongly articulated. The violent contrasts of scale, particularly between the two female nudes (Amphitritis and the nude on top of the small arch of triumph), the ambiguity of the sea horses that have the liveliness of real sea horses but are in fact the decoration of Neptune's throne—all this creates tensions that exceed courtly entertainment and the charm of an ornate object. In the saltcellar, one of the most successful works of the time, amusement becomes a pretext and a mask for seriousness. In a reversal of relation, the mock-heroic turns into a very elevated kind of poetry, although the elevation of tone is ostensibly involuntary, essentially unrelated to, and at odds with, both the scale and the purpose of the work. (p. 118)

Contrast this to the comment on the same work of a recent critic, Mary Ann Caws, in her *The Eye in the Text: Essays on Perception, Mannerist to Modern* (1981), who writes that "the extravagance of the gesture and the material value of the ornament in relation to its modest dimensions stress the very gratuity of the object in its sensual and next-to-useless elegance" (p. 55). Between the notion of a useless elegance and Shearman's elegance as its own justification, Zerner proposes the mean of *serio-ludere,* though it is the *serio* that predominates. I will postpone my own opinion on the saltcellar until the essay on Cellini that follows, but suffice it to say here that the problem of how to "take" it is essentially the problem of mannerism itself.

Also at the symposium Samuel Y. Edgerton, Jr., related high style in public execution to the broader subject of mannerism in the arts. Acknowledging both Shearman's stylishness and that "some sort of malaise probably did exist in the collective subconscious of the sixteenth century" (p. 68), Edgerton argued that "an essential quality of *maniera* was the attempt of sheer style to make agreeable even the most unsavory of subjects, to make what was substantially ugly not only palatable but even inventively fascinating and beautiful" (p. 69).

Two other papers, by Claude V. Palisca and Thomas M. Greene dealt in different ways with rhetoric, the former taking up the influence of Quintilian's oratorical theory on music composition, the latter analyzing Maurice Scève's use of periphrasis. Greene's illuminating study itself made an important contribution to the cause he pleaded, the working out of a mannerist poetic so that the concept of mannerism might have "its own integrity and independence as a properly *literary* tool" (p. 25). Greene also recalled Curtius, Hatzfeld, Weise, and Hugo Friedrich in his attention to a rhetorical figure, but with a difference that proves once again how inadequate it can be simply to note the presence of figures without asking, as Greene notably does, how these formal commonplaces function in a particular poetic text.

It is clear that although the Dartmouth conference did not pronounce on the final meaning of mannerism, there were signs of a synthesis in the making. And despite separatist yearnings, there was a consensus that, even if the different arts had always to respect their individual formal natures and to require unique critical criteria, ultimately the working synthesis that would emerge from the debate over mannerism would be an interdisciplinary one, to the mutual benefit of future studies of Renaissance literature, art, and music. Naturally, each of the arts would have not only its own kind but also its own degree of, or share in, the mannerist style that all seemed to agree *is* enough of a reality in Renaissance culture (or enough of a necessity for the *disegno interno* or idea we have imagined in order to understand it) to justify continued use of the term and concept.

Progress toward the ideal just adumbrated would not be linear, however, as two publications from 1970 make painfully clear. In one, an article entitled "Genre and Style," Morris Weitz subjects the opinions of six writers on mannerism (Friedlaender, Dvorák, Venturi, Smyth, Shearman, Freedberg) to a pitiless logical analysis. While conceding several areas of agreement, Weitz points to such conflicts as the irreconcilability of Friedlaender's "spiritualization" and Smyth's "art of pose and gesture" to conclude that the term *mannerism* is "irreducibly vague," but beneficially so: "It is consequently simply not true that without a true or real definition of 'Mannerism' its history remains chaotic. Indeed, with such a definition—a complete set of necessary and sufficient criteria—there would be no continuing history of Mannerism" (p. 211). In sum, Weitz vindicates Gombrich's argument that terms like *mannerism* function only as useful hypotheses in art history—they are merely concepts of style, not style-concepts.

The other retrogressive publication of 1970 is Robert S. Jackson's *John Donne's Christian Vocation,* whose author admits early on that "in Shearman's eyes and the eyes of those like him, I shall be adding to the confusions and contradictions" (p. 6). Jackson's notion of mannerism as "any style of disjunction between a pair of polar opposites where the way between the poles is invisible or, if visible, is vague, strained, twisted, or contorted" (ibid.) is applicable to both the "strained communication" between the author and John Donne (p. 8), and between inner life and external expression (p. 39). For Jackson, mannerism is not "fundamentally an aesthetic style; it is a style of life, and in this style of life the literary or other arts may have a meaningful function" (p. 50). He goes on in the same place to assert that "I connect the term also with depth psychology and certain aspects of existentialism and phenomenology." As for Donne, he was a "mannerist man" (p. 54).

In that same year of 1970, two veterans returned to the wars, with Rensselaer W. Lee publishing an essay that included mannerist illustrations of Tasso *(Poetry in Painting)* and Mario Praz devoting one of his published Mellon lectures, *Mnemosyne: The Parallel between Literature and the Visual Arts* to Renaissance and mannerism ("Harmony and the Serpentine Line," pp. 79— 107). Praz, who had written earlier on Donne and mannerist painting (1964), accepted "tension and counterpoint" as the main features of mannerism, and the *linea serpentinata* as their most common formula (p. 92), the latter illustrated in Salviati, Bronzino, Vasari, as well as Donne ("the nervous dialectic of his impassioned mind"), Della Casa, John Lyly, and Sidney. In the following essay on the baroque and rococo, Praz did not fail to include Crashaw, whom he and many others had treated earlier as a prime baroque poet. But in an article published also in 1970, L. A. Jacobus found "tension, shock value, distortion, and psychological pressure" in Crashaw's "The Weeper," and thereby a mannerist mode in the poet's arsenal (p. 80).

A year later, in his *Painting in Italy, 1500—1600,* published in the Pelican History of Art series (1971), Freedberg outlined the shape of a synthesis for visual mannerism that, insofar as it has valuable implications for literary criticism as well, deserves generous quotation:

> There is no suddenly-marked distinction in Florentine and Roman painting between the style into which the first generation of Mannerists matured towards 1530 and the dominating style of the years that followed. . . . In different degrees—Pontormo most of all, Perino del Vaga least—the early Mannerists had been concerned with problems of emotion that were highly personal. Their expression, furthermore, carried—again in different degrees—the effect of dissent

from the canons of High Renaissance classicism. Their achievement of Maniera represented, as we have seen, a partial reconciliation with classicism, especially in vocabulary of form. For the next generation, maturing into a more stable, but also a more restrictive atmosphere, the Maniera formed by their predecessors was a visible novelty of artistic resource, but also one that seemed reintegrated with the authoritative classical tradition. What was difficult and private within its expression was set aside; what was agreeable and generalizable, formally explicit, and related to traditional authority could be sympathetically received by the younger generation. It was the ornamental attitude towards both form and feeling and the formal apparatus that was its vehicle which were, to this generation, the accessible and workable matter in the Maniera that the early Mannerists achieved. . . . The attitude of the high Maniera towards the possibilities of art is, by comparison, restrictive. It inherits more than it invents, and what it invents of its own lies in a rare and specialized province of the powers of art. . . . The forms of high Maniera seem, even more than in the antecedent phase, to be commentary on appearance rather than description of it. Smaller forms especially—drapery, hair, or anatomical details—are transmuted into fine-wrought ornament like jeweler's filigree. . . . The high Maniera image is, beyond its precedents, stylized and purposely artificial, yet it conveys its own kind of intense convincingness. The fine and insistent technique of a high Maniera picture, and the care taken with often seemingly indifferent detail, sharply affirm all but the substance of reality. Fragments of an unreal whole may be given with the precision and the plastic emphasis of *trompe l'oeil*. The existence of the whole, essentially abstracting as it may be, is asserted by the extreme truth of the fragments of it; we are baited with the small variety to swallow the whole poetic lie. (pp. 421–22)[57]

Some of these ecumenical ideas also echoed on the literary front during the early years of the decade.[58] In 1971, Marcel Raymond's introduction to his anthology *La Poésie française et le maniérisme* and Aldo Scaglione's essay on "Cinquecento Mannerism and the Uses of Petrarch" both attempt to sketch out a poetic fusing rhetorical, anguished, and stylish mannerism, applicable especially to the lyric yet related to figurative art. Raymond, whose essay confronting mannerism and baroque had appeared the year before, here pointed to some uniquely mannerist elements, as in the following: "La thématique devient fonction du style, tout comme dans les arts figuratifs. L'apparence, une certain brillance verbale, se fait passer pour la 'realité,' et elle y réussira d'autant mieux qu'un doute planera sur la valeur ontologique de celle-ci" (p. 29: "Theme becomes a function of style, just as in the figurative arts. Appearance, a certain verbal brilliance, passes itself off as reality, and it succeeds in doing so the more doubt hovers over the ontological value of the latter"). Scaglione proposes that mannerism is "a fundamental aestheticism which, short of art for art's sake, seeks refuge in an aristocratic, hermetically sealed, introspective world of refinements, away from a troubled and disappointing external world" (pp. 127–28). He then goes on in his discussion of mannerist formalism to instance Renaissance correlative verse, so thoroughly studied by Dámoso Alonso in our time and trailing both classical and medieval antecedents. Though a matter of lyric structure rather than rhetorical figuration, traditional patterning devices of this kind again raise the question of how to differentiate current from recurrent models.

Also belonging to the bountiful year 1971 are two studies, by Tibor Klaniczay and Georg Weise, that vividly illustrate the interpretive polarities that haunt the concept of mannerism. The Hungarian scholar's essay, "La Crise de la Renaissance et le maniérisme," places its author squarely in the camp of those who regard mannerism not as an autonomous period of art but as a transitional cultural manifestation of social discord: "La crise économique-social de la Renaissance et la naissance de la nouvelle societé baroque du féodalisme tardif ont été accompagnées d'une crise intellectuelle générale" (p. 275). Such intellectual currents of the time as Platonism, Hermeticism, and neo-Stoicism, Klaniczay says, point to the dilemma, and also explain why, unable to wander long in a labyrinth, Renaissance man returned to the neofeudal authority of the baroque (p. 308). These views have been well received and widely circulated abroad, witness the Italian version of "La Crise" published in 1973 (with an introduction by Scrivano), and Klaniczay's presentation to the 1976 conference on *Tiziano e il Manierismo* of a paper on "Teorici antiaristotelici del Manierismo" that proposes anti-Aristotelian criticism as another aspect of the intellectual crisis he had earlier linked to mannerism.

Georg Weise, in contrast, attempts in his 1971 book, *Il Manierismo: bilancio critico del problema stilistico,* to "balance" formal and ideological considerations. Long an advocate of stylistic scrutiny of verbal and visual texts, Weise here recapitulated and extended his previous differentiation of visual mannerism from other contemporary artistic styles by focusing on its continuation of late gothic stylization, especially antithetical gestures and movement of an abstract, decorative kind. A pioneer historian of the word *maniera* itself and its usage, as we have seen, Weise has not dealt solely with visual figurative style in his rhetorical studies. Thus in 1976 he would assemble in his *Manierismo e letteratura* a series of articles published between 1960 and 1976 on "abstract antitheses" and "conceited metaphor" in English and European Renaissance and baroque literature. Weise's range of European texts and authors—from the late medieval lyric to Góngora—is impressive, as is his command of a wide repertoire of visual examples. As one of the few veteran scholars of mannerism thus doubly armed, and despite his somewhat relentless and reductionist formalism, Weise has been influential enough that his writings themselves have been the subject of scrutiny by such critics of mannerism as Scrivano (1966) and Ulivi (1972), among others.

The sociological approach to mannerism of Antal, Hauser, Klaniczay, and others, whether heavily laced or lightly sprinkled with Marx and Freud, sometimes turns up during the decade of the seventies in combination with recent literary and communication theory that also has its own roots in phenomenology, linguistics, and psychology. For example, Amedeo Quondam has published several articles and books that exemplify this blend and also echo Weise's rhetorical emphasis, but in a very different key. In his contribution to the festschrift for Natalino Sapegno (1975), Quondam argued that mannerism is the experience of "difference" with respect to a codified norm, a closed literary system, so that the poet, faced with writing only literature on literature, of being repetitive, becomes alienated and obsessive, as in mannered Petrarchism. In the introductions to both parts of the anthology they edited, La *"locuzione artificiosa": teoria ed esperienza della lirica a Napoli nell'etá del manierismo* (1973), Quondam and Giulio Ferroni argue that whereas in other genres there were classical models and theory to adapt in the modern vernaculars, the Renaissance lyric model was the modern vernacular poet Petrarch, whom Bembo and others had made into a cultural ideal; and there was relatively little antagonistic classical or modern theory. As a result, the lyric became a closed norm, only to be repeated or varied by rhetorical artifice, or *elocutio* ("locuzione artificiosa"). The "divine supremacy of the medieval universe" was thus replaced by the "sacredness of the text," with all of the social and ideological implications that still obtain (pp. 17–18). Following Hauser and other crisis critics, Quondam asserts that the theory and practice of the lyric as a pastime and reinforcement of courtly culture in the Neapolitan milieu during "the Mannerist age" became an alienating "search for the *other* in the *same*" (p. 226). Since I take up some of these matters in my later chapters on Petrarchism, I need not pause here to comment on Quondam's provocative view of Petrarchism, but the reader should keep it in mind also as a challenging though negative interpretation of literary mannerism. Finally, we should note that Quondam has the distinction of having edited the first real "casebook" or collection of critical essays on the concept of literary mannerism (by Panofsky, Curtius, Sypher, Hauser, Haydn, Weise, Battisti, Scrivano, Ulivi, et al.) in his *Problemi del Manierismo,* published in 1975, the same year as his related critical study, *La parola nel laberinto,* also appeared.

As the studies of Weise and Quondam certainly prove, discussions of mannerism inevitably take rhetoric into account. In addition, thanks to the revival of rhetoric in the critical theory of our time following upon the work of Kenneth Burke, and the interest shown in it by several "new" new critics as well as veteran scholars, it is possible to go beyond tropes and figures to larger philosophical and psychological matters. Apart from *elocutio,* there are in the theory and practice of rhetoric such central concerns as the shaping and presentation of a persona and the psychology of audience response. Identity formation, the fashioning of a self, and the manipulation of various real and fictive audiences have figured importantly in recent studies by Richard Lanham (1976), W. J. Kennedy (1978), and Stephen Greenblatt (1973, 1980), which do not deal with mannerism per se but provide valuable insights for future analysis of texts in a rhetorical key. At the same time, Gérard Le Coat's *Rhetoric of the Arts, 1550–1650* (1975) reminds us of another more historical but fertile interdisciplinary approach involving traditional rhetoric as it was shared by the arts in the late Renaissance. Modern studies of the relations between verbal and corporeal rhetoric go back at least as far as Rensselaer W. Lee's *Ut Pictura Poesis* of 1940, but could now be pursued with fresh vigor because of the current interest in linguistic and semiotic gesture.

There were other unresolved issues from the past still haunting the writing on mannerism of the seventies, especially those involved with mannerism in the national literatures. In Hispanic studies, the decade began typically with Orozco Diaz's *Manierismo y barroco* (1970) and concluded appropriately with the reprinting of Durán's "Manierismo en Quevedo" (1980), thus symbolizing the continuing preoccupation of these and many other studies published in between with accommodating the two concepts to the literature of the Spanish Golden Age. Some notable examples include Enrique Rodriguez Cepeda's "Manierismo y barroco en el Siglo de Oro español" (1972), Douglas P. Hinkle's "Literary and Pictorial Mannerism in the Spanish Golden Age: A Question of Definitions" (1976), and David A. Kossoff's "Renacentista, manierista, barroco: definiciones y modelos para la literatura española" (1977). Kossoff's essay is especially provocative in its attempt to align the production of Spanish literature and art with the chronology and the stylistic stages of the contemporary Italian development, with a consequent focus on Spanish literary mannerism in such sixteenth-century figures as Garcilaso and Herrera. This revisionist approach, also exemplified by Cayentano J. Soccarás's 1977 study of Herrera (subtitled "el rompiniento del equilibrio renacentista"), will be retrospectively glanced at and then explored further by David H. Darst in his "Mannerism in Sixteenth-Century Spanish Literature" (1982). Though he adopts the stylistic criteria of Friedlaender and Smyth to the scrutiny of a specific literary genre and a single work—the pastoral novel and Montemayor's *Diana*—Darst asserts boldly that "the vast majority of Spanish literature written during the period from 1556 to 1598 can be considered truly Mannerist" (p. 89).

In French scholarship Montaigne remains a favorite crux, as indicated by Pierre Bonnet's "Montaigne, le maniérisme et le baroque" (1973), which began by reviewing the "état de la question" (pp. 45 ff.). As Bonnet notes, Montaigne had been claimed for mannerism by Sayce, Raymond, Hatzfeld, Jean Starobinski, and Michel Butor, among others; but although he rejected the label "baroque," Bonnet was not confident enough about the claims for Montaigne's "maniérisme" to accept these either. Thus he ends by doubting the utility of either term since neither "fits" the *Essais* (p. 58). Ruggero Campagnoli's "Su Jodelle e il manierismo" (1972) is significant, on the other hand, because of its deployment of the terminology of the *nouvelle critique*—he analyzes a dozen or so sonnets of Jodelle with a modish critical vocabulary ("ulteriority," "grade zero," "metastylistic," "stylemes," etc.) and asserts his preference for a mannerist over a baroque Montaigne because of its salutary emphasis upon formal elements (p. 22). Montaigne also was featured at the eleventh Stage International de Tours on the theme "Renaissance, Maniérisme, Baroque," whose papers were published in 1972. Among the participants, Sayce reviewed the problem of mannerism and periodization with some irony but was forced to conclude that he had not found the philosopher's stone: "Au lieu de tirer les choses au clair, comme je l'avais promis, j'ai l'impression d'avoir plutôt ajouté à la confusion" (p. 54). Yet he went on to argue in a second paper that Montaigne's "mobilisme," contradictions, and narcissism conform to a mannerist hypothesis, as does his interest in ingenious machines, fountains, and so on manifest in the *Journal de voyage* (p. 145). While approving the utility of Hocke's "labyrinth" image for the *Essais,* Sayce concluded that Montaigne is mannerist only in some senses but that the label cannot contain him (p. 150). Three years later Sem Dresden's article "Montaigne maniériste" (1975) also expressed doubts about Montaigne's relationship to an aesthetic that embodied attitudes to art and nature fundamentally different from those found in the *Essays*.

As for the poets, Terence Cave's essay "Ronsard's Mythological Universe," in the volume of essays he edited entitled *Ronsard the Poet* (1973), invoked the "traditions and fashions in the visual arts" (p. 159) to elucidate his theme. Enumerating the features of the world of plastic decoration within which the French court moved, particularly at Fontainebleau, Cave noted the characteristic multiplicity and profusion of elaborate décor in Ronsard's milieu and in his poetry, where it has a similar function of transposing reality "into an ideal realm in which tensions are resolved and destinies consecrated" (p. 175). Cave would return to his theme in his later study *The Cornucopian Text* (1979), in which he confronts *nouvelle critique* and sixteenth-century topoi and texts; but neither in the earlier essay nor in the later book does he choose to use or discuss the label and concept of mannerism; yet there is no doubt that what he has to say is crucial for understanding its French variety. And since a year later (1974), Monga was to claim Bellau as a mannerist, thus extending the previous scrutiny of the Pléiade, Cave's terminological puritanism was a welcome though brief respite from the continuing controversy.

In English literature, several essays of the 1970s attest to the endurance of Sypher's initial inquiry, though not necessarily his approach. Cyrus Hoy's "Jacobean Tragedy and the Mannerist Style" (1973) departed from the premise of a crisis of the Renaissance and its relationship to "the anti-classical movement" in sixteenth-century painting and Jacobean drama. Juxtaposing acute analyses of Italian paintings and the plays of Shakespeare, Jonson, and others, Hoy emphasizes "formal distortion," the mingling of different spheres of reality and levels of style, the "grotesque discontinuities" and "bizarre and somewhat equivocal effects" of his examples. In treating masques, he argues that the victory of Inigo Jones over Ben Jonson, of spectacle over text, "marks a clear stage in the decline of mannerism and the advent of the baroque" (p. 58). A few years later Michael Neill, citing Sypher and Hoy, focused on Ford's *Perkin Warbeck* and its mannerist art. Ford's self-consciousness and his "elevation of style as an absolute moral principle" (p. 118) are adduced in support of a thesis that there is a mannerist style in tragedy characterized by self-referentiality.

In a different vein, Gordon R. Smith's "Mannerist Frivolity and Shakespeare's *Venus and Adonis*" (1971) instanced several visual examples of mannerist opulence and parody of classical myth that parallel Shakespeare's and Marlowe's treatments. A. D. Cousins's "The Coming of Mannerism: The Later Ralegh and the Early Donne" (1979), while dealing with poetry rather than drama, took a quite different tack. Cousins began with the assertion that "The basic questions about literary mannerism in England still have no decisive answers: people cannot agree when it occurs, what characterizes it, or even whether it exists at all" (p. 86). Arguing that around the early 1590s "the High Renaissance styles, which crown the Tudor aesthetic evolving from Elyot to Hooker, begin gradually to be supplanted" (ibid.), Cousins asserts that this was countered by "unformulated private aesthetics" that have "clear points of contact with theories and forms typifying in Italian art the mannerist response to the High Renaissance styles" (ibid.). In Donne and Ralegh he stresses skepticism, "calculated uncertainties" (p. 94), paradox, virtuosity, "an aesthetic of disorder" (p. 100), outer form as an enactment of inner movement of the soul (p. 105), as in the *figura serpentinata* of Michelangelo and its theoretical justification by Lomazzo. In contrast, Jill L. Levenson's 1976 essay, "Shakespeare's *Troilus and Cressida* and the Monumental Tradition in Tapestries and Literature," took up realizations of the Trojan myth in the gothic and mannerist modes.

Murray Roston's *The Soul of Wit* (1975), though primarily on Donne, also deals with drama, denying, for example, that *Hamlet* and *Lear* are mannerist. For Roston, only *Antony and Cleopatra* qualifies, because it espouses the spiritual transcendence of reality, the dematerialization of the phenomenal world (p. 94), thus confirming what he regards as the essence of mannerism, especially in Donne—"a refined, sensitive spirituality" (p. 29). Indeed, Roston argues, the final impression of Donne's "progression" from the *Songs and Sonets,* "with their teasing undermining of Renaissance perspective and logic" to the "dedicated writing of his last years" (p. 218) is one of "deep conviction rather than (to use a well-worn phrase) of 'unresolved tension'" (p. 204). Other signs of conflict in the English arena include Ronald Huebert's study of Ford as baroque rather than mannerist (1977) and Alastair Fowler's *Conceitful Thought* (1975), which surprisingly associated Spenser's *Prothalamion* with mannerist poetry and visual art. On the other hand, Orgel and Strong's sumptuous *Inigo Jones: The Theatre of the Stuart Court* (1973) established beyond doubt the indebtedness of Jones to mannerism for his designs of scene and costume: "If one had to place Inigo Jones within the context of the development of Renaissance art, it would be as an exponent of the late Mannerist school stemming from Parmigianino" (1:35). And if there is any doubt that he is our most deft and insightful interpreter of English literary mannerism, Louis Martz's contribution to the York Tercentenary Lectures on Marvell, his "Marvell and Herrick: The Masks of Mannerism" (1978) both makes its case and shows how to do so. Employing a definition of mannerism that includes using but deviating from High Renaissance norms, instability of design (Pontormo's *Deposition* as a "universal masque of sorrow"), "sweet fluency of parts," Vasari's "most graceful grace" and the effect of "staged performance," Martz adduces visual works and parallel texts by the two poets to support his claims for their being mannerist. He is especially intrigued by the tension between religious feeling and polished elegance or intellectual control in

Hesperides and in poems like "A Drop of Dew" and "To His Coy Mistress" (pp. 202–07), and by the mannerist fusion of "mask" and "masque," or performance and disguise (p. 209).

A few other samplings of the fascination with mannerism during the 1970s that recapitulated or extended earlier themes include Ernesto Grassi's essay on the philosophic significance of mannerism ("the mania for ingenuity") in the 1971 volume *L'umanesimo e "la Follia"*, and Scrivano's article on mannerism and rhetoric (1979). Branimir Anzulovic's survey of the discussion of literary mannerism (1974) was followed by Robert N. Nicolich's "The Baroque Dilemma: Some Recent French Mannerist and Baroque Criticism"(1976), Victor E. Graham's "Aspects du maniérisme et du baroque en littérature" (1976), and Sem Dresden's "La Notion de manière au XVIe siècle et dans la poètique moderne" (1977), all four reviewing the concept and historiography of mannerism. The other three critics would have disagreed, however, with Nicolich's conclusion that "mannerism has already fared far better than the baroque" (p. 32) in establishing its meaning. And while one historian, R. J. W. Evans, included a chapter entitled "Prague Mannerism and the Magic Universe" in his *Rudolf II and His World* (1973), another, Hessel Midema, was undermining some key assumptions in his "On Mannerism and *maniera*" (1978–79). Writing in the Netherlands quarterly for the history of art, *Simiolus*, Miedema chided Smyth, Freedberg, and Shearman for not grasping that *maniera* did not denote an aesthetic ideal but "a working method" (p. 34) and that its purpose was not to achieve a stylistic ideal but the "optimum processing of information and the ultimate in unity and naturalness" (p. 37). Were it not for the modern prejudice against content, literary or verbal meaning, he argued, there would not be a misplaced emphasis on style in the theoreticians mentioned above.

The decade of the seventies also saw the emergence of a host of musicologists on the battlefield of controversy over mannerism. Armed with terms and concepts borrowed from the art and literature historians, and feeling somewhat left out, they had to contend with both their late arrival on the scene and the intractability of the notion of mannerism in its application to Renaissance music. As had often happened in the other disciplines, the issue was contested at an international gathering, in this instance the congress taking place in Rome's Academy of Saint Cecilia in October 1973 (acts published 1974). Despite its announced theme, "Mannerism in Art and Music," and its intended international scope, the debate was dominated by music history and by the "big guns" of American academic musicology in considerable though polite disagreement with each other. In the obligatory opening assessment of the category of mannerism in relation to music, Enrico Fubini pointed out that music had no classical past and no violent changes or developments in the sixteenth century comparable to the events in the other arts. And in the papers that followed, dealing with both the theory and the possible application of mannerism, these doubts were to come up again or to be brushed aside by those participants who chose to focus on concrete examples like the works of Palestrina or Gesualdo, among others, or on the madrigal, or on specific formal and stylistic elements. Glenn Watkins, referring to his earlier book on Gesualdo (1973) and its fourth chapter entitled "The Question of Mannerism," renewed his argument by comparison and contrast of specific compositions by Gesualdo and others (pp. 55–74). Lewis Lockwood, after reviewing the terms *mannerism* and *Renaissance,* opted for the latter, whereas Edward Lowinsky, in by far the longest and most detailed presentation, attempted and affirmed a definition drawn from art history. In Lowinsky's view, the tensions and strains of anguished or crisis mannerism are discernible in musical theory and texts, so that they share a "plaint over the lost dream of the Renaissance" (p. 178). In opposition to this Sypherean or Hauserean interpretation, James Haar's "Self-Consciousness about Style, Form and Genre in 16th Century Music" took a Shearmenesque stance; and Claude V. Palisca's "Towards an Intrinsically Musical Definition of Mannerism in the Sixteenth Century" tried to limit the meaning of the concept to forms of rhetorical expression in terms that recall Curtius's literary topoi and verbal ornamentation.

Another important interdisciplinary symposium took place in June of 1977 at the University of Canberra in Australia. This gathering of scholars to treat the topic "Mannerism and the Manneristic Configuration in the Creative and Performing Arts" has not been widely noticed by European and American specialists in literature and art. The explanation lies not with the remoteness of the site but with the fact that the papers were published in 1980 in the Australian journal *Miscellanea Musicologia,* even though only five of the total eleven deal with music. They deserve a better fate, as I hope the following summary will prove.

The first of the papers, by John Shearman, is about "The Galerie François Premier: A Case in Point" (pp. 1–16). Shearman's "case in point" refers to his familiar argument that mannerist artists did not rebel against their predecessors. Reconstructing the original plans and appearance of the gallery at Fontainebleau, he proposes that "Rosso's Galerie François Premier is more logical and less capricious than it appears at first sight" (p. 12), because later structural changes have obscured Rosso's quite "normal" plans for its decoration. Robert Smith then takes up "Mannerism and Modernism" (pp. 17–27) in an attempt to clarify this perplexing issue through what he calls a "genuinely comparative approach to causality" (p. 24). Mannerism in the sixteenth century shares with modernism a recourse to aesthetic abstraction and "a distancing from its ostensible content" (pp. 22—23), but similar causes do not produce similar styles in a crudely deterministic way. Nor do stylistic resemblances "necessarily involve correspondence of causal factors" (p. 26). Since both periods are preoccupied with style, there will be incidental resemblances, but the specific conditions prevailing in each period assure that mannerism does not "recur" or reemerge in modernism.

Richard Chaney's "The Problem of Mannerism in Sixteenth-Century French Literature" (pp. 28—48) begins with a review of recent approaches, with particular attention paid to Marcel Raymond's use of analogies drawn from rhetoric, then proposes three varieties of French mannerist poetry: the emotionally expressive (Jodelle, Sponde, La Ceppède, d'Aubigné, du Bartas); the rhetorically oriented and aesthetically self-sufficient type (exemplified by Desportes); and the self-protective, intellectual, and skeptical mode (Scève, Montaigne, Chassignet). Walter Veit's paper entitled "Mannerism and Rhetoric: Some Aspects of the History of the Concept in Literary Criticism" (pp. 49—65) explores nothing less than a whole tradition of opposing classical norm and mannerist degradation, "the cult of the disharmonic" (p. 52) from Aristotle to Curtius and Hocke. Michael Neill's "Styles of Greatness: The Hero in English Mannerist Drama" (pp. 66—83) has the more modest aim of showing how, in Shakespeare and his contemporaries, the "hero-as-actor" of Marlowe becomes the "actor-as-hero" (p. 69). Instancing Ford, Massinger, Cartwright, Beaumont and Fletcher, and Shakespeare (Antony and Cleopatra), Neill shows how their protagonists are "makers and denizens of their own self-sufficient realm of art" (p. 68). Livio Dobrez begins his "Mannerism and Baroque in English Literature" (pp. 84—96) by asserting that the term mannerism is here to stay because it is useful, then goes on to analyze Donne's "The Sun Rising" as representing "a major shift of sensibility in the history of English literature" (p. 88). Othello's speech from act 1, scene 3, beginning, "Her father loved me, oft invited me" is likened to Tintoretto's "melodramatic grandeur firmly erected on a basis of complex and surprising perspectives" (p. 92).

The first of the papers on music, Steven C. Whittington's "The Two Faces of Mannerism" (pp. 97—104), distinguishes between stylish and expressive mannerism, the latter associated with chromaticism, short note values, and abrupt contrasts of sonority or rhythm. For Whittington, the baroque was to resolve the ambiguity of the mannerist Janus (p. 103). Gordon A. Anderson focuses on "Mannerist Trends in the Music of the Late Thirteenth Century" (pp. 105—10) and Carol Williams, on "Two Examples of Mannerist Notation in the Late Fourteenth Century" (pp. 111–28), thus evoking Curtius's perennial mannerism and the centrality of figurative play. Anderson writes of "techniques of configurations . . . being used for their own sake and not as integral parts of the composition" (p. 107), and Williams refers to an oscillation between "preciosity of style" and classicism, and to "a showcase for intellectual games" (p. 111). Though concerned with a single composer, John Steele's "Marenzio—from Mannerist to Expressionist" (pp. 129–53) echoes the larger debate over mannerism in his favoring of Shearman's approach and his references to dissonance, chromaticism, homophonic declamation, and "polished but emotionally neutral music" (p. 131). Steele finds Marenzio to have been a mannerist in his middle period but argues that his later madrigals have an austere and serious gravity contrasting notably with the "cultivation of elegance" characteristic of the mannerist compositions (p. 133). Finally, Andrew D. McCredie's "Some Aspects of Late Cinquecento Musical Mannerism in Munich and Augsburg" (pp. 154–71) emphasizes the influence of Petrarchism, rhetorical theory, and a flourishing publishing trade in accounting for the travel north of the style. In referring to musical settings, he asserts that "the *disegno interno* of a text to be reproduced musically would correspond to the composer's interpretation of its rhetorical structure" (p. 166).

A year later still another symposium was held in Pennsylvania at the West Chester State College, with the papers published in 1980 as *Essays on Mannerism in Art and Music*. Here Watkins and Haar returned to the fray, with the former offering a "reconsideration" of Gesualdo as mannerist and the latter pursuing the idea of a musical *maniera,* with Malcolm Campbell's "Mannerism, Italian Style" and Thomas Da Costa Kaufmann's "The Problem of Northern Mannerism" balancing the slate from art history. This last essay was particularly notable for its "contractionist" argument and its skeptical attitude toward the reality of a Northern mannerism, not to mention its conclusion that the concept of mannerism is "a dark sun obscuring as much as it illuminates" (p. 107).

A year later, in 1979, there appeared Maria R. Maniates's provocative *Mannerism in Italian Music and Culture 1530–1630,* marking a return to the bold panoramic survey, but now with music as the central concern. Maniates argues, in ecumenical language, that "stylization can be facile virtuosity of both the elegant and tortured variety, or sincere intensity of both the graceful and dramatic type. *Maniera* or self-conscious stylization underlies all other qualitative values" (p. 34). Later, she avers that "during the mannerist period, music not only keeps pace with other developments, but also stands in the vanguard of stylistic trends" (p. 512). In order thus to have musical developments march along with the other arts, however, she must take her musical mannerism well into the seventeenth century, with the witty poetry of Marino and the later works of Monteverdi, beyond the usual sixteenth-century topics of the genre of the madrigal, chromaticism, dissonance, monody, and musical theory. The insistence on rhetorical wit, by which she assimilates Curtius to the harmony of mannerisms thus established, raises the inevitable dilemma of the distinction between mannerism and baroque.

Still another international gathering occurred in 1976—77, this time in Venice, and focused on the theme of "Titian and European Mannerism" (published in 1978 as *Tiziano e il manierismo europeo*). Sponsored by the Cini Foundation, this assemblage of some of the leading theoreticians of mannerism (Hocke, Ulivi, Klaniczay) lacked only the presence of Hauser, who had indeed been invited but was unable to attend. Of special interest were three of the papers presented: Jean Starobinski's "Montaigne et la polemique contre les apparences" (pp. 389—413), Klaniczay's discussion of the anti-Aristotelianism of the theorists of mannerism, already referred to above, and Hocke's "Aion e Chronos: L'espansione dell'imaginazione" (pp. 435—57). Hocke associates the "expansion of imagination" of his title with anticlassical mannerism of the sixteenth and twentieth centuries, symbolized for him by the liberating labyrinth, as we know from his earlier writings. As he admitted himself, the meeting signified for Hocke a return to the past, and indeed there was a retrospective tone in several of the presentations and perhaps, too, an unadmitted flagging of energy in defense of old positions.

In contrast, that same year of 1978 saw the publication of Paul Barolsky's *Infinite Jest, Wit and Humor in Italian Renaissance Art,* which incorporates an illustrated chapter on mannerist *Bizzarie* (pp. 101—57), a welcome relief from the solemnity with which the topic is usually debated and provocative in its suggestion that some of the works discussed by modern critics in such serious fashion were actually intended and taken as jeux d'esprit (including, for example, Rosso's *Madonna and Child with Saints* as well as Bronzino's celebrated *Allegory*).

We begin the last part of our survey of the 1970s with a contrast of the kind usually considered baroque rather than mannerist. On the one hand, there is continuing interest in mannerism on the part of exponents of a sometimes abstruse *nouvelle critique* (as the book mentioned earlier by Caws attests); on the other hand, there are indications everywhere of the spreading popularity and general knowledge of mannerism through various cultural productions. To the first category belong two examples from the late seventies: James Sacré's *Un Sang maniériste: étude structurale autour du mot "sang" dans la poésie lyrique française de la fin du seizième siècle* (1977), and Claude-Gilbert Dubois's *Le Maniérisme* (1979). Sacré's book examines the use of "sang" by Sponde, Ronsard, d'Aubigné, Desportes, Chassignet, and Théophile de Viau, with the help of tables, diagrams, and sets of binary opposites (interiority and exteriority, constancy and inconstancy, presence and absence), to reveal that four of the poets studied, but not Ronsard or Théophile, show mannerist "conflict permanent" (p. 161). Dubois's study, though not bristling with Sacré's technical linguistic and semantic terms, is equally lavish with illustrative material, in this case diagrams of pyramids, faces, and hands. These serve Dubois's argument that mannerist works should be described not as products of an aesthetic but of a "mode of production" (p. 9), according to the theory of "morphogenèse" of René Thom. On the basis of what is alleged to be a more scientific analysis than hitherto, mannerism is said to be a "dynamic creator of forms" because of psychic energy released by subversive allegiance to the model or parent (p. 11). Dubois's biological and psychological approach is saved from debilitating abstraction and dense terminological strangulation by his focus upon individual motifs: "La manière et la main" (pp. 16–18), for example, takes up the topos that is the subject of my fourth chapter. Elsewhere, however, in his zeal to see mannerism as "cet art de cultiver les variations et les différences" (p. 57) and in universal terms, he can state that "Les dandies, les jazous, les beats, les punks sont a leur façon des maniéristes: ils veulent attirer l'attention par l'excès ou par l'écart: appâter et épater" (p. 22).

Of the more certain popular manifestations of a widespread interest in mannerism there are exhibitions such as the elaborate Parisian one on the School of Fontainebleau in 1972–73, as well as an outpouring of art books—introductory histories of Renaissance and mannerist art or mannerism alone—all richly illustrated, of course. Indeed, some individual mannerist works, especially paintings, have become as well known as the High Renaissance and masterpieces of Leonardo and Raphael. John Ashbery's collection of poems and his title poem (1975) reinforced the fame of Parmigianino's *Self-Portrait in a Convex Mirror;* and the summer 1973 issue of *Horizon* magazine, containing an introductory article on mannerism by J. H. Elliott, bore on its cover, in color, the enigmatic portrait of Lucrezia Panciaticchi by Bronzino. That artist's famous *Allegory,* already a central symbol in Iris Murdoch's *The Nice and the Good,* gained greater visual circulation by its inclusion in Lina Wertmüller's film *Seven Beauties* (1977), where it is seen leaning against the wall of the prison commandant's office, a silent witness to the sexual consummation that occurs there between bulky commandant and scrawny prisoner, its cool, polished eroticism in stark counterpoint to the grotesque overflowing physicality it observes.

To the decade of the seventies belongs also the publication of the facsimile edition of *The Farnese Hours* of Giulio Clovio, a stunning masterpiece of its kind that can serve as an index to the motifs and forms of visual mannerism—and a work of publishing art that made all those who received it as a Christmas present instant Renaissance aristocrats and patrons of mannerist art! Here was further proof that the popular dissemination of mannerist images via exhibition and book was continuing alongside scholarly study and critical exegesis. When one takes into account both the popular and scholarly manifestations, and adds the doctoral dissertations written and the courses offered in the academic environment, it is no wonder that the Studing and Kruz bibliography of multidisciplinary mannerism (1979) ran to well over sixty pages.[59] Such intense interest and energetic activity argue that any future history of our century's culture will have to come to terms with the spell our subject has cast over us for the past fifty years, with no sign that its fascination is waning. And since expressionism and surrealism in the arts have been succeeded by abstract and neorealist movements since World War II, it will not suffice to say that current interest in mannerism still reflects the mood of the early twentieth century. Indeed, when one considers that mannerism has been analyzed in terms of both its tendency to abstraction and its realism of detail, as well as its emotional expressivity, one answer the future cultural historian may give to the question of why mannerism has had a grip on us is that, if it has not directly inspired, it has at least curiously confirmed the succession of styles in the arts that has marked our century thus far. Certainly several recent neorealist works of painting or sculpture that have borne such labels as super realism, photo realism, magic realism, and stylish realism remind one of mannerism in their fidelity to the texture of flesh and cloth, and in their "cool" detachment. Thus, whereas mannerism may once have appealed to our sense of anxiety, its continued attractiveness may well be based upon our renewed hunger for the representation of the posed human figure and our predilection for the cool and detached attitude or stance that may or may not conceal underlying strain or torment. Although I have in mind certain specific portraits by Chuck Close and Alfred Leslie, and some sculptures of the seventies by John De Andrea and Duane Hanson, many other specimens of the new realism could be invoked as apposite evidence.

Nor have the first years of the present decade given any sign that the enthusiasm for our subject is waning, as the following sampling will attest. If the decade may be said to begin in 1980, there is Michael O'Regan's *The Mannerist Aesthetic: A Study of Racine's "Mithridate,"* which attempts to rehabilitate that controversial play by analyzing its allegedly mannerist features. These include duality, juxtaposition rather than unity, addition rather than subordination, distortion, shifting perspectives, frustrated expectation, a rich variety of attitudinizing, extravagant posturing—all found in Parmigianino, Bellange, the *figura serpentinata,* and so on. While refusing thereby to label Racine a mannerist ("The question is unanswerable, even meaningless"), O'Regan allows that, as "one of the available styles," mannerism as he defines it can occur in a single work in which the sole unity is a "concordance of disharmonies" (p. 88). And he concludes that "If the Mannerist aesthetic is seen as one of the formative elements in French classicism, and if the *Mithridate* in particular is considered with this in mind, much that seems strange in this rather neglected masterpiece falls into place" (ibid.). In contrast to this monographic and traditionalist approach there is Marc Bensimon's 1980 article entitled "La Porte étroite: essai sur le maniérisme (Le Greco, Saint Jean de la Croix, Sponde, Chassignet, d'Aubigné, Montaigne)" in a decidedly neo-Freudian mode. Departing from an analysis of El Greco's *Burial of Count Orgaz* with its tension between the temporal and spiritual realms, Bensimon goes on to explore in the painting and the authors of his title the necessary conflict between downward and upward movements, of birth and rebirth, and the narrow passageways that must be traversed in both cases, with a consequent blending of maternal and paternal roles. Thus a characteristic of mannerism is the affirmation of the self through ambivalent expression and gesture (p. 274).

In the following year (1981), Lucy Gent's *Picture and Poetry, 1560−1620,* dealt with English literature and art, including mannerism. Also, a collection of essays entitled *Monstres et prodiques au temps de la Renaissance* included a surprising treatment of Spenser's animals in the *Faerie Queene* as a "bestiaire maniériste." Guy Demerson's anthology of critical essays entitled *Poétique de la métamorphose: de Pétrarque à John Donne,* on the other hand, proved the continuing attraction of mannerist texts to the *nouvelle critique,* and in the instance of Betrand Schmidt's contribution, "La Métamorphose et les 'Objets de Madonna' " (pp. 81−94) on Petrarchist conceits, showed that it is possible to illuminate such texts without fretting over the conceptual problem. In art history, we have already noted David Summers's important study of Michelangelo's theory but not yet mentioned Joy Kenseth's revisionist article on "Bernini's Borghese Sculptures: Another View"—that other view being the argument that the most baroque of all artists so labeled may actually have intended those famous statues to be seen from the multiple viewpoints commonly associated with mannerist sculpture! In 1981 also, although in a sister discipline, another young scholar entered the lists when Yvonne Jehenson published her *The Golden World of the Pastoral,* which contrasted Renaissance Sidney and mannerist D'Urfé.

Some of the materials published in 1982 reveal some unexpected reversions to and revisions of the past. For example, Lance Donaldson-Evans recalled Sypher's book in the title of his essay "Two Stages of Renaissance Style: Mannerism and Baroque in French Poetry" but began with a sigh of relief that there was a lull in the by-now tedious discussion of French baroque. Nevertheless, he went on to propose a new periodization scheme, based upon a synthesis of Shearman's argument and the more recent delineation of the baroque by John R. Martin (1977), according to which mannerism would run from Marot to Desportes, or 1520 to 1580, and be understood as the stylistic norm that the Italian Renaissance exported beyond the Alps. The baroque would then begin around 1580, with certain figures (Sponde, d'Aubigné) situated on the borders. If nothing else, this was a scheme guaranteed to end the lull its author had earlier welcomed! There was also a curious and unexpected echoing of Curtius's perennial mannerism in Walter R. Johnson's excellent study, *The Idea of Lyric,* in which Vergil is referred to as a "young lyrical Mannerist" (p. 167). However, Johnson's emphasis is not upon verbal ornament but the response of the poet to his pastoral source, the eclogues of Theocritus, which he renounces in his own, although "as he grows older, he will partially accept and will then be able to adapt to his own *maniera*" (ibid.).

To 1982 belongs also the largely traditionalist but impressively comprehensive two-volume study completed in that year by the Danish scholar Esther Nyholm, written in Italian and bearing the title *Arte e teoria del Manierismo.* This major work surveys the whole subject, from sixteenth-century art and art theory to modern conceptual debates (her two volumes being topically divided into "ars naturans" and "idea"). In literary studies, there was other evidence, taking us into 1983, of both continuity and innovation in the work of young scholars. For one example, Martin Elsky's "John Donne's *La Corona:* Spatiality and Mannerist Painting" continues a line of interdisciplinary speculation on a familiar set of juxtaposed texts. Another is Richard Helgerson's *Self-Crowned Laureates,* a study based in semiotics that invokes the mannerist hypothesis to characterize the English Cavalier poets as a generation "in which the *sprezzatura* and *virtù* of that manual of mannerist behavior, *Il Cortegiano,* found at last their purest English manifestation" (p. 195). But he also finds the Milton of the 1645 *Poems* "as much a Mannerist as any of his cavalier coevals" in his pursuit of *maniera* and display of virtuosity as a feature of his self-presentation (p. 262). Helgerson's argument, drawing heavily upon Martz and Shearman, is both retrospective in its pursuit of a mannerist Milton and contemporary in its application of recent linguistic and sociological theory, reminding us again of the stubbornly persistent lure of the question of mannerism in

English and other literatures. Thus, another 1983 publication, *German Baroque Literature, The European Perspective,* a collection of essays by different scholars, opens with Gerald Gillespie's "Renaissance, Mannerism, Baroque," still another obligatory survey of the criticism (pp. 3—24).[60]

In 1982—83, an exhibition of the works of El Greco toured the nation and was everywhere received with an enthusiasm that must have owed something to the spreading popularization of our subject that we have already noted. In the academic world, the year 1983 also saw the return of S. J. Freedberg to a theme he had done so much to clarify when he published a lecture entitled *Circa 1600: A Revolution in Italian Painting.* Appropriately for him and for the conclusion of our survey, the study charted the end of mannerist painting in Italy and the coming of the baroque.

Having arrived at our own day, I would add finally that even at the level of mundane contemporary speech we still employ both *manner* and *style* in English usage, and sometimes even distinguish between them; and we still speak of good and bad *manners.* We hear both the primitive and complex meanings of *maniera,* or manner, in such expressions as "I can see Smith's hand in this operation," or "I'd give anything to have a work from his hand," which involve both the literal hand and the metaphorically extended notion of style. But we also hear the behavioral and artistic meanings in such criticism as "Smith's way of dressing and talking is terribly *mannered,*" or "Smith's latest painting is lacking in freshness; it is terribly *mannered,*" though we do not as readily accuse anyone or any work of having *too much style,* or of being *too stylish.* The closest we come to negative usage with style is our *stylized* or *stylization,* which imply the conventional, the self-conscious, the unnatural, even the quasi-parodic. However, our *mannered,* if we may trust current dictionaries and our own verbal experience, perhaps reflecting the hostile attitudes to mannerism that prevailed after the Renaissance and up to our own time, seems reserved for occasions or instances of excessive or peculiarly intense stylization, with thoroughly negative connotations. Thus, in addition to the insights into the culture of our own time which an awareness of mannerism may bring, there is also the bonus of increased sensitivity to the rich connotations of two of our handiest contemporary words.

Toward a Mannerist Poetics

A reader of the preceding account may well wonder with Thomas M. Greene whether "the pursuit of a mannerist literature is itself a mannerist enterprise—given to nervous self-questioning, abstraction, tension, and instability" (p. 25). Or, with Antonio Illiano, "fall back, with some relief, on the function of Mannerism as a useful concept, an instrument of research and a tool for the description and classification of artistic phenomena" (p. 164). For, as he adds, "as long as art history and literary history have a need for description and classification, the pursuit of these praiseworthy objectives will have to rely upon the use of instrumental concepts." Thus, in his view, the Dartmouth conference on "The Meaning of Mannerism" seems to have concluded that "it is better to have concepts—however elusive, misguiding, or tyrannical—than to have no concepts at all" (ibid.).

I have already argued above that we need not be discouraged by wrangles over terminology, since with some nudging on our part they tend to settle down into consensus. And I have implicitly and explicitly endorsed throughout my preceding discussion of the debate over mannerism the usefulness of the concept as an instrument of research, description, classification, and criticism. Yet this latter seems to me to be a desperately minimalist justification for the study of our subject, born out of an understandable frustration with what appears to be a hopeless confusion of opinion and theory. It should be enriched by another way of looking at the phenomenon I have just surveyed—by reference to the history of the concept of the baroque—that puts forward its more positive features. In favorite Renaissance terms, the *utile* or usefulness of the concept of mannerism should be supplemented by an awareness of its *dulce* or delightful rewards.

As the revival of the baroque has taught us, a fresh look at the past spurred by conceptual revisionism does promote the revival or revaluation of hitherto ignored or undervalued artists and works. In some instances—Pontormo, Donne, Monteverdi, Bernini—the artist's work has taken its rightful place among and enriched the company of the supreme exemplars of human creativity. At the same time, overly familiar artists and works may earn a new and fresh viewing or reading from us, to their and our benefit. Also, a concept that is multidisciplinary in scope and therefore encourages, nay requires, interdisciplinary or intermedia criticism, however risky, does compel us to put our own discipline within its largest context. At a time when we deplore excessively narrow specialization and lament the lack of communication between students of the same cultural period, we should welcome an opportunity to see it whole. Finally, let us not forget that many previous conceptual blueprints of the past, although apparently endangered by such concepts as baroque and mannerism, as though chaos would follow their dislodgement, were themselves never either adequate or stable. One has to think only of the obvious examples: Early, High, and Late Renaissance, Counter-Renaissance, Platonism, Petrarchism, Bembism, euphuism, Metaphysical, Marinism, Góngorism, preciosité, not to mention the various classicisms and anticlassicisms proposed by Ciceronianism and anti-Ciceronianism, the pure or mixed-genre-derived labels of pastoralism, the heroic, the tragicomic, the naturalistic. Disturbing as it may be to introduce new concepts either as additions or replacements, surely much of what was there before was no model of clarity or precision. And equally surely, the rewards I have mentioned above far outweigh the undoubted inconvenience of adjusting our received terminology and conceptual maps.

As to the special problem of literary mannerism, I believe our approach must be flexible enough simultaneously to sustain a dialogue with the visual and musical works of the time and to develop a particularly literary analysis and specifically literary criteria derived from scrutiny of carefully selected texts. Obviously we will have the other arts in mind, as Renaissance authors themselves did, but we are not bound to their sometimes schematically facile comparisons, just as we are not doomed to our own impressionistic intermedia generalizations. We can avoid these without ignoring the genuinely close relations between literature and the other arts in the sixteenth and seventeenth centuries. These include not only mutual inspiration and abundant cross-references, but also similar personal and professional frustrations and social obstacles. Indeed, to take one example I have had occasion to note earlier, literary and rhetorical theory enjoyed a primacy that stimulated budding artistic and musical theory, which then in turn fed back into its source. From the time of Vasari and his contemporaries and into the next century, an age of literary criticism, art theory and history are also abundant and also preoccupied with the "literary" problems of defining the essence and purpose of imaginative creation; imitation (of nature and other artists); the relationship to classical tradition; the role of nature and nurture in the creative process; the social role and obligations of the artist; and a host of generic, formal, and stylistic issues. What is more, critical discourse is conducted in the same formal ways, by dialogue and treatise, by juxtaposition of classical and contemporary works, and through comment upon and accumulation of authoritative critical sources. One should not be surprised, finally, to discover that actual literary and visual works of the time may be both fully or only partially explained by the generally abstract theory—and sometimes not at all, as when Sidney does not account for Shakespeare and Vasari does not satisfactorily explain Parmigianino.

Thus the pursuit of a literary mannerism must include among its assumptions that the specifically literary conclusions it may reach will bear some relationship to the other characteristic artistic products of Renaissance culture. There are, however, several additional, less ecumenical assumptions that should also guide critical activity. Mannerism in the visual arts is now a well-established phenomenon, and despite some continuing disagreement it has a definite enough physiognomy to claim status as an autonomous sixteenth-century style. Literary mannerism has not achieved, and may never achieve, such a status—or at least it has not yet been demonstrated to exist in the same substantial way. Hence, whatever the origins and fate, the motives and meaning, of visual mannerism, and whether it is regarded as a stage of, reaction to, or departure from Renaissance style, the student of literary mannerism should be prepared to find a different historical status or pattern of development as well as a different "formal" situation—my own use of *mode* rather than *style* is intended to embody this caution. I think it also advisable that we apply an Occamite razor to unwieldy notions of a universal mannerism, of an age of mannerism, of a mannerist soul or psychology, and even of mannerist authors and total output. The working assumption I would prefer is that there is a particular artistic sensibility that expresses itself in certain formal and stylistic ways, on occasion, and is therefore best sought in individual literary works as a modal variety of Renaissance literary style rather than a separate, autonomous phenomenon. As such, it may dominate a part of or a whole work and even appear in a series of poems or plays; but we had best assume that statements such as that Donne is a mannerist, or that Tasso's *Jerusalem Delivered* is mannerist, or that the Jacobean drama reveals a mannerist mentality, are at this stage of our understanding so frustratingly vague as to be almost meaningless.

As an art that comments upon art, that reveals rather than conceals art, mannerism is likely to be found, everyone seems to agree, whenever and wherever the Renaissance artist confronts the obligation to imitate both nature and art, and in the case of art, to contend with, to quote but not ape a predecessor whose achievement in a particular genre or form has been declared supreme or unsurpassable, or simply *the* norm. Characteristically, and in contrast to his baroque successor, the Renaissance creator may opt for the mannerist style or mode by preferring to dwell more intensely in the realm of art to innovating by pouring fresh pailfuls of experiential reality into the received artistic mold. This is why, for example, and again in contrast to the baroque, so much sixteenth-century love poetry courts mannerism by eschewing thematic expansion and settling for stylistic refinement or modulation, with the inevitable mixed results that range from the merely mannered and stylized to the more effective and appealing kind of mannerism we take up below. This is why, also, literary mannerism is so often sought in those literary phenomena, such as Petrarchism, where there is parodic juxtaposition to, even a parasitic dependence upon, a thematic and stylistic model. But as the negative implications of *parasitic* and the ironic overtone of *parodic* imply, there are several possible outcomes for such a creative situation, and the chances of sterile imitation are uncomfortably great. Hence it comes about, in the visual arts, for instance, that both the norms of a Raphael and the innovations of a Caravaggio will seem to cast the stylizations of a Pontormo and a Bronzino into bloodless shadow. And both the sober moral realism of a Spenser and the sensuous, visionary ecstasies of a Crashaw may move us more than the stylish amatory utterances and graceful formal gestures of much Elizabethan lyricism.

I would argue, following Freedberg's formulation and adapting it to the literary situation, that we can postulate three different results, or products of imitation, given the artistic sensibility and the creative obligation or dilemma posed above. First, there is the *mannered,* analogous to *di maniera* or *manierato,* which I would define as exploitation—rather than renovation—of the model or normative tradition. It exploits either by giving undue prominence to the model's superficial features, or by upsetting its fine balance through distortion or reversal of an essential feature, thematic or stylistic. An example of the latter would be the literalizing of a Petrarchan metaphor and its use, by extended conceit, as the witty subject or point of the whole poem, as in the exercises of a Serafino. Another example would be the image-by-image and argument-by-argument parody of counter-Petrarchism, as in the well-known poems by Berni, du Bellay, and Shakespeare.

A second possible outcome would be, whether in reaction to the first seen as abuse of the model, or as an activity justified on its own, a version of the model that echoes its purity of language, its polished form, its serious tone, its sententious statement, its total artistic finish. This is typical, of course, of the Bembist approach to Petrarchism. And it is no wonder that Shearman seizes upon it as a literary counterpart of visual stylishness, for like the art works he instances, this kind of Petrarchism is more than an opportunity for personal artistic expression and can mean more than a limited literary exercise. What with its social and linguistic as well as aesthetic implications—it being intended to purify not only the language but also the manners, and even the morals, of a cultivated society—it promotes a community of taste. I would propose that this kind of imitation is therefore *stylized* rather than *mannered,* what Shearman calls "stylish." It has *maniera* in the sense of elegance and refinement; but unlike the mannered or *manierato,* with which it shares a dependence upon a recognizable model or norm, it is not content with mere literary reminiscence, the titillation of recognition, or clever virtuoso display. Instead, it aims at an aesthetic existence of its own; its beauty is not merely a reminder of Petrarch and its author's skill in imitating him, but contributes to the aestheticization of personal and social life. Hence it may even pass as a significant gesture within a reform movement. Unlike the mannered, too, the imitation with *maniera* may or may not conceal or suppress beneath its polished surface anxiety or tension of a psychological or ideological sort. But one suspects that if strain is there, it is always difficult to find or prove because, precisely as in graceful social deportment, it was certainly not intended to show.

If it were possible at this late stage of the discussion, the term *mannerist* could profitably be reserved for only a third product of literary imitation, since it is the least *mannered* of all, does not depend exclusively on *maniera* for its effect, and out of the obligation to echo other art creates an important, if not always impressive, comment on the sensibility and creative dilemma involved in the mannerist mode itself. Because mannerist imitation so defined dwells completely in but can also talk about the realm of art, because the poet is totally absorbed in but also self-conscious about his creative situation, he can include complex perspectives and meanings, and even allow strain to show, whereas mannered or stylish works cannot. He may sacrifice some *maniera* to do so, but he is thereby less likely to create merely *di maniera*.

Finally, it may be said that the mannerist work as just briefly defined, and perhaps at its best, may *seem* to move wholly within an aesthetic world and apparently is determined to remain faithful to the norm or model; however, its way of defending or justifying both is to prove the paradoxical point that, when totally absorbed in art, one discovers that he is not roaming freely in an attractively autonomous realm but traveling along a path that opens onto nature again. That discovery may involve the realization, as Sidney's Astrophel is shown to grasp, that art will not suffice, precisely because it may be either awkwardly mannered or merely stylish. At its most interesting, it seems to me, the mannerist work is thoroughly of its own time in its risks of being *di maniera* and in its display of *maniera;* yet it can also speak to us about the universal dilemma that any artist faces when he comes to terms with, or pits his individual talent against, normative tradition and impinging external reality. But again, not every Renaissance work is thus engaged, either at the level of subject or theme, or in the local stylistic modulations and manipulations that constitute the formal expression of the theme. Not only is literary mannerism a mode of, rather than *a* or *the* Renaissance style, it is occasional rather than omnipresent, even within the literary kinds (autobiography, Petrarchan lyric, pastoral) I take up in the chapters that follow. It is one important way in which Renaissance literary creation responded to its underlying assumptions and demands in the larger context of an artistic culture that had social and political, as well as aesthetic, causes and aims.

These are, of course, generalizations that cry out for demonstration, but since they do embody the working principles as well as the conclusions of what follows, and since they respond in part to the discussion of mannerism I have surveyed, I have put them forward here and now, in the hope that the reader will not be so convinced by them as to concede their rightness in advance! I am aware, of course, that what I have just stated is the logical equivalent of a ride on a hermeneutic carousel—working principles chasing after texts to reach conclusions that turn out to validate the principles. Now some important scientific discoveries have apparently come about precisely that way, but it also seems to be inevitable in historical research that Gombrich's general theories and cherished particulars travel in tandem. In any event, it is not the ride on the carousel that counts but the number of rings—clarifications, insights, meanings—one can snatch as he goes round. Of these I hope the reader will find enough in the remaining pages of this book to justify the ride.

The Mannerisms of Benvenuto Cellini (1500—1571)

he plural in the above chapter title refers to the several ways in which Cellini's *Autobiography* is a crucial document in the study of visual and literary mannerism.[1] For one thing, he was an example of the double talent, a sculptor and goldsmith as well as an author. For another, he lived and created in exactly those decades during which Italian figurative and verbal mannerism came into existence and flourished. In addition, he was personally involved with mannerist artists and their patrons of both the first and second generations and toiled prominently in the centers of culture—Florence, Rome, Paris—where mannerism took root and bloomed into an international style. Indeed his introduction of Rosso, Giulio Romano, Primaticcio, and Vasari himself, among others, makes his book valuable for the historian who wishes to recreate the cultural milieu in which the artists of the time produced the mannerist masterpieces. Apart from their reflection of the contemporary world of art, his works and especially his book reveal an artistic sensibility that, despite or perhaps because of outrageous exaggeration and enormous egotistical inflation, is a precious index to the attitudes that underlie the mannerist style or mode.

There has not been much doubt that Cellini's works as sculptor and goldsmith are prime examples of visual mannerism.[2] As we have seen, the saltcellar for Francis I is likely to turn up in discussions of the concept, and most art historical surveys of mannerism will also include at least the *Perseus* and the *Nymph of Fontainebleau* from among his extant statues, medals, and decorative objects. But less attention has been paid to the *Autobiography*, not as a source book for the world of mannerism but as a literary work in the mannerist mode. One problem has certainly been the fact that it is written in an informal prose style that reveals oral dictation, hence cannot be classified according to either the rhetorical criteria of stylish mannerism or the tension-packed compression of anguished mannerism. If anything, its style, seen as a reflection of its author's "primitive" personality, continues to be praised, in nineteenth-century fashion, for its wonderful naiveté. And Benedetto Varchi is still praised for refusing to revise it out of worry that he might polish its rugged spontaneity into a correct and deadly stylishness.[3] However, Benvenuto's so-called naturalness is no less artful than that of Saint Teresa and Montaigne, and is no less a conscious deviation from the norms of formal prose, with similar literary concern to present a particular verbal image of the self. Thus, because his oral style does not qualify him as a stylish mannerist, and because its overflowing energy, which reflects his robust personality, cannot easily be argued to indicate unresolved tension and tormenting anxieties—unless one mechanically psychologizes its hyperbolic excessiveness—Cellini demonstrates the fragile nature of polar views of mannerism.

In analyzing the *Autobiography,* then, I propose to touch but not to dwell upon the fact that it is a crucial cultural document for the sociologist of mannerism. For I will emphasize that Cellini's is not only a great auto-biography but a fascinating exemplar of literary mannerism, both for its revelation of a Renaissance artistic sensibility and for the particularly liter-ary ways in which that sensibility expresses itself. Nor, I might add, is its literary mannerism unrelated to its effectiveness as autobiography.

Cellini reveals a mannerist sensibility in his fictionalizing of the world he lived in and of the role he played in that world, while baiting us into accepting the reality of both. He tries to convince us that he is reporting his milieu accurately by focusing on events that involved specific times—his life began with the sixteenth century and therefore runs parallel with it—well-known and therefore verifiable places, and the most important person-ages of the day. Even his frequent claim to report in detail only those events having to do with his professional activity supposedly guarantees, by its allegedly exclusive emphasis on artistic commissions and creations, that the *vita* will be a valuable sociological document cast in the form of memoirs. And by insisting in his inimitable voice that he is simply an honest man blessed by God with a great talent that insidious fate prevents him from exploiting and sharing with the world, Benvenuto almost persuades us that even if he exaggerates and distorts, this too is part of his personality, rendered directly and utterly without self-consciousness.

But in taking up the text and inquiring into its origins and aims, the reader soon discovers that matters are far more complex than our author would have us believe. For example, in his treatise on the goldsmith's art, he says at one point that because Duke Cosimo unaccountably turned against him, he was left without work to do and therefore began to write his vita and technical treatises: "Solo per giovare al mondo, e per esser lasciato da quello scioperato, veduto che m'è impedito di fare, essendo desideroso di render grazie a Dio in qualche modo dell'esser io nato uomo, da poi che m'è impedito il fare, cosí io mi son messo a dire" (Solely to be useful to the world and because it had left me unemployed, and since I was prevented from making, and being desirous of rendering thanks to God in some fashion for my having been created a man, and because I was prevented from making, I thus betook myself to saying).[4] This does indeed make practical sense as an explanation of why a busy and committed sculptor and goldsmith who is also pious would take time out to write or dictate his memoirs or set down the principles and techniques of his craft. In the sonnet preceding the autobiography, which begins "Questa mia Vita travagliata io scrivo" (I write this wretched Life of mine, p. 3), he also asserts the pious motive of thanking God but adds regretful awareness of the precious time lost in vanities (8–11), clearly in imitation of Petrarch's opening sonnet of the *Rime*. In the prefatory remarks to the actual vita, which explain how and why he came to initiate the task, he says that he began by writing himself but, finding it time-consuming and excessively vain, shifted to dictating while he worked, thereby combining the *fare* and the *dire* in a pleasurable way that increased the quality and tempo of his artistic production (pp. 3–4). Thereby he also convinced many future readers, who were swayed by the fact of oral dictation, that the result is a loose but fresh and spontaneous assemblage of reminiscences off the top of the head and from the tip of the tongue of a garrulously charming personality which comprised genius and roguishness, and was capable of both delicate aesthetic taste and the instinctive, unbridled violence of a ruffian. In short, here is Renaissance individualism with its most attractive and repulsive features curiously and fascinatingly combined.

In the prefatory remarks to the first book, however, Benvenuto goes on to give a different reason for writing or dictating his memoirs, thereby suggesting that however spontaneous, sparkling, and effervescent his chatter, it was filtered through or screened by a very present literary consciousness:

Tutti gli uomini d'ogni sorte, che hanno fatto qualche cosa che sia virtuosa, o sí veramente che le virtú somigli, doverieno, essendo veritieri e da bene, di lor propria mano descrivere la loro vita; ma non si doverrebbe cominciare una tal bella impresa prima che passato l'età de' quarant'anni. Avvedutomi d'una tal cosa, ora che io cammino sopra la mia età de'cinquantotto anni finiti, e sendo in Fiorenza patria mia, sovvenendomi di molte perversità che avvengano a chi vive; essendo con manco di esse perversità, che io sia mai stato insino a questa età, anzi mi pare di essere con maggior mio contento d'animo e di sanità di corpo che io sia mai stato per lo addietro; e ricordandomi di alcuni piacevoli beni e di alcuni innistimabili mali, li quali, volgendomi in drieto, mi spaventano di maraviglia che io sia arrivato insino a questa età de' 58 anni, con la quali tanto felicemente io, mediante la grazia di Dio, cammino innanzi.

Con tutto che quegli uomini che si sono affaticati con qualche poco di sentore di virtú, hanno dato cognizione di loro al mondo, quella solo doverria bastare, vedutosi essere uomo e conosciuto; ma perché egli è di necessità vivere innel modo che uno truova come gli atri vivono, però in questo modo ci si interviene un poco di boriosità di mondo, la quali ha piú diversi capi. Il primo si è far sapere agli altri, che l'uomo ha la linea sua da persone virtuose e antichissime. Io son chiamato Benvenuto Cellini, figliuolo di. . . . (pp. 7–8)

[All men of whatever sort who have done something that is worthy or truly similar to worthy things should, being truthful and of good disposition, describe their lives with their own hand; but one ought not to begin such a beautiful enterprise before passing the age of forty. Aware of this obligation, and now that I am traveling beyond my age of fifty-eight completed years, and being in my native Florence, calling to mind the many adversities that come to those who are alive, I find myself plagued by fewer such adversities than ever before up to my present age. Indeed, it seems to me that I am enjoying a greater contentment of soul and health of body than ever before in the past. And remembering some pleasurable good things and some inestimably evil ones that, looking back, shock me with wonder that I have arrived at this age of 58 years, and that I am able to bear them, and so happily, thanks to the grace of God, go forward.[5]

Although those men who have labored with some small sign of achievement have given notice of themselves to the world, and that should suffice, seeing themselves both men and recognized, nevertheless because it is necessary to live as one finds that others do, it comes about in this fashion that worldly vanity intervenes with us and manifests itself in several ways. The first is to let others know that one traces his lineage from ancient and worthy persons. I am Benvenuto Cellini, son of. . . .]

This remarkable preamble deserves careful scrutiny. The motifs of piety and humility persist but are forced to yield to the demands of the real world, the necessity of living as others do and letting others know. Paradoxically, to let others know violates humility but is the only way the grace of

God can be praised and demonstrated to those others. Another ideal, the Renaissance humanist insistence on the dignity and the potential for high achievement of man, is also trotted out to endorse the beautiful enterprise of describing one's life. The frustration of enforced leisure, the discomfort with saying rather than making, the pain at the continued malignity of fate in the form of his patron's gratuitous displeasure are here sublimated. What could be said to and understood by fellow craftsmen addressed in a technical treatise would not do for the larger audience envisioned for the vita.

What rises to the surface, then, is the obligation to undertake, in the fullness of age and experience, and for the sake of truth and goodness, the "beautiful enterprise." Benvenuto even claims that he has never felt better spiritually and physically, and so the time is ripe in every way. The reader who knows the facts of his turbulent life wonders whether our author is being giddily optimistic here, but of course he was not. For just as the word *beautiful* in the phrase *bella impresa* implies idealization of events, so the word *enterprise* tells us that Cellini, in thinking of the ripe time for beginning his narrative, was alluding to the ideal moment at which chivalric and amatory quests begin, here transposed to autobiographical recollection seen as a perilous journey through troubled times.

Even as he apologizes for the bragging that he is about to do, the proud "I am Benvenuto Cellini, son of . . . ," and the subsequent tracing of his lineage to a distinguished Roman captain Fiorino who settled in and may have given his name to Florence, fairly trumpet forth his real aims. Benvenuto must tell his story in order to proclaim the personal worth and notable achievements of a man endowed with unyielding moral character and prodigious artistic talent, and to defend both against the wicked slander that would besmirch them. To do so effectively, however, he must, reluctantly, have recourse to words, to saying, for the public medium of language and the persuasive literary forms it can take reach an audience which no product of "making" can hope to attract. In his world, a beautiful work made with the hands could silence detractors of an artist's talent but could not in and of itself justify or condone an antisocial mode of existence. As much as Cellini himself at times implies or has others suggest that artists are special creatures standing above the laws of man if not of God, he knows that a reputation for honesty, hard work, and just dealings—in sum, character—is as essential to lasting fame as the creation of masterpieces. Thus Pope Clement's remark, "Tuo padre è stato cosí virtuoso, buono e dabbene uomo, quanto nascessi mai, e tu punto non traligni" (your father was as talented, virtuous, and good a man as ever was born, and you have not degenerated from him in any way, p. 99) should be juxtaposed to the more famous words of Pope Paul: "Sappiate che gli uomini come Benvenuto, unici nella loro professione, non hanno da essere ubrigati alla legge" (You should know that men like Benvenuto, unique in their art, are not to be constrained by the law, p. 160).

Having thus, like Vasari in his biographies of the illustrious artists of the past, made the connection between talent and character, and, also like that contemporary chronicler of the art world, having stressed ancestry as a source from which character is in strong measure derived, Benvenuto could argue that he was not only a great artist but also a good man. Since the chief vehicle of slander throughout his life was evil words, spoken and believed, Benvenuto had to counter with words that prove what he was and what he did. His discomfort with the recourse to language persists, so that even the act of dictating rather than writing his memoirs is acceptable because it allowed him to continue working with his hands in an idealized blend of making and saying. And if he exaggerates, if he presents his background and mature life with the help of humanist ideology and historiography, myth and legend, lyric poetry, novella, and romance, it is no more than an appropriate response to the distortion of language employed by his enemies in their lying slanders. The beauty of his artworks and the "beautiful enterprise" of his narrated vita will silence them forever.

Having established his purposes and method, his Roman origins and the family tradition of martial prowess, Cellini proceeds to the more immediate past with his grandfather and father, in whom the inheritance of military valor begins to be infiltrated (or better, diluted) by knowledge and performance in architecture, music, and design (in actuality, engineering, instrument making, and jeweling). Though inflated, these reports of ancestral and paternal skills help to explain why Benvenuto is gifted with artistic talent, but also why, despite his duty as eldest son to pursue a craft, he would have preferred to be a soldier like his younger brother. Distinction in the arts does not erase the inherited violent temperament, the penchant for fighting that cannot be absorbed by artistic creation. Instead, the appetite for martial glory transforms not only his street brawls but also his execution of artworks into incidents of heroic action, as we shall see.

Even as a child, Benvenuto tells us, there were signs—omens and prodigies—that he was destined for greatness. After all, he was born on All Saints' Day in the year 1500, both his arrival and his sex were a happy surprise and therefore most welcome ("benvenuto"). At the age of three, he happily played, Hercules-like, with a scorpion; at the age of five, he saw the first salamander that anyone had ever seen; and soon he began to show precocious skill in playing the flute. Thereafter he fiercely resisted his father's passionate desire that he play the cursed flute as a profession. Indeed, he tells with relief how, at the age of fifteen, against his father's wishes, he put aside the flute and undertook apprenticeship in the less effeminate goldsmith's craft. A year later, he defended his younger brother with his sword in a street fight—against impossible odds of course (pp. 12–18). And this early episode involving his courage and skill in arms is only the first of several subsequent demonstrations of how he employed them in daring and heroic fashion, not excluding incidents of homicide that he shows to be justified, if not warranted. It would seem that the goldsmith's trade was a compromise between the life of a soldier and the playing of the flute, the latter a symbol from antiquity through the Renaissance of unpleasant performance because it required ugly distortion of the face, as Cellini would have known.[6]

Once having launched his career as goldsmith and jeweler, Benvenuto encountered another great frustration that underlies his narrative and explains its formal manipulation. This was not so much a matter of a career he could not follow professionally as a problem of status within the one he did choose. As we have seen, artists and their work were enjoying a new prestige, social acceptance, and even awed deference in Benvenuto's day. Yet within the arts themselves there were hierarchies, so poetry reigned over the figurative arts and painting was often held to be superior to sculpture in the *paragone,* or contest, between them, with sculpture much above jeweling and goldsmithing.[7] The latter was considered inferior, a mere craft, more suited to small, simultaneously utilitarian and decorative objects than to great works for public display. Hence Cellini had to contend, not only with his status as artist, which did not have the heroic glamour his society admired in its soldiers, but also with his low status within the artistic hierarchy. Since mental activity was considered superior to mere manual skill, as both poets and painters argued in extolling their respective crafts, making one's own designs was proof of artistic learning, talent, and stature; thus Benvenuto often insists that he is not merely a craftsman executing the ideas of others. Then, too, in competing with other artists and oneself, one had to compete with and surpass the *ancients* in order to be validated as a genuine artist for all time and not simply a transitory hack. The creation of a monumental sculpture like the *Perseus* was therefore both a proud reply to critics and a bid for eternal fame.

All of these motifs—affirmation of character and talent, frustration over choice of career and status, over the need to say as well as do, and the need for validating competition among and between the arts—appear in and give piquancy to the following three scenes:

Ancora m'aggiunse il Cardinale, insieme con quei dua sopra ditti, ch'io gli dovessi fare un modello d'una saliera; ma che arrebbe voluto uscir dell'ordinario di quei che avean fatte saliere. Messer Luigi [Alamanni], sopra questo, approposito di questo sale, disse molti mirabil cose; messer Gabbriello Cesano ancora lui in questo proposito disse cose bellissime. Il Cardinale, molto benigno ascoltatore e saddisfatto oltramodo delli disegni, che con parole aveano fatto questi dua gran virtuosi, voltosi a me disse—Benvenuto mio, il disegno di messer Luigi e quello di messer Gabbriello mi piacciono tanto, che io non saprei qual mi tòrre l'un de' dua; però a te rimetto, che l'hai a mettere in opera—. Allora io dissi—. . . 'l primo che io vi mostrerrò, Monsignor reverendissimo mio patrone, sarà mia opera e mia invenzione; perché molte cose sono belle da dire, che faccendole poi non s'accompagnano bene in opera—. E voltami a que'dua gran virtuosi, dissi—Voi avete detto e io farò—. (pp. 290–91)

[Then the Cardinal asked that in addition to the two works mentioned above I should make for him a model of a saltcellar, but that he would wish it to be different from the ordinary ones made hitherto. Messer Luigi [Alamanni] then improvised many marvelous things on the theme of this saltcellar; messer Gabbriello Cesano also said many beautiful things on this same subject. The Cardinal, a very attentive listener and extraordinarily satisfied with the verbal designs these two great virtuosi had made, turned to me and said: "My Benvenuto, the design of messer Luigi and that of messer Gabbriello please me so exceedingly that I would not know how to choose between them. Therefore I rely on you, who must execute it in a work." Then I said, ". . . the first I will show you, most reverend monsignor, my patron, will be my work and my invention; for many things are beautiful when rendered in words which, when they then have to be made cannot be well reproduced in a work." And turning to those two great virtuosi, I said: "You have said, and I shall make."]

In the second account, Michelangelo himself appears:

. . . e in mentre che io lo lavorava, venne Michelagnolo Buonarroti piú volte a vederlo; e perché io mi v'ero grandemente affaticato, l'atto della figura e la bravuria de l'animale molto diversa da tutti quelli che per insino allora avevano fatto tal cosa; ancora per esser quel modo del lavorare totalmente incognito a quel divino Michelagnolo, lodò tanto questa mia opera, che a me crebbe tanto l'animo di far bene, che fu cosa inistimabile. Ma perché io non avevo altra cosa che far se non legare gioie, che se bene questo ere il maggior guadagno che io potessi fare, non mi contentavo, perché desideravo fare opere d'altra virtú che legar gioie; . . . (p. 94)

[. . . and while I was working on it, Michelangelo Buonarroti came several times to see the work. And because I had labored greatly, the attitude of the figure and the ferocity of the animal were different from all such things done to that time. And also because that method of working was totally unknown to that divine Michelangelo, he praised this work of mine so much that the longing that grew in my soul to do well was incredible. But since I did not have anything else to do than to set jewels, though it was the work that brought me the most profit, I was not content with it, because I desired to do other works of a different worth from the setting of jewels; . . .]

And in the third instance, Pope Clement comments on a finished medal:

Era un giorno doppo desinare del mese di aprile, ed era un bel tempo: il Papa era in Belvedere. Giunto alla presenza di Sua Santità, li porsi in mano le medaglie insieme con li conii di acciaio. Presele, subito cognosciuto la gran forza di arte che era in esse, guardato messer Piero in viso, disse—Gli antichi non furno mai sí ben serviti di medaglie— (p. 154)

[It was a day in the month of April, after dinner, and the weather was pleasant; the pope was in the Belvedere. Arriving in the presence of His Holiness, I placed the medals along with the steel dies in his hands. Taking them, he quickly recognized the great power of art they displayed. Looking messer Pietro in the eye, he said: "The ancients were never served by such medals."]

Shortly afterward occurs the famous scene in which the dying Pope Clement, unable to see, fingers the reverse of the medal Cellini had just completed and sighs deeply (p. 156). Thanks to the reputation the medals had brought him, however, Cellini is confident that upon the death of this pope another will provide him with patronage and pehaps even greater rewards! The conjunction of reputation and reward, or as it usually occurs in the phrase *l'onore e l'utile* (of honor and profit), is one of his ideal goals; but it is also another of the paradoxes in Cellini's personality that the stated aims of his life conceal and his choice of words reveals.

What seems paradoxical to us, however, may not have been an unresolved tension or stress-ridden situation for Benvenuto and his world of art production. True, a work of art was evaluated and paid for in money, but the worth and the payment depended upon how beautiful it was, how much "power of art" it showed according to the opinion of experts. Pain and conflict arose over failure to provide promised preliminary funds for material and added help, over the length of time needed to complete the work, and over neglected or insufficient final payment. It seems to have been understood on all sides that this haggling was inevitable, just as it was understood that the monetary details of commissions were ordinarily left to subordinates and the artist to wrangle over, while the noble patron and the artist discussed mainly aesthetic matters of design and execution. In sum, art was both high culture and serious business.

There is nevertheless little doubt that Cellini harbored a great deal of bitterness as a result of his dealings with noble patrons and influential, interfering members of their entourages. But here, too, the autobiography—with its exposure of their gullibility, greed, duplicity, and faithlessness—provided a means of exposing and thereby avenging himself upon his enemies unequaled by any single work of figurative art. If there is an unresolved tension in the vita, it exists between this obviously fulfilled longing to get even and the loss of credibility that results from Benvenuto's presentation of the facts and of himself in a thoroughly prejudiced manner. He sees the world as divided sharply into the forces of good and evil, with no middle ground. And he is always in the right, always just, ever the innocent victim of wicked men and a pernicious fate. Granted, the *Vita* did not see publication until the early eighteenth century and did not become well known until the nineteenth, and it may have been suppressed because of its attacks on the character of the mighty. And granted, too, that in the treatise on goldsmithing cited earlier, Cellini explicitly says he once fearfully tore up and threw into the fire what had been written about his service to Duke Cosimo.[8] Still, the *Vita* is not a private diary; however much Benvenuto may have worried about its publication and the offense it might give, he proclaims it to be for the world to know, and writes or dictates his story in full consciousness of its intended wide audience, as we have seen.

There was a problem, more literary than social or psychological, that our author may not have successfully resolved. Simply put, it is that at the time Cellini did so, there was no real precedent for an artist who wanted to write his autobiography as heroic narrative. Earlier, Ghiberti and Lotto had written about themselves and the making of their works, it is true. But neither of them could offer him anything like the heroic model Cellini needed. Therefore, in order to present himself as artist and sculptor alongside those models of human virtù whom the Renaissance admired, he had to adapt to his self-portrait existing literary types that featured the warrior, the saint, the poet-lover, and even, at a lower social level, the clever bourgeois who outwits fate in many a Boccaccian novella, or the humble, Bible-reading, unchivalric Christian knight promoted by Erasmus and his followers.[9] Perhaps the only model Cellini did *not* follow was the recently arrived tale of the picaresque hero, despite a certain resemblance in the elements of meandering plot and confrontations with the law in crowded city streets.

Unlike other literary mannerists, then, Cellini is pioneering rather than imitating a literary genre or model. His literary mannerism; his sensibility and practice as a verbal creator, lie less in the manipulation of a norm than in the adaptation and fusion of several literary types in telling his story, and of his telling that story in such thoroughly literary terms. And just as the fictional worlds in which Renaissance heroes define themselves are very fragile—as Don Quixote and Sancho Panza can testify—so the world Cellini delineates as the real one of the sixteenth century, while consistently aestheticized in order to serve as the appropriate backdrop for his artistic exploits, frequently arouses suspicion both by its hyperbole and by its slippage into verisimilitude. That he does not succeed in convincing us that the backdrop and the exploits are either literally true or fully imagined is, of course, related to the very nature of the autobiographical genre. But it is also related to the typical mannerist contention between reality and art.

If Cellini's *Vita* does not juxtapose itself to a great model in the way, for example, Saint Teresa's *Vida* imitates Saint Augustine's *Confessions,* the same cannot be said for his visual works. There seems to be general agreement that these are not of the very first rank, that they are mannered, or at best possess *maniera*.[10] One reason is, as we have noted, the overwhelming presence of Michelangelo. Benvenuto is so obsessed with the typical mannerist dilemma of validating his talent with reference to an acknowledged master that he offers not only the scene quoted earlier but several others, equally suspicious, in which Michelangelo himself is said to have confirmed it.[11] We thus have an interesting split: there is Benvenuto the visual artist, who can achieve only a stylish mannerism, in part because he is preoccupied with the goal of outdoing others and himself within fixed aesthetic boundaries; and there is the literary artist, who can move beyond stylishness into the more complex and meaningful arena where the creative process and the relations of art world and real world are problematic, in part because he did not have a single literary model but several literary types that he could adapt rather than imitate fully.

Given what we have learned thus far of Cellini's aims and the motives that shaped his narrative, the crucial issues would seem to be the fictionalizing of his world and his self and the conviction it carries as such. In the remainder of this chapter, therefore, I would like to focus on these issues not only because of their relevance for his mannerism but also because they are essential to his achievement as an autobiographer.

After the establishment of his early character, and beginning with his first departure from Florence, Benvenuto tells a tale of three cities—Rome, Paris, Florence—in each of which he completes a climactic work that is an aesthetic triumph and a moral vindication. In Rome, as we have seen, it is the medals for Pope Clement; in Paris, it will be the saltcellar, although the *Nymph of Fontainebleau* relief and a few other sculptural projects of small and large scale were also completed. Back in Florence, the statue of Perseus, large-scale, monumental, for public display and admiration, is the master-piece that will validate and justify him for all time—even though he completed other works afterward, between the time when the autobiog-raphy breaks off with his departure for Pisa in 1562 and his death in 1571. He insists countless times that the facts of how he came to create these works is all that concerns him, though he may digress occasionally in order to encompass his character as well as his artistic performance:

> Con tutto che io esca alquanto della mia professione, volendo descri-vere la vita mia, mi sforza qualcuna di queste cotal cose non già minutamente descriverle, ma sí bene soccintamente accennarle. (p. 52)

> [Even though it means departing somewhat from my profession, since I want to describe my life, I am compelled to take up these things, not to describe them in detail but to allude to them briefly.]

> . . . voglio riserbare queste parole a parlare de l'arte mia, quale è quella che m'ha mosso a questo tale iscrivere; e in essa arò da dire pur troppo. (p. 53)

> [. . . I want to save these words to talk about my art, which is what has moved me to write this; and even then I have too much to say.]

> —O isciocconi, io sono un povero orefice, il quale servo chi mi paga, e voi mi fatte le baie come se io fussi un capo di parte. (p. 195)

> ["O you idiots, I am a poor goldsmith, who serves whoever pays me, and you jeer at me as though I were the head of a political faction.]

According to Benvenuto, the exclusive, amoral preoccupation with the world of art production, its rivalries and intrigues, afflicted even those well above him in station:

> Abbattessi ad essere fatto legato di Parma quel ditto cardinale Salviati,
> il quale aveva meco quel grande odio sopraditto. In Parma fu presso un
> certo orefice milanese falsatore di monete, il quali per nome si doman-
> dava Tobbia. Essendo giudicato alla forca e al fuoco, ne fu parlato al
> ditto Legato, messogli innanzi per gran valente uomo. Il ditto Car-
> dinale fece sopratenere la esequizione della giustizia, e scrisse a papa
> Clemente, dicendogli essergli capitato in nelle mano uno uomo il
> maggior del mondo della professione de l'oreficeria, e che di già gli era
> condennato alle forche e al fuoco, per esser lui falsario di monete; ma
> che questo uomo era simplice e buono, perché diceva . . . suo confes-
> soro aveva dato licenzia che le potessi fare. Di piú diceva—Se voi fate
> venire questo grande uomo a Roma, Vostra Santità sarà causa di
> abbassare quella alterigia del vostro Benvenuto, e sono certissimo che
> le opere di questo Tobbia vi piaceranno molto piú che quelle di
> Benvenuto—. Di modo che il Papa lo fece venire subito a Roma.
> (p. 130)

[It came about that this Cardinal Salviati, who had that great hatred
for me referred to above, was made legate of Parma. In Parma there
was seized a certain Milanese goldsmith, counterfeiter of money, who
bore the name Tobias. Sentenced to be hanged and burned, his cause
was pleaded to the Legate on the grounds that he was a very worthy
man. The said Cardinal had the execution of justice delayed and wrote
to Pope Clement, saying that there had fallen into his hands a man
who was the greatest in the world in the profession of goldsmithing,
that he had been condemned to be hanged and burned for counterfeit-
ing money but that he was a simple and good man, for he said . . . his
confessor had given him permission to do so. He said further: "If you
have this great man come to Rome, Your Holiness will have the means
to humble that arrogance of your Benvenuto, and I am certain that the
works of this Tobias will please you much more than those of Ben-
venuto." Hence the pope made him come to Rome quickly.]

The implication of this last quoted episode is startling: not only does
Benvenuto try to persuade us that he cares about little except his profession,
he also would have us believe that cardinals and popes had little else to do
than dabble amorally in the politics and economics of art production,
intriguing against him to boot. The sense of unreality, or at least distortion,
which such an episode arouses—as though it were a scenario for a poem by

Robert Browning—must be countered, however, by awareness that the interpenetration of art, business, and politics was often real and serious in those days. Witness the famous *Saltcellar of Francis I,* which we observe came to life as a design requested by the cardinal of Ferrara for an ingratiating gift he intended to give the French monarch, though eventually he failed to provide the resources and was forced to watch Cellini smoothly extracting them from the king himself. Because of its destination and cost, from the time of its creation as a design in wax until Benvenuto showed the finished work to the king, the making of the saltcellar was a political and economic as much as an artistic affair. Even when it was finished, after all the fuss, it was cheerfully used for the first time by Benvenuto and his cronies on his own supper table (pp. 356–57), the king having asked him to keep it until further instructions—that is, until he was able to reward him properly for it, there being at the moment a wartime shortage of money! Perhaps we need to take a closer look at this small but portentous object.

Cellini has left us three separate accounts of his work and its meaning, the first as a model (pp. 291–92), then again as a finished work (pp. 356–57), and a third time in his treatise on goldsmithing (pp. 1030–31). Since these differ from each other and from the final product in a few details, one needs to conflate the three passages and check them against its actual appearance in order to come up with a working, if not entirely satisfactory, description of the saltcellar.

It is oval in shape, measures only 10¼ by 13⅛ inches, and is made of gold and enamel. If we are to believe its creator, it embodies a *disegno interno,* or idea, that is nothing less than an elaborate mythological conceit of cosmic import. Because salt and pepper come from the sea and land, respectively, and these elements are crucial to the fertile economy of nature, Benvenuto extrapolates from them a decorative program by which a holder of condiments is turned into an exquisite and complex assemblage of symbolic images. Thus the sea and the land are represented by seated male and female nudes facing each other with legs intertwined, because sea and land do thus interpenetrate; and each has one leg bent and one extended to signify the high and level places of the earth. On his, the ocean side of the saltcellar, sea, or Neptune, holds a trident in one hand and some sea plant in the other; he sits upon a floating throne or, as Cellini describes it, "un nicchio marittimo, fatto in forma di trionfo, con i sua quattro cavagli marittimi, i quali erano cavalli dal mezzo innanzi e pesci dal mezzo indreto" (a sea shell, made in the shape of a triumphal car, with its four sea horses, which were half horses in front and half fish behind, *Trattato,* p. 1030). In

Benvenuto Cellini, *Saltcellar of Francis I*. Vienna, Kunsthistorisches Museum.

other words, the sea horses are both real *and* serve as decoration because they so position themselves about the sea vehicle they are towing; there is really no ambiguity, in Zerner's sense, in the fact that they seem alive but are actually the inert decoration of the throne (see above, p. 46). Beneath Neptune, on the sea-half of the saltcellar, several different marine creatures cavort in an enamelled sea. Finally, beside Neptune and under his sway is a ship for holding the salt, with incised depictions of battling sea monsters on its side.

Land, the female nude, sits opposite, with one hand holding her breast and the other stretched down grasping a cornucopia of leaves, fruit, and flowers at the side of a miniature Ionic temple made to hold the pepper. In actuality, this temple is really a triumphal arch, and other indications— Cellini's neglect to mention the miniature nude reclining on the top of the arch, the sustenance-motif of Land holding her breast, and his confusion about the right and left hands and what they are doing—suggest that he was merely recollecting the final product, or looking only at an eventually modified or different model or second version of it when he wrote his descriptions. In any event, in symmetrical fashion Land's side of the saltcellar emphasizes earthly fertility through the creatures and minerals located around and beneath her.

Benvenuto concludes his descriptions by referring to a black ebony base or block with only a tiny strip showing in effective contrast to the gold, and fitted out with ivory balls that allowed the saltcellar to be rolled around on the table. On a small bevel between the base and the platform for the main scene described above, he created niches for eight figures of gold and enamel in bold relief: Night, Day, Twilight, Dawn, and representations of the Four Winds or Seasons. The former figures echo, of course, the great sculptures of Michelangelo in the New Sacristy of San Lorenzo in Florence! No wonder the French king was stupefied and could not take his eyes from the saltcellar.[12]

There is a danger in reacting to the *Saltcellar of Francis I:* one may be tempted to take it either too seriously or not seriously enough. There is no doubt that the work is preposterous in the disparity between its size and function and its cosmic iconography; not only can you have the fecund universe at your fingertips, but you can also roll it playfully around the dinner table! Yet it will not do to see in the work a rescuing ironic or ambiguous meaning, a blend of amusement and seriousness. Both the work itself and Cellini's abundant chatter about it do not imply any kind of ironic amusement or witty undercurrents whatsoever, nor does anyone responding to it in Cellini's texts even hint otherwise. Although I believe we can "read" the saltcellar in any way that best explains it to us or gives it meaning for us,. I would argue in this instance that we should begin, and may have to be satisfied, with its meaning for Cellini and his time, if only to avoid the real risk of imposing on it more ponderous interpretations than its fragile nature can bear. For in these respects the saltcellar was also preposterous to its creator and his contemporaries: he challenged himself to do the impossible, and they responded flatly that it could not be done; he proudly asserted that no such thing had ever been done before, and they proclaimed it to be nothing less than a miracle.

Part of its miraculous achievement, of course, was precisely that it accomplished the impossible feat of saying so much in such small creative space, exquisite detail being, as we know, a crucial feature of stylish mannerism. As a *decorative* item—it was surely not intended for the actual, mundane uses of a condiment holder—and at the same time an intellectual treat and virtuoso performance of the goldsmith's craft, it has its raison d'être. Like other examples of the high *maniera,* it *is* elegantly, exquisitely, and impossibly beautiful, and Shearman is right to insist that we accept these values as such; but we must hesitate to say with him that this is all we know or need to know. For while we can believe that it is *not* reductive to see only the sheer beauty of an object, and that such objects should not be burdened with profound interpretations they cannot bear, we are not obliged to ignore the possibility that the sheer beauty may have been achieved at a price—namely, the integrity of the total work, its truth to itself rather than its formal unity and coherence—or that the exquisiteness and elegance may be of the surface, a matter of detail and finish rather than formal integration. For me, at least, there is also the problem of the mannered or *manierato* that lurks threateningly in all *maniera* works, and which I believe surfaces in Cellini's *Saltcellar.*

I base this opinion on three of its elements, the profusion of tiny visual detail, the density of symbolic allusion, and the quotation from other art, particularly the monumental sculpture of Michelangelo. The first two should be obvious objections, but it may be argued that the forces and products of nature can be appropriately rendered and symbolized at any scale and in any density because these permeate the universe at its grandest and most minute. But the quotations of Michelangelo are not art representing nature but art commenting on other art, turning in on itself and finding its referential reality within its own aesthetic realm. Nor is there any mannerist sense of the creative tension or dilemmas involved. Cellini wanted to quote his great model and to have viewers enjoy recognizing the imitation in small, the allusion to the times of the day being merely a gesture toward the integrity of his cosmic theme. Were it not for this disturbing *manierato,* we might well accept the saltcellar for its *maniera,* contemplating it as its two protagonists, the figures of Land and Sea, contemplate each other across its length, lone and silent rulers of a self-enclosed miniature universe.

In more practical terms, the saltcellar certainly fulfilled its creator's sacred dual goals of *honor* and *profit,* but under the circumstances it was destined to be seen and admired by few; hence the zest with which Cellini turns to the new medium of the printed word and proudly describes it, in the treatise on goldsmithing, for his fellow craftsmen and, in the autobiography, for the larger world of patrons, connoisseurs, and consumers of art. As we return now to the *Vita* in the last part of this chapter to focus upon Benvenuto's literary projections of himself as lover, warrior, and saint, we will find that the making of the saltcellar and his other visual creations is not finally a separate activity of "the artist," but rather that he utilizes the established modes of heroic action in order to blend them into and initiate a new tradition of artistic heroism.

We begin with Cellini as lover because this was the most complex and problematic of his self-dramatizations. We know that he eventually married and that he had an assortment of some eight legitimate and illegitimate children. In the autobiography, however, there are only a few brief and, with one exception, quite detached references to children, and no evidence that he loved anyone with the intensity of devotion he gave to his art.[13] Perhaps in response to occasional charges or slanderous remarks alleging unnatural sexual behavior with apprentices or models,[14] he takes great care to present himself as a robust heterosexual by narrating incidents of gratified lust and utter indifference to sexual partners who are said to be desperately enamored of him. Early in his story, when he tells about the escapades of a brilliant gathering of artists in Rome, he unfolds with deft narrative skill the novella-plot centering on the beautiful boy Diego (pp. 62−66), whose head was "more beautifully shaped than the ancient one of Antinous" (p. 63). Adorning him with his art, Benvenuto transforms him into a stunning female beauty who is able to fool the dinner party into believing that he is our author's companion, until gross physical proof exposes the fraud. In its typically Renaissance feeling about male beauty, its invocation of classical precedent, the motif of transvestism and sexual ambiguity, and finally the contrast between the power of artful deception and the disillusion of exposed reality, the episode is a crucial one in that it reveals the intertwining of the erotic and the aesthetic in Benvenuto's sensibility.

At another point in his story, Benvenuto recounts that, prompted by his youthful age of twenty-nine, he took on as a servant "una giovane di molta bellissima forma e grazia, questa tale io me ne servivo per ritrarla, a proposito per l'arte mia: ancora mi compiaceva all giovinezza mia del diletto carnale" (a young woman of beautiful and graceful form, so that I was able to make use of her as a model for the purposes of my art: also she satisfied my youthful desires for carnal pleasure, p. 117). One can perhaps make too much of the cool tone here, not to mention the order of value the young woman—and others who succeed her—has for him, but it is typical of Benvenuto's priorities. In another place, he says about his tempestuous and passionate affair with a Sicilian girl who had been taken from him: "per essere invaghito tanto innella medaglia, io non mi ricordavo piú né di Angelica né di null'altra cotal cosa, ma tutto ero intento a quella mia opera" (because I was so enamoured of my medal, I no longer remembered Angelica or anything else, for I was completely absorbed in that work of mine, p. 145). For Cellini it seems there was urgent physical gratification at one extreme and complete devotion to art at the other, with little or nothing in between. For him the work of art is the master/mistress of his artist's soul, the equivalent of the Petrarchan beloved whom one serves totally as inspiration and ideal; and every creator of masterpieces must be and, if successful, has been, a lover in this sense. Never mind that the by-product of such devotion will be profit as well as honor. Never mind either that, unlike the love poet who struggles to sublimate physical desire, Benvenuto insists that love is simply a physical need, like eating, that must be met as safely, cheaply, and conveniently as possible so that the artist can get on with his truly important business! Hence for him venereal disease is not moral retribution but a stupid, if inevitable, mistake that costs him in interrupted work (p. 129).

In contrast, Cellini's self-dramatization as warrior is quite straightforward: he usually depicts his soldierly deeds as artistic performances—a deftly delivered thrust of the knife into the body of an enemy, followed by swift and safe escape, is a feat of artistic proportions, a beautiful deed previously unheard of in the annals of glorious homicide.[15] On the other hand, the creation of a work of art incomparable in its display of bravura craft and its overcoming of previously insoluble artistic problems marks a new stage in the human achievement of beautiful art, surpassing even the ancients.[16] The motive, as we have seen, is clear enough: the rejection of music, the appetite for soldiering revealed in dress and in street brawls and homicides, the instant offense taken and the swaggering threats, the violence and brutality of his revenge on those who would sully his honor or threaten his profit—all reveal not so much the quirks of one who is essentially a confident and committed artist as the frustrated responses of one who is not sure that his profession is recognizably heroic enough.

Apart from some street fighting, Benvenuto's first full-scale display of martial prowess came during the Sack of Rome, when he claims to have killed both the constable of Bourbon and the prince of Orange, slaughtered a great many of the enemy, and saved the Castel Sant'Angelo through his direction of the artillery from its highest point: "Io, che tal volta più era inclinato a questa professione che a quella che io tenevo per mia, la facevo tanto volontieri, che la mia veniva fatta meglio che la ditta" (I, being sometimes more attracted to this profession than my own, did so willingly, and therefore did better at it, p. 79).[17] At one point he shot and killed a Spanish officer in the presence of the pope, who was observing the siege with him from the castle's keep. His falconet shot, striking the soldier's sword worn across the front of his body, actually cut him in two! Pope Clement, who, like us, was startled by this deed, "ne prese assai piacere e maraviglia" (derived a good deal of pleasure and wonder from it, p. 84), then absolved Benvenuto of this and any other homicides that he might commit in defense of the church. Our multitalented author next tells us that he exercised his other profession by removing from their settings and melting down papal jewels and gold—thus saving both the church and its treasure!

Here, in contrast, are some apposite quotations illustrating Benvenuto's martial conception of his "other profession" as competitive duel:

. . . per esser venuto in Roma un certo maestro Giovanni da Castel Bolognese, molto valentuomo per fare medaglie di quella sorte che io facevo, in acciaio, e che non desideravo altro al mondo che di fare a gara con questo valentuomo, e uscire al mondo adosso con una tale impresa, per la quale io sperava con tal virtú, e non con la spada, ammazzare quelli parecchi mia nemici. (pp. 144–45)

[. . . since there had arrived in Rome a certain master John of Castel Bolognese, a man very talented in making the kind of medals I made, in steel, I wished nothing else in the world other than to compete with this talented man, and assault the world with an enterprise such that I hoped would enable me, not with the sword but with my talent, to slaughter my many enemies.]

. . . il detto diamante era il piú difficile che mai né prima né poi mi sia venuto innanzi, e quella tinta di Miliano era virtuosamente fatta; però la non mi sbigottí ancora. Io, auzzato i mia ferruzzi dello ingegno, feci tanto che io non tanto raggiugnerla, ma la passai assai bene. Dipoi, conosciuto che io avevo vinto lui, andai cercando di

vincer me, e con nuovi modi feci una tinta che era meglio di quella che
io avevo fatto, di gran lunga. (p. 201)

[the said diamond was the most difficult that has come to my atten-
tion before or since, and the tint of Miliano's was brilliantly made; but
that did not frighten me. Sharpening my wits, I did such that I not
only equaled but surpassed him by good measure. Then, knowing that
I had conquered him, I set out to beat myself, and with new tech-
niques accomplished a tint that was better than the one I had made,
and by far.]

The tension in Benvenuto's life between warrior instincts and artistic
activity is but one instance of a widespread Renaissance preoccupation with
the juxtaposition and reconciliation of arms and letters, the sword and the
pen. No mere debating topos, it appeared prominently in the works of
Castiglione, Machiavelli, Rabelais, Montaigne, Shakespeare, and Cer-
vantes, among many others, because it presented these authors and their
time with a supposed ideal that was in fact an awkward choice. Although
the physical skills of the new "art" of sculpture and goldsmithing would
seem to make it lean toward arms, the necessary emphasis on the mental
effort also involved pushed it into the arena of letters. Benvenuto's desire to
have it both ways, to be a fighting artist and an artistic fighter, was another
idealistic solution that in actuality often came down to painful choice or,
because of unwillingness or inability to choose, punishing consequences.
But there was another heroic ideal available to Cellini and his society, one
even held to be above the others, though most difficult of all to attain
because it required cooperation from God as well as individual character and
aptitude. I refer, of course, to the saint, whether as passive martyr or
Christian warrior, visionary mystic or militant activist on behalf of the
church. Although he might have chosen this as his final synthesizing role,
Cellini preferred instead to draw upon this tradition of Christian heroism to
add still another dimension to his composite self-portrait, complicating and
inflating it even more, so that we must also take into account his fictionaliz-
ing of the artist as saint.

The best guarantee we have of the sincerity of Benvenuto's piety is the
recurrence in the autobiography of countless expressions and many incidents
that show him to be keenly aware of supernatural influences. Whether
grossly superstitious or loftily spiritual, his attitudes toward these forces are
always couched in terms of genuine fear and respect. He cannot make up his
mind, of course, whether "the stars not only influence but compel us"
(p. 34) or God "keeps account of good and evil, and gives to each what he
deserves" (p. 76). And he dabbles in the art of necromancy, requesting evil

spirits raised through incantation in the Colosseum to unite him with his Angelica (pp. 140–41). But he never doubts that, because of his faith, God has inspired him in his art and has kept watch over his affairs, and will continue to do both.

The great test of faith Cellini does endure begins with his imprisonment in 1537 on charges of filching papal jewels during the Sack of Rome. This fantastic episode reads like a saint's legend (pp. 225–85). The protagonist at first attempts to escape (too soon?) from his prison and a mad castellan, with miraculously successful results; then, finding himself again incarcerated and nursing a broken leg, on the day after the feast of Corpus Christi in 1539 he decides to trust in his God and die—unjustly, like his Savior, even forgiving the church for its ungrateful treatment of him! His life again being spared, his sufferings increase until he contemplates suicide, especially when he can no longer read his Bible at night; but before he can take his life he is lifted up and hurled away from danger by a mysterious force. He then experiences a vision in which an angelic being urges hope of salvation, after which he prays, sings psalms, reads his Bible, and composes dialogues between body and soul and other poems, when not worshiping before certain sacred images he has drawn with a piece of charcoal on his prison wall. After further conversations with his guardian angel and God, and another narrow escape from execution, he prays to Christ for a glimpse of the sun and vows to visit the Holy Sepulchre in return.[18]

Miracles and wonders now begin to multiply. The angel, playing Virgil to his Dante, offers him a brief tour of the afterlife and a stupendous vision of the sun as Christ crucified, then as the Madonna and Child—both, like the aforementioned sketches on his cell wall, chief subjects of religious art in his day. Finally, after his release, Benvenuto tells us that he experienced "the greatest thing that has ever happened to any man" (p. 279), for from the time of his prison vision to the present, it has pleased God that a marvelous brightness, a kind of glory or halo, can be seen above his head—though only by those he wants to see it, and which, in accord with the theological dictum that grace does not alter nature, is visible only at certain times of the day and under certain weather conditions—hence one can see it more clearly in France, where there is more mist, than in Italy!

Thus concludes Benvenuto's account of his suffering and salvation, the favors his Lord has shown him as one of His elect. The allusions to Dante, the Bible, and other religious texts, as well as the pious iconography, can be read literally, of course, as an inevitable, confused outpouring of the contents of Cellini's mind under extreme physical and mental stress; but it is more pertinent to our analysis to realize that in dictating what happened many years later, it is Cellini the author who is recalling those events and shaping them according to a literary tradition of hagiography that he must rely on to give them artistic coherence and meaning in and of themselves and also in relation to his entire story. The pattern of martyrdom, of suffering and gradually acquired sanctity, consistent in itself, also fits into the larger scheme of justifying man and artist to a world in which intense Counter-Reformation spirituality had revitalized the values of faith.[19]

The climax of Cellini's career, and the moment when his adapted literary forms came together in a composite rather than a cumulative portrait of the artist, is the casting of the bronze statue of Perseus. This, the greatest of his *imprese* or res gestae, coming near the end of his story, is a supreme test of his love for his mistress art, his martial prowess, and his staunch faith. He says flatly that he expects all of his miseries to cease and happiness to reign upon completion of this work (p. 423), the first of its size made in Italy by him and therefore bound to arouse skepticism, disbelief, and finally, wonder. One must believe, too, that the subject of Perseus and the slain Medusa, the conquest of evil by youthful heroism, satisfied yearnings for victorious revenge in our sculptor: "Se Iddio mi dà tanto di grazia che io finisca la mia opera, spero con quella di ammazzare tutti i mia ribaldi nimici; dove io farò molte maggiori e piú gloriose le mie vendette, che se io mi fussi sfogato con un solo" (If God allows me sufficient grace to finish my work, I hope by means of it to slaughter all of my scoundrelly enemies, and thus my revenge will be greater and more glorious than if I had vented my anger at one alone, pp. 410–11).

In its conception, preliminary modeling, and beginning execution, the *Perseus* is typical of Cellini's previous works in their psychic meaning for him as well as the practical difficulties encountered. The statue was to stand between the works of Donatello and Michelangelo in the Loggia of the Florentine Piazza della Signoria, thus reminding us of the earlier motif of artistic competition and validation, especially since this was to be no miniature saltcellar but a monumental, full-scale sculpture. As usual, too, the patron, here Duke Cosimo, proved less supportive than at first promised in the midst of the now familiar court intrigue and backbiting of and by other artists. Naturally, there was doubt from the start that the statue could be made at all, since it would require a technical miracle, the impossible, and the previously unheard of, far surpassing anything the ancients had known—and so on.

In the event, Cellini has to overcome a series of seemingly hopeless obstacles: he falls mortally ill with fever, the workshop catches fire, wind and rain sweep in from the garden, the furnace cover blows open, and the casting apparently fails. But Benvenuto, rising from his deathbed like Lazarus, and letting forth a tremendous howl that is a trumpet call to arms,

Benvenuto Cellini, *Perseus with Head of Medusa*. Florence, Loggia dei Lanzi.

proceeds to rally his discouraged workmen. Like a general, he reverses the tide of battle; like a saint, he brings the corpse of the dead statue back to life, proclaiming it to be nothing less than a miracle of art, for which he promptly and piously thanks his God (pp. 425–29). Having somehow, during this frantic action, also recovered from his allegedly mortal fever, he can now sit down with his troops, his harassed workmen, to enjoy a hearty victory dinner!

The statue that emerged from this tumultuous action shows the hero Perseus holding aloft the severed head of the Gorgon, her body writhing beneath his feet. In his other hand he grasps a curved sword horizontally along the vertical of a taut, weight-bearing leg, while the other leg is bent in the classical manner of contrasting function. His winged helmet and sandals recall his protector Mercury, who gave him his sword and also appears as one of the four small bronze statues set in niches in the marble pedestal: the others are Minerva, the other protector of Perseus and the donor of his shield; his mother Danaë, holding the hand of the hero as a child; and Zeus, his father. A bronze bas-relief depicting the rescue of Andromeda, his other famous feat, completes the scheme of visual allusion to the Perseus myth. The rest of the pedestal is nearly overwhelmed with decorative motifs of all kinds, drawn from classical sources but executed with little classical restraint. But even if we focus only on the hero above, we may feel that, despite his Michelangesque muscularity and his serious engagement in the climactic moment of a memorable deed, this version of Perseus has more *maniera* than power or energy, is more a statue commenting upon statues than a vivid representation of its mythic subject.[20]

The aftermath of the Perseus casting was, like the statue itself, initially dazzling but eventually disappointing. Upon unveiling his masterpiece, Benvenuto enjoyed the plaudits of the people, the rulers, and, most important, the artists of his native city—not only did Pontormo and Bronzino praise it, but the latter wrote poems about it, some of which he sent to the sculptor and others of which he affixed to the statue's framing posts. In a state of euphoria over this praise and grateful to God for still another manifestation of His favor, Cellini determined to ask leave of the duke to go on a brief pilgrimage:

> Domattino mi partirò e me n'andrò a Valle Ombrosa, di poi a Camaldoli e a l'Ermo, e me n'andrò insino ai bagni di Santa Maria e forse insino a Sestile, perché io intendo che e' v'è di belle anticaglie: dipoi mi tornerò da San Francesco della Vernia, e ringraziando Iddio sempre, contento mi ritornerò asservirla. (p. 456)

> [Tomorrow I shall leave and I shall go to Vallombrosa, then to Camaldoli and to Eremo, and I will go as far as the Baths of Santa Maria and

perhaps as far as Sestile, because I understand there are some beautiful antiquities there; then I will return by San Francesco della Vernia, and, ceaselessly thanking God, return, content, to serve you.]

Soon afterward, however, the old problems recurred: intrigue, neglect, failure to pay, and sudden loss of favor. Unable to return gracefully to France (by now he had idealized his stay there into an artist's dream of extravagant patronage), Benvenuto remains at the end of his tale in an unhappy state, going off to Pisa to try once again to please his fickle patron.

And so once again Cellini's total devotion to art and to the exhausting creation of masterful works does not suffice to mitigate the harsh realities of the actual milieu in which they were consumed. Nor could Benvenuto seek true solace in religion as a separate experience, as he claims to do, for if he did, he would not be trying to combine that pilgrimage of thanks for the miracle of the Perseus with a side-trip to Sestile to see the antiquities! To insist on bringing God into the aesthetic realm was also to risk blaming Him for its vagaries, which Cellini was reluctant to do, hence when things artistic went wrong he had to curse his malignant stars. Nor could he see or admit that art creation is art production, that beautiful objects become commodities, hence he states that it is only evil men prompted by selfish motives who ruin the holy and heroic enterprise of making masterpieces of creative genius.

As an apologia claiming that both he and art are faultless, Cellini's autobiography served him well and almost convinces us. For by writing he could justify himself and his art to a larger public persuaded to see him whole. Instead of judging him by one work of art here, one act of violence there, one rumor about his shady behavior in still another place, the reader of the printed book could hear it all, see the pattern of events, and ponder the divine plan and favor underlying the scattered incidents of his life.

Like other mannerist literary works appropriately so designated, the autobiography is about the supposed self-sufficiency of the realm of art, but also about the inevitability of the intrusion upon that realm of the reality from which it has abstracted itself. The very literariness of Benvenuto Cellini's self-dramatizations, his determination to present us with a heroic portrait of himself and his profession, arouse suspicion even more than the congenital hyperbole and the realistic details of milieu, behavior, and speech that suddenly bring to life the sights, sounds, and smells of sixteenth-century Italy. Of course, it is as autobiography that Cellini's narrative has its broadest appeal and literary worth, and its mannerist credentials are perhaps of interest only insofar as we are deeply curious about Renaissance culture and, in particular, the artistic currents that made it so rich and complex.

Nevertheless, I would propose, on the basis of the foregoing analysis, that his mannerist sensibility and the literary modes he adapted to convey his heroic sense of himself and his life as an artist enrich Cellini's narrative with additional layers of ironic meaning; and further, that these have contributed no small share, however unacknowledged, to the success which Benvenuto's story has enjoyed. In any event, it *has* reached that wider audience he hoped would listen to, believe, exonerate, and then applaud him, just as the people of Florence did on that day in April 1554 when he finally unveiled his *Perseus* in the soft early morning light that suffused the great piazza.

3
Visage and Veil: The *bel viso* and the *bel velo*

A veil, or the lack of one, declared a woman to be unmarried, married, or widowed. . . .[1]

his chapter is about veils and the gestures of veiling and unveiling in the normative love poetry of Petrarch and his progeny. Because its intention is to demonstrate the potential for *maniera,* both mannered and mannerist, in Petrarch's *Rime* by focusing on a single theme, it is complemented and completed by the succeeding chapter on the theme of hand and glove, the *bella mano* and the *caro guanto.* As we shall see, this second theme is pointedly linked by Petrarch with that of the veil, for it also plays off the complex motif of covering and uncovering a part of the lady's anatomy that is aesthetically and erotically stimulating, disturbing yet also suggestive of moral or spiritual meanings. The enormous appeal of the *bella mano* theme to the Petrarchists of Renaissance Europe requires and accounts for a shift of emphasis in the next chapter from Petrarch himself as norm or model, to his imitating followers. Here I shall adduce mainly a few Italian sixteenth-century examples, literary and visual, of Petrarchism as a cultural force that permeated the social life and artistic consciousness of the time.[2] In this regard, the portrait by Andrea del Sarto of *A Girl Holding a Volume of Petrarch* is a fitting visual prelude to both chapters. It images the social diffusion of Petrarch and, insofar as it is a work of art that was imitated by Bronzino, announces the key theme of mannerist response to an authoritative predecessor.

Thus I shall begin by glancing at the Petrarchan model, then return briefly to Benvenuto Cellini as we pursue our inquiry into sixteenth-century mannerist veils, for he can serve us again as a transition and introduction to the aesthetic psychology of veiling and unveiling. The portrait by Agnolo Bronzino of the poetess Laura Battiferri holding a volume of the *Rime* (see Frontispiece) also serves to illustrate that psychology and aptly summarizes

Andrea del Sarto, *Portrait of a Girl Holding a Volume of Petrarch*. Florence, Galleria degli Uffizi.

in visual imagery the tradition established by Petrarch's veiling and unveiling of Madonna Laura's *bel viso*.

When we peruse the *Rime* of the founding father, we learn that his veils were at once more real and more richly symbolic than they were to become in either High Renaissance or mannerist portrait iconography, where aesthetic concerns often took precedence over moral or religious meaning. At the same time, there is already present in Petrarch a tendency to associate the veil with art, and in particular with the art of poetry. While there is no doubt that we are to understand the veil worn by Laura to be a real and ordinary one, an item of clothing worn to cover and protect head and face, we are also expected to note that the veil is beautiful, whether in and of itself or by transference, and is therefore an embellishment. Added to this aesthetic suggestion is the fact that veils in Petrarch's time had accumulated symbolic freight and were subject to metaphoric usage, hence could not avoid emitting moral and spiritual signals.

Chief among the figurative resonances of veiling was an association with allegory, as Michael Murrin has demonstrated in his study of the development in *The Veil of Allegory*.[3] It is well known that classical hermeneutics and biblical exegesis combined to convince the Middle Ages that the true meaning of a sacred or poetic text was not to be found on its historical or fictional surface, which was thought of as an opaque veil to be penetrated or drawn aside. Thus Dante, in the *Inferno,* book 9, says: "mirate la dottrina che s'asconde / sotto 'l velame de li versi strani" (ponder the doctrine that is hidden below the veil of the strange verses, ll. 62–63). And Boccaccio was to argue that the essence of poetry is "velamento fabuloso atque decenti veritatem contegere" (to conceal truth under a veil of fitting fable). Because allegory as concept, analytical tool, and formal or generic type persisted, despite opposition, into and through the Renaissance, we can still hear echoes of the veil metaphor in Donne's "curtaines of allegories" or Bunyan's admonition to "put by the curtains, look within my veil."[4] And as late as Shelley, whom Murrin quotes as an instance of a romantic revival of allegory (p. 199), the tenacious image occurs—except, of course, that Shelley's "Veil after veil may be undrawn, and the inmost naked beauty of the meaning never exposed" attributes an inexhaustibility and mystery to poetic truth that would have baffled earlier critics, who held that one veil was enough, and that, once penetrated, a truth would be found behind it.

According to Thomas M. Greene's study of imitation in Petrarch, this confident notion of penetrable veil and discoverable truth was already yielding in the poet to a new humanist hermeneutic based on his frustrating experience of reading resistant, because remote, classical texts that required "archeological" subreading (pp. 93–95). Not only is meaning elusive for and in Petrarch, Greene argues, but there also looms before him an ominous alternative to the literary text as veil: it is a text that exists and has value only as "an autonomous universe of autoreflexive signs" (p. 115). As implied by John Freccero's insightful juxtaposition of Augustinian fig tree and Petrarchan laurel, such a self-contained text, with the self-absorption it thematizes, would be idolatrous in the Augustinian sense of being a mere phantasm.[5] Thus Greene joins those many modern critics of the *Rime* who see them as embodying or sublimating considerable tension and strain.

At first glance these ontological, epistemological, and theological concerns would seem to have little relevance to sixteenth-century *maniera* and mannerism. But insofar as the poems of Petrarch reflect a dilemma or crisis of creativity, they can perhaps be seen as proleptic in more than the obvious sense of being thematic and stylistic models for his successors. As I have argued earlier, the mannerist artist bent on accommodating both nature and other authoritative texts and images may succeed in creating a richly complex work that creatively exploits his dilemma. But he may also achieve only the aesthetic equivalent of an "idolatrous" work, in my terms one that is merely mannered, or Petrarchistic. In Petrarch himself, for whom no single classical or medieval author was the kind of overwhelming and absolute authority in lyric poetry that he was to become for his followers, authorial anxieties and poetic solutions could be stirred by the tension between the desire and the inability to imitate distant predecessors. In contrast, his followers, not having to contend with a hopeless historical and linguistic gap between themselves and Petrarch's normative poems, felt obliged to both echo and recycle them. If Petrarch himself, isolated in his pioneering imitative venture, feared that he might be creating nonreferential, autonomous universes of linguistic signs, his followers, participants in a later ripe and crowded literary culture, feared that their texts would refer back only to his, and have no other value. In the language of Berni's rebuke, they would stand accused of uttering merely pretty *parole* instead of profound *cose*.

As Petrarch makes clear in his poems about Laura's veil, he is aware of and occasionally expresses these attendant ideas and dilemmas. But it is the real veil worn by the real woman, not the veil of art, or Dante's veil hiding doctrine, or Boccaccio's fable concealing truth, that primarily concerns him. The whole point of the amatory scenario of the *Rime* is the integrity of the surface of Laura's being, the value she represents before exegesis; one must come to terms with and acknowledge her physical reality before interpreting her as a sign.

One way the poet insists upon Laura's historical reality is to tell us that his friend the Sienese painter Simone Martini actually painted her portrait:

> Per mirar Policleto a prova fiso
> con gli altri ch'ebber fama di quell'arte
> mill'anni, non vedrian la minor parte
> de la beltà che m'ave il cor conquiso.
>
> Ma certo il mio Simon fu in paradiso
> (onde questa gentil donna si parte),
> ivi la vide, et la retrasse in carte
> per la fede qua giú del suo bel viso.
>
> L'opra fu ben di quelle che nel cielo
> si ponno imaginar, non qui tra noi,
> ove le membra fanno a l'alma velo.
>
> Cortesia fe'; né la potea far poi
> che fu disceso a provar caldo et gielo,
> et del mortal sentiron gli occhi suoi.[6]

[If Polyclitus and the others who were celebrated for the art of sculpture were to compete for a thousand years in observation, they would not see the smallest part of the beauty that has conquered my heart. But certainly my Simon must have been in Paradise, from which this gentle lady has come, and there he saw her and portrayed her on paper, to testify down here to her beautiful visage. The work was surely one of those that can be imagined in Heaven, not here among us, where the body veils the soul. It was a courtesy, nor could he have done it after descending to our realm of heat and cold, his eyes returned to mortal sight.]

As it has not survived, we do not know if the painting showed Laura veiled, and if it did, as seems likely, precisely what kind of veil she was wearing. However, we can make a case, based on contemporary painting and Petrarch's other texts, that Laura's veil was of the fully enveloping kind (resembling, if not in fact, the hood of a cloak) that does not merely frame the face but partly covers and conceals it. Perhaps, too, at moments of alarm the folds of the veil could be drawn closer together by a gloved or bare hand—a gesture that can be observed in Simone Martini's celebrated *Annunciation* in the Uffizi, where the Madonna gathers her cloak and its hood more tightly about her in surprised response to the angelic intrusion. Some such gesture may even partly explain the conjunction of face and hand in

Petrarch's cluster of veiling motifs:

> In quel bel viso ch'i' sospiro et bramo,
> fermi eran li occhi desïosi e 'ntensi,
> quando Amor porse, quasi a dir "che pensi?"
> quella honorata man che second'amo. (257, p. 321)

[My desirous and ardent eyes were fixed upon that beautiful visage for which I sigh and hunger when Love, as though to say "What are you thinking about?" extended before my sight that honored hand, my second love.]

I have stressed that the veil is imagined by the poet as real and that its reality must not be automatically dissolved into doctrinal allegory or poetic fable, but also that it does send out metaphoric signals that command attention. The reference to the body as veil of the soul in the poem about Martini's painting of Laura is certainly one of these, for it proposes that Laura's veil reveals and conceals another veil, that of the body vis-à-vis the soul, the essential and eternally real element of being. Though the veil worn by Laura is thus twice removed from the soul, a metaphor of a metaphor, it happens to cover and uncover that part of her body—face and especially eyes and mouth—where the soul is mirrored or issues forth in breath and words. The veil can thus mediate between body and soul as well as conceal or reveal both. As a metaphor for poetry, the veil would then suggest the potential of the love lyric for conveying the complexities of both art and being, but also the danger of becoming absorbed in and enclosed by its own metaphoric folds, as in mannered Petrarchism. As a metaphor for the earthly body that is apparently beautiful and pleasing but barely reflects the pure beauty of the soul or the resurrected body, it poses a similar danger of indulgence in desiring an alluring but perishable shell.

In the very first poem of the *Rime* to take up the motif of the veil, also the first *ballata* of the collection, the poet says that, to his great loss, his lady has worn it ever since she first became aware of his love—that is, ever since he revealed his previously concealed thoughts through his expression of them in his avid glances, perhaps, or better, through his words or poems. That revelation has led to her cruelly concealing the source of his inspiration:

> Lassare il velo o per sole o per ombra,
> donna, non vi vid'io
> poi che in me conosceste il gran disio
> ch'ogni altra voglia d'entr'al cor mi sgombra.

> Mentr'io portava i be' pensier'celati,
> ch, ànno la mente desïando morta,
> vidivi di pietate ornare il volto;
> ma poi ch'Amor di me vi fece accorta,
> fuor i biondi capelli allor velati,
> et l'amoroso sguardo in sé raccolto.
> Quel ch'i'piú desïava in voi m'è tolto:
> sí mi governa il velo
> che per mia morte, et al caldo et al gielo,
> de'be'vostr'occhi il dolce lume adombra.
>
> (11, p. 13)

[I have never seen you lay aside your veil in sun or shadow, Lady, since you recognized in me the great desire that puts to flight all other wants. While I bore hidden my beautiful thoughts, which have vanquished my mind with desire, I saw you adorn your face in pity; but then, when Love made you aware of me, your blond tresses were veiled and your amorous glance gathered back into itself. That which I most desired in you has been taken from me: thus the veil treats me, for at the cost of my death, in both heat and cold, it hides the sweet light of your beautiful eyes.]

But Petrarch makes it clear in the following sonnet, addressed to Orso dell'Anguillara, that the veil now concealing Laura's face and especially her eyes, like her upraised hand performing the same function, deprives him of a sight that, however painful when revealed, is better to contemplate in awed frustration than to be deprived of entirely:

> Orso, e' non furon mai fiumi né stagni,
> né mare, ov'ogni rivo si disgombra,
> né di muro o di poggio o di ramo ombra,
> né nebbia che'l ciel copra e 'l mondo bagni.
>
> né altro impedimento, ond'io mi lagni,
> qualunque piú l'umana vista ingombra,
> quanto d'un vel che due begli occhi adombra,
> et par che dica: Or ti consuma et piagni.
>
> Et quel lor inchinar ch'ogni mia gioia
> spegne o per humiltate o per orgoglio,
> cagion sarà che 'nanzi tempo i' moia.
>
> Et d'una bianca mano anco mi doglio

ch'è stata sempre accorta a farmi noia,
et contra gli occhi miei s'è fatta scoglio.[7]

(38, p. 55)

[Orso, there were never brooks or ponds or seas into which every
stream pours itself, nor any shadow cast by wall, hill or branch, nor
any cloud that covers the sky and bathes the world, nor any other
obstacle, no matter how much it impedes human sight, that I lament
as much as a veil that hides two beautiful eyes and seems to say: "Now
waste away and weep." And that lowering of theirs, which extin-
guishes all my joy, whether through humility or pride will be the
cause of my early death. And I complain also of a white hand, always
ready to harm me, that has made itself an obstacle to my sight.]

This should be contrasted to a madrigal, the first of its kind in the *Rime,*
that invokes classical myth and realistic amatory psychology to portray the
sensual experience of the lady seen *without* her veil:

Non al suo amante piú Diana piacque,
quando per tal ventura tutta ignuda
la vide in mezzo de le gelide acque,

ch'a me la pastorella alpestra e cruda
posta a bagnar un leggiadretto velo,
ch' a l'aura il vago et biondo capel chiuda,

tal che mi fece, or quand'egli arde 'l cielo,
tutto tremar d'un amoroso gielo.

(52, p. 71)

[Diana did not please her lover as much—when, by a similar chance,
he saw her all naked in the midst of icy water—as did my cruel
mountain shepherdess me in the act of washing a lovely veil that
protects her charming blond tresses from the breeze, such that even
under a burning sky she makes me shiver all over with an amorous
chill.]

At another extreme from Laura unveiled and overwhelming in her stark
physical presence is Laura totally absent in death, but now even more
powerfully envisioned as a source of personal and spiritual consolation.
Earlier the poet had recalled seeing her eyes "a l'ombra d'un bel velo" (in the
shadow of a beautiful veil, 127, l. 62, p. 172). In death, her "invisible
form" can be found in Paradise,

> disciolta di quel velo
> che qui fece ombra al fior degli anni suoi,
> per rivestirsen poi
> un'altra volta, et mai piú non spogliarsi,
> quando alma et bella farsi
> tanto più la vedrem, quanto più vale
> sempiterna bellezza che mortale.
>
> (268, p. 337)

[loosened from that veil that here cast a shadow over the flower of her years, to be dressed in it once again, and never again to be unclothed, when we see her become as much more kindly and beautiful as eternal is worthier than mortal beauty.]

Typically, the shadow cast by the veil over her eyes has anticipated the shadow of death, and the resented veil itself has become in retrospect far less significant than the veil of her body, which "shadowed" her young life and which she will don again in its resurrected form. The body he thought beautiful turns out to have been veiled by Laura to his benefit, for he now knows the difference between beauty that is "sempiterna" and that which is merely "mortale."

In another place, the poet imagines Laura in heaven taking him by the hand and saying,

> "Mio ben non cape in intelletto humano:
> te solo aspetto, et quel che tanto amasti
> e là giuso è rimaso, il mio bel velo."
>
> (303, p. 376)

["Human intellect cannot grasp my good: I wait only for you and that which you loved so much and has remained down there, my beautiful veil."]

But he also has her assert indirectly that his poems have not been written in vain, that they are not mere verbal veils, perishable like her body and lacking eternal beauty in their "unresurrected" or un-spiritualized state. Rather than esteem in silence "the truth that conquers every style" (309, ll. 12–13, p. 383) or risk divine song, in which he is experienced and for which he may be unworthy, the poet is advised by his beloved through Amor that he should not extinguish her fame by failing to sing, but rather to both glorify her and make his name illustrious by continuing to write (268, ll. 677, p. 339). An added implication is that, by continuing to sing of her, he may also soon reach, and lead others to reach, an understanding of her untimely death. Yet, despite his attempt to rebuff any "velo che mi fea non veder quel ch'i 'vedea" (veil that made me not see that which I saw, 329, ll. 13–14, p. 408) the poet persists both in his grief and in his writing, expressing his inability to be consoled in poem after poem and reporting recurring visions of a very human Laura dealing kindly and lovingly with him from her heavenly seat. These visions seem to affirm his earthly experience of her and to validate his poetic record of that experience. It appears that ultimately he rejects neither the veil of her flesh nor the veil that is his poetry. But his raising the issue and associating the two veils in the first place, and the long struggle he records as he tries to justify them, inevitably suggest an exhausted and fragile resolution.

The veil of living Laura is thus paradoxical and complex in its function, effects, and meanings. On the one hand, it relieves Petrarch of the full impact of an inspiring but troubling sight, the face and eyes that arouse physical desire which cannot be satisfied, and thus provoke anguished poetry. On the other hand, since the veil does not obliterate the memory of that sight, the poet remembers and suffers, and his antagonism toward the veil because it compels such suffering memory also provokes poetry. But the same face and eyes that arouse unruly desire also mirror the lady's virtuous soul. The veil that has blunted the source of erotic stimulus has also switched off the reflecting light of her inner and restraining spiritual power—he is left with a mere covered body, a veiled veil, an adumbration of her dead as yet unresurrected body. As both a real veil that conceals a desired object and an irresistible stimulus to lyric creativity, the veil is thus peculiarly frustrating in that it forces the poet to turn inward, to rely on memory, to meditate upon rather than notate reality, to recall rather than call up both the lady and poetic resources, to write poems that are themselves veils insofar as they may conceal rather than reveal both erotic and moral experience, and may therefore perhaps be fated to inhabit an aesthetic realm in which, like Laura's earthly body, they are only their own justification.

That Petrarch's veil poems contain *in nuce* the paradoxes, complexities, and conflicts—moral, spiritual, and artistic—that dominate the *Rime* as a whole is not surprising. Nor is their potential for both literary *maniera* and *manierato*, stylishness and style-for-style's sake, as their later imitators will easily prove. But if Petrarch himself is not the first *manierato* it is because he is able to avoid the dual dilemmas of sterile adherence to his vernacular and Latin lyric models, and total immersion in a self-sufficient and totally enclosed aesthetic world. By accommodating a wide range of empirical as well as aesthetic experience, by continually transacting between nature and art, between real and imaginary veils, his poems achieve a saving tension that asks no resolution, for it is a chief source of their appealing wholeness.

Turning now to consider the fate of Petrarch's veils in the sixteenth century, we shall call upon Benvenuto Cellini again, this time to act as our guide to the aesthetic sensibility of his time. As we have seen, the climax of Cellini's career is undoubtedly that moment when he finally unveils the *Perseus* in an early morning light to an admiring crowd of spectators in the Florentine Piazza della Signoria. This gesture, with its managed lighting, suspense, and surprise, its sheer theatricality, tells us again what we have already learned from earlier incidents in his narrative: works of art inhabit their own exclusive realm of existence and therefore must be presented to the so-called real world on their own artistic terms. In effect this means that art and artfulness must be employed in order to state emphatically that the work is, essentially and finally, an aesthetic object, art about art rather than art about life. And we have associated this attitude with the mannerist sensibility, which values an art that reveals art while clinging to and exploiting classical mimetic norms and paying lip service to the classical ideal that the greatest art conceals art. But if Benvenuto's dramatic gesture of unveiling and revealing his *Perseus* reminds us of this tension between the classical norm and the claims of his aesthetic sensibility, it is also true that the actual covering he removes from the statue is unambiguously opaque and temporary, intended to conceal it completely until the right moment, unlike another veil of his we shall turn to shortly. Because it is quickly cast aside and has no lasting effect on the appearance of the *Perseus,* Cellini's covering trivializes the ideal of concealed art, which should be a permanent quality of the statue, of course. As a mere prop in the staging of a transient inaugural effect, the covering serves to enhance the statue by the sudden surprise it creates in the viewer when it is removed. Indeed, as I have indicated, the *Perseus* strikes one as a sculpture that lacks communicative power; perhaps it would be consonant with its nature, and therefore to its benefit as an appealing work of art, if it were seen even now, first covered, then uncovered.

Earlier, at the court of Francis I, Cellini tells us that his enemy and the king's mistress, Madame d'Etampes, had persuaded the French monarch that his newly finished statue of Jove ought to be placed in the corridor or loggia at Fontainebleau, which, thanks to the work done there by Rosso Fiorentino and other imported Italian mannerists, had become a magnificently decorated gallery. Among its treasures were some artfully displayed bronze casts of antique statues that even Benvenuto feared would threaten the impact and evaluation of his modern sculpture. Having delayed the king's arrival until nightfall, Madame d'Etampes found her evil purpose frustrated when Benvenuto used the artificial lighting of a taper held by his statue to enhance its appearance dramatically, then made it seem alive by moving the work slowly toward the king—and away from the antiques. Undaunted, Madame still insisted on the superiority of the antiques to modern "stupidities," went on to argue that Benvenuto's work would not hold up in the light of day, and finally, says our aggrieved author, charged

> . . . che io avevo messo un velo addosso alla ditta figura, per coprire gli errori. Questo si era un velo sottilissimo, che io avevo messo con bella grazia addosso al ditto Giove, perché gli accrescessi maestà: il quale a quelle parole io lo presi, alzando per di sotto, scoprendo quei bei membri genitali, e con un poco di dimostrata istizza tutto lo stracciai. Lei pensò che io gli avessi scoperto quella parte per proprio ischerno. (p. 366)

> [. . . that I had put a veil over the said statue in order to hide its faults. This was indeed a very thin veil that I had placed over the said statue of Jove with beautiful grace to increase its majestic appearance; so that, upon hearing those words, I began to take it off, lifting from below, and thereby revealing those beautiful genitalia; and then, with a bit of evident annoyance, tore the whole thing off. She was convinced that I had uncovered those parts in order to scoff at her.]

Madame's charge was not entirely unfair, for Benvenuto himself admits that he had placed a diaphanous or translucent veil over the statue, "to increase its majestic appearance," that is, to enhance its art with artfulness. But a thin veil, no matter how translucent, does conceal as well as reveal by simultaneously softening contours, edges, and surfaces and casting over the object a crystalline shade that increases its "artificiality"—the mannerist predilection for nature seen under glass. By his defiant lifting of the veil, Benvenuto of course was quite consciously aiming at Madame's discomfiture, as the sequence of his action alone confirms. But also, perhaps more than he was aware, his gesture makes a comment on the vexing problem of how to make art about art without being victimized by increasingly reflexive aesthetic demands. If even genitalia are beautiful, then it cannot be really shocking to reveal them. The statue of Jove has not survived, but one suspects that it was, if not mannered, a work of high *maniera,* lacking that mannerist contact with other kinds of reality that might have rescued it from the perpetual and exhausting contest with antiquity and one's more recent masters to make the work even more beautiful than its predecessors. By tearing the veil completely away, Benvenuto proudly asserts that his flawless statue does not need it, but also that people like Madame do not understand true art and its enhancement, hence do not deserve to have its refinements wasted on them. At the same time, however, his act is also a small explosion of the creative tensions aroused by the competitive presence of those bronze casts of antique statues in a place beautified by illustrious contemporary Italian artists. It may very well be that Madame was not too far off the mark when she raised some doubt about the purposes of that veil.

Sometime between 1555 and 1560, the mannerist painter Agnolo Bronzino painted the portrait of Laura Battiferri (1523–89) that serves as the frontispiece of this book. Laura was a poetess and from 1550 the wife of the sculptor Ammanati. Bronzino, it may be recalled, was one of the Florentine artists who praised in verse the statue of Perseus upon its unveiling. Ammanati had succeeded Bandinelli as a rival and hated enemy of Benvenuto at the Florentine court, and both he and his wife are treated scornfully in the final pages of the autobiography. Indeed, at one point Benvenuto refers sarcastically to Signora Ammanati's several lovers, though his praise of her virtue in his own verses is closer to the truth about her.[8]

As John Pope-Hennessy has pointed out, the portrait belongs to a type that shows the sitter holding an open book, and in particular a volume of Petrarch's poetry.[9] We have seen another example in Andrea del Sarto's earlier *Portrait of a Girl Holding a Volume of Petrarch* that precedes this chapter and contrasts in several interesting ways with the Bronzino version. There is disagreement among scholars about the identity of del Sarto's sitter, who may or may not be his stepdaughter, Maria del Berrettaio, but there is no disagreement about the painted text she is holding and pointing to while smiling coquettishly at the viewer. Del Sarto has gone to the trouble of indicating clearly enough that her copy of Petrarch's *Rime* is open to pages 67–68, and that on page 68, which we can see, two sonnets are printed: "Ite, caldi sospiri, al freddo core" ("Go, heated sighs, to her cold heart"), above, is number 153 in modern editions; "Le stelle, il cielo, et gli elementi a prova" ("The stars, heaven, and the elements vied"), below, is number 154, hence in sequence. Pope-Hennessy, arguing that "it is very hard to associate the emotional tension of the first sonnet or the hyperbole of the second with the placid girl sitting in front of us," concludes that the Christian name of the sitter must have been Laura, hence the pose (p. 235). John Shearman, who finds the girl "impish and archly secretive," notes that the girl's index finger seems to be pointing to the lower poem on the opposite page, which we do not see but chronologically would be number 152, "Questa umil fera, un cor di tigre o d'orsa" ("This humble wild beast, with heart of tiger or bear"). We thus have "a fully intentional paradox," in that sonnet 152, not seen but easily known and expressing the despair of the poet over his frozen paradoxical state ("between fear and hope"), is the real message and is intended for her viewing lover (1:123–24). Shearman admits that his interpretation makes for considerable psychological and ironic complexity. And I would have to modify it on the grounds that, at most, the conceit of such an obviously young and pleasant girl sending so "ferocious" a message with so disarming a smile can only be an elaborate and sophisticated literary joke. But insofar as the painting remains intelligible, Shearman adds, like the developing portraiture of Andrea himself, it stops short of mannerism.

The connections between the del Sarto and Bronzino portraits are more than iconographical. We should recall that Bronzino's teacher was Pontormo, who was in turn a pupil of Sarto, so that there is the weight of an inherited mantle on Bronzino's shoulders. Apart from this typical mannerist creative situation, there was a need to convey a much more fully charged emblematic theme. Laura Battiferri is a complex subject not only because of her first name but because of the fact that she herself was a poetess—a Laura who might have responded to Petrarch's *rime* with some of her own. Thus, though her head is turned and her gaze directed away from the book, the latter attracts attention because of the way her typically mannerist hands hold it open and on her lap. Those exquisite hands, with their marblelike texture and color and their long, tapered fingers engage the book in an elegantly posed rather than a naturalistic way. What is more, the two poems printed on the open pages are not in the usual sequential order, so that they too have been posed for the artistic occasion. The first, Petrarch's "Se voi poteste per turbati segni" (If you could ever, by any agitated signs, 64, p. 86) is a sonnet that protests against the lady's disdain. The other, "I'ò pregato Amor, e 'l ne riprego" (I have pleaded with Love, and pleaded with him again, 240, p. 304) also begs for pity, as her beauty consumes him and he cannot help loving her. Like the Laura addressed by Petrarch in the two poems, the poetess is depicted here as meditating in a distant and detached fashion, but also with a hint of melancholy, on the poet's meaning, perhaps pondering and reflecting on the conflict between the moral and literary imperative to maintain a virtuous, even haughty stance in the face of the poet-lover's unruly passion and the troubled awareness that her beauty has inflicted intolerable suffering on him. There is an undoubted tension between the "cool" pose and gestures of the sitter and her implied thoughts.

Finally, and of special interest to our theme, we note that this Laura wears a veil that frames her face and falls onto shoulders and breast. It is a diaphanous veil of the kind Cellini manipulated to increase the majesty of his statue of Jove, and is intended artfully to reveal rather than conceal the visage of Madonna Laura Battiferri while at the same time softening its angularity and distacting attention from other of its less-than-attractive features. As such, the veil joins other symbolic elements—book, hands, and visage—in proposing that this is not so much a portrait of its subject as a flattering pictorial essay on the significance of her name and profession, a visual equivalent of the literary Petrarchism that flourished as both verbal style and social custom at the time.

A comparison with another portrait of a veiled woman, the *Donna velata* or *Veiled Lady* (1516) of Raphael, is instructive. The sitter, traditionally held to be the painter's mistress, wears a veil that Pope-Hennessy quite aptly describes as forming a niche behind her head (p. 114). Though gauzelike in substance, the veil is not transparent enough to reveal the shoulders it drapes, and it shares in the shadows that predominate on the right side of her face. Though Pope-Hennessy comments that "never was an expression of physical affection so purged of passion and so intellectualized" (p. 117), the Raphael *Velata* certainly yields at least in the latter of these qualities of expression to the Bronzino portrait, in which self-conscious artistry abounds and thereby affords an excellent mannerist contrast to or adaptation of the High Renaissance style of Raphael. Raphael's pictorial motif of a generous gossamer veil that fully frames his pensive yet very human sitter has been translated by Bronzino into a thin, frugal, and transparent curtain over his sitter's brow and parts of her face, neck, and shoulders, ambiguously covering yet not covering them, and thereby contributing to the rendering of Laura Battiferri as the embodiment of an abstract, intellectualized concept, as we have noted.

We should contrast also the manner of representation of the sleeves in both portraits. In *Donna velata,* according to Pope-Hennessy's acute observation, "the head, classical in structure and realized with breath-taking simplicity, is placed like a jewel in a setting of unrestrained and almost willful elaboration. Hither and thither run the folds of the white gold-embroidered sleeve, as though they were looked on by the painter as an area where he could give free rein to his pictorial fantasy" (p. 114). The sleeves of Laura Battiferri, while evidencing Bronzino's own also typically mannerist penchant for and skill in rendering silks and velvets, are far more subdued. One has to wait for the baroque, with its flying and fluttering garments, to see the full exploitation of Raphael's exuberantly errant folds.

Although it has sometimes been associated with stylish mannerism, a "delight in disorder" is not really a key to its sensibility, as it often prefers, as here with Bronzino's sleeves, to confine potential unruliness within decorative pattern.

As portraits by Bronzino and other painters confirm, by the mid-sixteenth century in Italy almost every habit and gesture of cultivated existence, from the use of verbs to the wearing of veils, had been penetrated by and subjected to the authority of Petrarch's *Canzoniere*. Aesthetic ideals were extracted from its forms by literary and art critics, while social norms

Raphael, *La Donna velata* (The Veiled Lady). Florence, Palazzo Pitti.

were distilled from its style by arbiters of behavior, costume, and taste. Even churchmen, forced to contend with a rival religion of love, and painfully aware that the Petrarchan text was better known to many of its readers than the Bible, "converted" it by sacred parody into a *Petrarcha spirituale*.[10] But whereas painters might vie with each other in trying to replace that lost painting of Laura by Simone Martini, wittily posing and flattering contemporary Lauras by showing them with their "sacred" volumes of Petrarch in hand, poets had to confront the very present texts of the master, known by heart if not held in the hands of scores of sophisticated readers whose numbers had been vastly increased by the outpouring of editions of the *Rime* from the printing press.

One result was a flood of mannered poems on veiling and unveiling that are content merely to provide such readers with tiny shocks of recognition. For the apprentice or amateur lyric poet who had cut his creative teeth on the Petrarchan texts, it was both necessary and desirable to display what he had learned and what he could do by imitating the master's *maniera*. For the veteran or professional lyricist revising or supplementing his earlier output, it was essential to demonstrate that the lesson of the master had been thoroughly absorbed and an advance of sorts made beyond him, if only in freshness and vitality. As happened with painters, however, the advance often amounted to no more than the achievement of a smooth facility of style, a lyric *maniera* that at its best was gracefully eloquent but at its worst, irritatingly bland. As for conceptual freshness or innovation, the spectrum ranges from startling insight through mere cleverness to silly punning and word juggling, with too many of the Petrarchist poems clustered at the wrong end.

A poem that certainly belongs there, and aptly illustrates why, is the following madrigal by Battista Guarini (1538–1612) on the unveiling motif. As a text inviting if not intended for musical setting, it reminds us of still another territory invaded by Petrarchism. But this does not affect its exemplary status as a mannered poem staking its life on a venerable if not exhausted Dantesque pun on the word *salute* (which can mean "greeting," "health," or "salvation") and the Petrarchan cliché of an armed Amor launching inflammatory arrows at a disarmed lover:

> Donna, per salutarmi
> scopriste il volto, ov'era armato Amore,
> e mi feriste il core.
> Che fareste pugnando,
> aspera guerrera, poi, se salutando
> voi mi fate nel cor mille ferute?
> O saluto crudel senza salute![11]

[Lady, to give me your salutation you uncovered your face, where Love
lay armed, and you wounded my heart. What would you accomplish
combatting me, harsh warrior, if in saluting me you wound my heart a
thousand times? O cruel salutation without salvation!]

Far more interesting than Guarini's witless exercise is a *canzone* by
Giovanni della Casa (1503–56) in which he imagines his lady fleeing like a
frightened deer at the very sound of his "parole d'amor." 'If she were to pity
him and listen, however, he would confess

> tutte le insidie e i dolci furti miei.

> Né taccio ove talor questi occhi vaghi
> sen van sotto un bel velo,
> s'avvien che l'aura lo sollevi e mova,
> e come il dolce sen mirar mi giova
> (non che l'ingorda vista ivi s'appaghi),
> e qual gioia il cor prova
> dove 'l bel piè si scopra anco non celo:
> cosí gli inganni miei conto e rivelo, . . .
> né questo in tanta lite anco mi giova.[12]

[all of my stratagems and sweet thefts. Nor would I be silent about
how at times these my hungry eyes peer under a lovely veil if it comes
about that a breeze lifts it up and away, and how it pleases me to stare
at a sweet breast (not that my greedy sight is thereby contented), and
what joy my heart feels when a beautiful foot reveals itself I will not
hide either: thus I relate and reveal my deceits, though it hardly helps
to do so in the midst of such anguish.]

Here echoing with sophisticated irony Petrarch's veil poems and their motif
of the *bel viso* covered or uncovered, della Casa manages effectively to play
off Petrarchan syntax, amatory psychology, and "rhetorical strategies of
voice and address" aimed at the fictive and real audience of readers.[13] The
first nine lines of his stanza, beginning "Né taccio ove talor questi occhi
vaghi," wind their way haltingly to the period, negotiating a series of
delays—the unexpected *anco non celo* and the detours of *nor, if, not that,
but*—which mirror his creative struggle and reveal how fragile his chosen
strategy really is. In contrast to the Petrarchan model of a tormented
poet-lover who suffers nobly the tragic dilemma of finding no relief and, at
best, fitful inspiration whether he sees the lady veiled *or* unveiled, della
Casa's persona, less lofty-minded, is willing to admit his frankly erotic

feelings and how they have expressed themselves in less-than-decorous vi-
sual thefts—especially if such a confession will be more successful than
previous ploys! The poem, then, is about how to convey and discriminate
between real and feigned passion in *parole* that will neither disappoint with
their seemingly artless honesty nor fail to convince because of their blatant
conventionality. And so the poet is in that quintessentially mannerist liter-
ary and amatory bind so aptly encapsulated in Suckling's well-known
couplet:

> So we false fire with art sometimes discover
> And the true fire with the same art do cover.[14]

Della Casa's strategic rather than psychological or moral resolution of these
conflicting impulses and desires is noteworthy. After dutifully echoing and
tentatively posing the solution of Petrarchan contraries suspended in per-
petual tension, he ends his *canzone* instead with a *congedo* that artfully, or
artificially, balances her, and his, fault—his last and best ploy:

> Canzone, tra speme e doglia
> Amor mia vita inforsa, e ben m'aveggio
> che l'altrui mobil voglia
> colpando, io stesso poi vario e vaneggio.
>
> (p. 67)

[Song, Love suspends my life between hope and grief, and I under-
stand well that, blaming another's changeable will, I myself then
waver and rave.]

Many of the *Rime* of Torquato Tasso (1544—95) have, among their other
merits, a welcome context of actual social settings and situations against
which he deploys his exploitation of traditional amatory motifs. This con-
text is expecially welcome because so many of the poems would otherwise be
totally arid courtly panegyrics; their obvious intention to praise and please
at any literary cost, an unrelieved embarrassment. For example, the follow-
ing madrigal, in praise of Lady Marfisa d'Este, departs from the actual social
fact that Ferrarese women wore veils until, Tasso affirms, they ceased to do
so on her initiative.[15] Because unveiling is traditionally an erotic gesture or
an act of bold defiance, or both, Tasso has to find a way to chide and praise
simultaneously:

> Portano l'altre il velo;
> voi le chiome dorate
> forse per alterezza al sol mostrate.

> Ma s'a sdegno prendete
> ogni esempio terreno,
> con altri esempi il ciel vi mova almeno:
> col vel l'Alba vedete
> e lei che nacque in Delo,
> e l'Iri il suo colora anco nel cielo.

[Others wear a veil; you display your golden tresses to the sun perhaps out of pride. But if you disdain every earthly model, let Heaven move you at least with other models: you see the Dawn veiled, and she who was born in Delos, and Iris also color the sky with hers.]

Marfisa is, of course, already literary insofar as she is named after the Este heroine of the Orlando *romanzi* of Boiardo and Ariosto, where she is depicted as a warrior maiden of considerable, and haughty, independence. Yet, it should be noted, Tasso says her unveiling is only "perhaps" an act of pride. It may be arrogant to scorn all earthly models, but, then, a superior person like Marfisa should. Lest she be too scornful, however, and thereby not only rank herself above all mortal women but act like the aloof goddess frustrated poets sometimes claim she is—a capital crime according to the code of love—she is reminded that even the Dawn, Diana, and Iris wear veils at times. However, that one can adduce the example of such goddesses to her is simply another way of saying that she belongs in their company! And so, like an intricately designed and exquisitely finished little piece of jewelry, Tasso's poem, offered as a gift to Marfisa, crams a good deal of subtle reasoning and normally expansive imagery—rosy dawns, clouded moons, and rainbow skies—into a tiny poetic space. It ignores as inappropriate to panegyric the latent tensions of its theme and must and does opt instead for a precious display of verbal *maniera* that is undoubtedly *manierato*.

We may recall that there is another Petrarchan veil—apparently and distractingly real but ultimately insubstantial—which the poet meditated upon: the body of Laura as the cover of her soul. In the following widely anthologized sonnet by Bernardino Rota (1508—75), this and a medley of other images culled from the *Rime* are interestingly deployed:

> Candida notte e più che 'l dì serena,
> che 'l ben mi dai, che già morte mi tolse,
> ahi perché l'alma ancor teco non volse
> girsen col sonno, e con sua dolce pena?
>
> Ritorna, prego, e quel piacer rimena,
> che dolcemente i miei spirti raccolse

dispersi e vaghi; e nel partir poi sciolse
in caldo vento, in lagrimosa vena.

Scender da Dio, ripreso il suo bel velo,
parea madonna, e al suo cerchio menarme,
e tutto intento a riverirla il cielo.

Che potea più la notte e 'l sonno darme?
O caro inganno! Il meglio io taccio e celo:
resti pur la memoria a consolarme.[16]

[Night incandescent and more serene than day, that gives back to me
the good that death once took from me, alas why did my soul not yet
wish to depart with you in sleep and with its sweet pain? Return, I
pray you, and bring back that pleasure which sweetly gathered in my
scattered and hungry spirits; and when parting loosened them in hot
sighs and tearful floods. My lady seemed to descend from God, taken
on again her beautiful veil, and to guide me to her sphere, with all of
heaven intent on honoring her. What more could Night and Sleep
give me? O dear deceit! I am silent about and conceal the best: let the
memory remain to console me.]

Here is a veritable mosaic of Petrarchan rhetorical, thematic, and stylistic
motifs: to begin with, there is the conventional address to Night and Sleep,
recalling an extraordinary dream in which the dead beloved returned briefly
to console the grieving poet. He pleads for its and her return, but is also
aware that all he can have is the memory of that experience. We quickly
note that he has given both rhetoric and reasoning their due in dividing and
apportioning his argument among the quatrains and tercets of the sonnet
space. We recognize easily, too, the antithetical balancing, the oxymora,
and the word patterning of lines 1, 2, 4, 5, 8, and 13; the persistent
doubling of nouns, verbs, adjectives, and phrases; the subtle modulations of
rhythm within and across the fourteen lines; and the orchestration of al-
literative, assonant, and pitch sound values. Now all of these lyric devices
can be found in any workmanlike Petrarchist poem of the time, hence
would not by themselves give this sonnet any distinction. Yet we might be
led to expect something different from a poet like Rota, who is often singled
out as being unusual in that he wrote his poems about a "real" lady, and his
wife at that! His beloved consort, Porzia Capece, died in 1559, and our
poem is one of those he wrote "in morte" and published between 1560 and
1572.

However sincere Rota may have been in his grief, it would have been
unthinkable that he express his sorrow and honor his wife's memory by

breaking out of the Petrarchan tradition to seek new rather than fresh creative grounds for doing so. Not only his wife's soul and his own psyche, but also his reading audience and his reputation could have their different needs satisfied only by his echoing of the quasi-sacred texts of Petrarch's *Rime*. What is significant about the poems "in morte" of Porzia is not that they uniquely recall her as beloved wife, but that they assimilate her to the dead Laura, as our selection proves. Even his hint, in the last triplet, of some secret joy experienced beyond that of seeing his wife again in the flesh, with its clearly sensual overtones, is not a "domestic" touch, as Petrarch himself had suggested in several poems that the dead Laura was kinder and more approachable, even more physically present, in vision and dream than she had ever been when alive.[17]

What characterizes Rota's poem as mannerist rather than mannered, despite its conventional features, is its curiously abstract, almost surreal quality, due in part to the sense it gives us of an uneasy tension between apparent order and actual flux. This feeling is not simply a reverberation of its nocturnal theme but a resonance of the poem's language and structure, which suggest that it inhabits a transitional space between worlds. There is a restlessness and a shuttling back and forth suggested by verbs of leaving and returning, coming and going, giving and taking back, gathering and loosening, spiritually rising and physically descending, telling and not telling. Despite the formal control evident in the stylistic features mentioned above, there is a strain against and overflow of barriers evident in the hesitant and full enjambments of lines 3 and 4, 6 through 8, 9 and 10. And at the end of the poem, the poet-lover must admit that he cannot tell us the best of what happened in his vision, that his consolation must be a deeply private memory, so that he and we are left with a final frustration—the inadequacy of art. In this instance, at least, the montage of Petrarchan clichés does not deprive a poem of its own life, for Rota has deliberately evoked another poet mourning another dead beloved and has hinted that there are limits to the possibilities of filtering one's own grief through that of another, and therefore a limit to the ordering and healing power of poetry. At the same time, the Petrarchan tradition and its conventions do provide a guarantee that the grief will be understood and its object honored.

If, as I believe, the poems discussed thus far are fairly representative, it may be useful at this point to hazard, with their help, a very tentative categorization of Italian Renaissance veil poems of a recognizably mannerist stamp into three groups. The first, and by far the largest, would include poems that are mannered in the wholly negative sense—that is, clever rearrangements of Petrarchan clichés without interest or value other than as historical phenomena. An analogy might be drawn with contemporary paintings in which Michelangesque muscles or poses and Raphaelesque suavity and grace are quoted for their own sakes, or heroic images and profoundly meaningful symbols are taken out of appropriate contexts and scaled down to purely decorative uses. The second group would consist of poems that combine an elegant facility and witty intricacy of form and content that makes them attractive precisely because of, and not despite, their ingenious recycling of Petrarchan or classical resources—in other words, possess *maniera* in a positive sense. One thinks here of certain contemporary visual works that similarly achieve *maniera* as their intended goal rather than as a result of a failure of nerve or creative powers: the statues of Giambologna and the paintings of Parmigianino would be appropriate examples to consider in this light.

The third and smallest group would comprise those poems I would exclusively label mannerist, if such usage were now practicable, in order to distinguish them from others on the basis of their transcending the limits and limitations of *maniera*. Such poems, as I have argued earlier, do not fully inhabit an isolated aesthetic realm; they do not rest entirely on other poems as their mimetic base. Hence the characteristic ways these poems have of acknowledging reality, or other realities. They may thematically and formally embody the creative dilemma. They may try to negotiate between outer and inner worlds by means of the manipulation and modulation, or straining, of experiential and literary norms in the interest of gaining and conveying perceptions and insights not otherwise available or reproducible. Obviously the visual analogues here would include many of the works—by Pontormo, Rosso, Giulio, Tintoretto, and El Greco, among others—that we have seen discussed in terms of anguished mannerism. But if, as I have argued earlier, we define *mannerism* in the broader sense I have proposed, this third group of literary works would also allow analogues from among visual examples that are not expressive of crisis and tension and strain.

It is not surprising that mannerist works of this third kind have seemed modernist, but their preoccupation with the creative dilemma and their tendency to abstraction from and disarrangement of norms, the interplay of inner *disegno* and external reality they favor, must not be confused with vaguely analogous modern concerns. A Renaissance poet could conceive, for example, that poems are desperately needed to shore up cultural ruins against existential chaos, but not that the structures of poems should mirror that chaos or that complete abstraction, a "pure" poetry aspiring to the autonomy of musical composition, should be the goal of their imaginative efforts. Granted that if, as I am sure, mannerist poems are more interesting than mannered poems, a crucial reason is their greater complexity, a notable modernist trait. Still, it is Renaissance complexity, not the modern variety, that accounts for their appeal.

As for the poems just analyzed, the verses of Tasso and Guarini certainly belong to the first and second categories, respectively, of mannered veil poems I have posited. The selection by della Casa, though perhaps less obviously so, can certainly claim a place under the third rubric on the basis of its exploitation of the mannerist creative quandary. The sonnet by Rota joins it there for similar reasons, but also because it mediates between art and reality in its struggle to filter and order psychic experience through a literary tradition that can satisfy several of its audiences but not finally encompass the poet's complex grief.

Veil poems continued to be written, of course, well beyond the chronological limits established for this inquiry, but mostly and notably in the seventeenth-century baroque style. It will be appropriate, therefore, to conclude this essay with a few examples that signal the final flourishing of the tradition and also anticipate the attempt in my final essay to clarify the difference between mannerism and baroque. No better guide exists for this purpose than the indefatigable Giambattista Marino (1569–1625), whose sonnet "A un velo che copriva le chiome e 'l petto della sua donna" addresses "a veil that covered the tresses and the breast of his lady":

> Candido vel, ch'al più leggiadro oggetto
> ch'abbian quest'occhi t'attraversi e spieghi,
> e di madonna ingiurïoso leghi
> l'òr crespo e celi il terso avorio e schietto;
>   perché del biondo crin, del bianco petto
> il vago lume ai vaghi lumi neghi,
> e d'onesto desio sprezzando i preghi,
> copri a lei la bellezza, a me 'l diletto?
>   Se quindi, di mia gioia invido e scarso,
> non ti rimove Amor, tosto cadrai
> da'miei sospiri incenerito ed arso.
>   Vienne, ed asciuga il mio gran pianto omai;
> si poi, sicuro, di quest'acque sparso,
> tra le mie fiamme e tra 'suoi raggi andrai.[18]

[White veil, who obstruct and unfurl yourself before the loveliest object these eyes have, and injuriously bind my lady's golden curls and hide her bright and pure ivory; why do you deny the loving light of her blond tresses and white breast to loving eyes, and, spurning the pleas of honest desire, cover her beauty and my delight? If henceforth, envious and greedy for my joy, you are not removed by Love, you will soon be burned to ashes. Come, now, and dry my flood of tears; so that then, dampened by those waters, you may make your way safely between my flames and her beams.]

Especially noteworthy here is the aggressive tone, the dramatic setting, and the physical realism—methods that baroque poets employ to invigorate what had come to seem the flaccid and cerebral poetry of their mannerist predecessors. Thus Marino's poet-lover denounces and threatens, cajoles and comforts the veil. The physicality of that once quasi-sacred image and portentous symbol is bluntly asserted: it can burn, get wet, and dry tears, like any cloth. And in contrast to the wittily ambiguous or imperfectly suppressed sexuality of mannerist veil poems, the erotic impulse of Marino's sonnet is unmistakable: he wants the rival and intrusive veil taken off! And if the lady removes her veil—yields to him—out of pity for his tears, it can henceforth safely negotiate the passionate space between them—in other words, it (or she) will find it easier from now on to uncover and re-cover herself regularly.

The Marino poem also reminds us that he was instrumental in promoting on a European scale a flurry of poems on still another kind of veil, namely, that worn by widows. Although Bronzino has a *Portrait of a Widowed Lady* in the Uffizi that shows her wearing a diaphanous veil,[19] there is little if any evidence in mannerist veil poems of an interest in either the widow or her veil. But there is no question that for baroque poets the widow comes into her own as a theme. What is more, her veil is not transparent but dense and dark, as these opening lines of Marino's celebrated *canzone* on the theme of *la bella vedova* affirm:

> Quest'animata Notte,
> ch'avolta in nera veste,
> ricopre il biondo crin di bruno velo,
> non da le stigie grotte,
> ma dal balcon celeste,
> non d l'abisso vien, ma vien dal cielo.

> (pp. 59—62)

[This animate Night, who, enveloped in black garments, covers her bright tresses with a dark veil, comes not from Stygian caves but a celestial balcony, comes not from the abyss, but from the heavens.]

We should also note that the gestures of veiling and unveiling, or covering and uncovering, may be associated with other veil surrogates, for example, cornets, fans, and masks. If one were to study the history of such gestures in English Renaissance love poetry, for example, he would find that for reasons of national cultural differences, they replace veils and veiling gestures with their own appropriate ones. And so at the very beginning of our hypothetical history one might place Surrey's translation of Petrarch's earlier cited "Lassar il velo o per sole o per ombra" in the sonnet beginning "I never saw youe madam laye aparte / Your cornet black, in colde nor yet in heate," a cornet being a headress with a veil.[20] In Sidney's sonnet from *Astrophel and Stella,* which starts "In highest way of heav'n the Sunne did ride," we are told that as the sun shone brightly on some ladies out riding, they shaded themselves with fans, all except for Stella, who "with face unarmed marcht" to meet her rival. In a mannered adaptation of the uncovering motif, Sidney then says she escaped unscathèd because the Sun, "which others burn'd, did her but kisse." As for masks, we may glance at the opening stanzas of Thomas Randolph's "A Mask for Lydia":

A Mask for Lydia

> Sweet Lydia, take this mask, and shroud
> Thy face within the silken cloud,
>   And veil those powerful skies;
> For he whose gazing dares so high aspire
>   Makes burning-glasses of his eyes,
> And sets his heart on fire.
>
> Veil, Lydia, veil, for unto me
> There is no basilisk but thee:
>   Thy very looks do kill.
> Yet in those looks so fixed is my delight,
>   Poor soul, alas, I languish still
> In absence of thy sight.[21]

Obviously not a landmark of English literature, Randolph's poem still can serve to reinforce for the reader both an awareness of a tradition of veil poems stemming from Petrarch and an appreciation of how vital that tradition was because it could still inspire poets hundreds of years after Petrarch began it. The same reader, noting the mannered quality of the Randolph verses, can also see in them evidence that by then the tradition had exhausted itself.

4

Hand and Glove: The *bella mano* and the *caro guanto*

See how she leans her cheek upon her hand!
\ O that I were a glove upon that hand.
That I might touch that cheek!
—Shakespeare, *Romeo and Juliet*

Who sings thy praise? onely a skarf or glove
Doth warm our hands, and make them write
    love.
—George Herbert, "Love I"

As Parmigianino did it, the right hand
Bigger than the head, thrust at the viewer
And swerving easily away, as though to protect
What it advertises. A few leaded panes, old beams,
Fur, pleated muslin, a coral ring run together
In a movement supporting the face, which swims
Toward and away like the hand
Except that it is in repose. . . .
—John Ashbery, "Self-Portrait in a
    Convex Mirror"[1]

I have illustrated this chapter with Parmigianino's celebrated *Self-Portrait in a Convex Mirror* and quoted from the three works above as a concise means of introducing its subject and intent. Parmigianino's prominent hand can serve to suggest the emphasis placed by him and other mannerist painters on the *belle mani* of their figures. Romeo's observation of Juliet culminates in a Petrarchan amatory motif; George Herbert protests against and thereby affirms the diffusion of that motif in secular poetry; and a contemporary poet offers and invites interpretation of its meaning.

Unlike bold Romeo, who touches Juliet's hand and kisses her lips upon their first encounter, most Renaissance poet-lovers considered the mere sight of the beloved's uncovered hand an overwhelming event, a recapitulation of the *innamoramento* that might promise but certainly would not be followed quickly by physical contact with the *bel viso*. But there is an unspoken division of meaning in some of these poets between veiled visage and gloved hand. It allows the former to retain its Petrarchan mystery and spiritual significance, remaining loftily remote, while it attributes to the latter considerable and unalloyed erotic force. Undoubtedly, the fact that

125

Il Parmigianino, *Self-Portrait in a Convex Mirror*. Vienna, Kunsthistorisches Museum.

the face containing the beloved's eyes was the original source of enamour-
ment, and the eyes and mouth, respectively, the mirrors and the exit point
of the soul, whereas the hand commanded the lesser sense of touch, affected
this division. Although it is located lower in the body, as is the *bel piede* or
beautiful foot of the beloved, the hand contrasts with both face and foot in
that it is the only part of the anatomy that is normally seen with frequency,
and unclothed. Furthermore, its mobility and its gestures—utilitarian,
social, aesthetic, and expressive—far more than the face, enable the hand to
mediate between parts of her body and between the beloved and the external
world. As for the *bel piede*, it had received comparatively little attention
from Petrarch, who was content mainly to invoke the ancient topos of the
lady's "generative footsteps" arousing inert nature wherever she walks.[2]
Thus the hand could represent not only the sensual appeal of the beloved
but also a range of other personal virtues and social values she might
possess. At the same time, as a surrogate or instrument of the beloved's
death-dealing cruelty, it could be the focus of frustrated aggression directed
toward the beloved and the darker side of amatory experience.

It is no accident that the favorite terms which Renaissance poets used for
gestures of covering or uncovering the hand with a glove were drawn from
the act of dressing and undressing, of being generous (morally lax) or
niggardly (morally strict), and of being aggressive or passive in or toward
acts of theft, seizure, violent crime, and bloody warfare. Unlike the veil,
which is sometimes regarded as an enemy but never as a fetish or trophy,
the glove that sheathes the hand can be both a focus of desire and a sign of
conquest. In some rare cases, it is even thought of in the contrary sense, as a
guarantor of chastity and a protector of the flesh, rather than as an envied or
hated obstacle to its enjoyment. For these reasons, I believe, and because of
its very small size and yet complex structure—five fingers basically alike
though different from each other in length and shape, with the contrasts of
hard fingernails emerging from soft flesh and of lined palm and veined
back—the hand offered a challenge to competitive poetic exploitation.
Thus we find that it was one of the most widely diffused of motifs in
European Renaissance lyric poetry. And in its Petrarchistic variety, as we
shall see, mannered and mannerist hands, verbally rendered, are dominant
in this poetry, as are their visual counterparts in contemporary painting.

As we saw in the previous essay on veils and veil poems, to begin at the
beginning is to search through Petrarch's *Rime*. There we will find the
following sonnet, surely one of the most influential in the entire collection:

> O bella man, che mi destringi 'l core,
> e 'n poco spatio la mia vita chiudi;

man ov'ogni arte et tutti loro studi
poser Natura e 'l Ciel per farsi honore;

di cinque perle oriëntal' colore,
et sol ne le mie piaghe acerbi et crudi,
diti schietti soavi, a tempo ignudi
consente or voi, per arrichirme, Amore.

Candido leggiadretto et caro guanto,
che copria netto avorio et fresche rose,
chi vide al mondo mai sí dolci spoglie:
Cosí avess'io del bel velo altrettanto!
O inconstantia de l'umane cose!
Pur questo è furto, et vien chi me ne spoglie.

(199, p. 255)

[O beautiful hand that clasps my heart and encloses my life within a
small space, hand in which Nature and Heaven have demonstrated all
of their art and concern in order to honor themselves; fingers sweetly
trim, colored like five oriental pearls and only bitter and harsh toward
my wounds, Love now enriches me by agreeing to let you be naked a
short time. Luminous, lovely, and precious glove, that covered limpid
ivory and fresh roses, whoever saw in this world such sweet spoils?
Would that I had as much of the beautiful veil! Oh the inconstancy of
human affairs! For this too is theft, and she comes who will despoil me
of it.]

Here we have the seeds of the tradition, including the juxtaposition of
hand and face, glove and veil (line 12), the beautiful hand as synecdoche for
the body in its beauty, erotic appeal, and tyrannical sway. The pearl-like
color and texture of the fingers suggest a precious and unmovable chastity,
the red of "fresh roses" implies the pulse of vital blood racing through
them. Though normally hated because it conceals so much beauty, the
glove is also envied because it usually enwraps that same desired flesh. This
latter idea, already found in classical sources,[3] takes on a fresh complexity in
Petrarch because, unlike his predecessors, he has Christian scruples about
preoccupation with the nakedness of a transitory body. Thus he has the
poet-lover temporarily displace his passion to the hand, but its nakedness is
short-lived and pemanent possession is disallowed. The reference to the veil
may be interpreted to mean that the poet wishes he could enjoy the sight of
the rest of his beloved's body as well as her hand, but in the context of the
other *Rime* it can also signify that however joyous this glimpse of her naked

hand and brief possession of her glove, the attainment of similar joy with face and veil is more difficult because it is a higher goal.

Petrarch reinforces and enlarges upon these images in the two poems that follow (200–01, pp. 256–57), extending his denunciation and praise of Laura's ungloved hand to the rest of her body in the first sonnet, while expressing deep regret that he did not abscond with the glove in the succeeding one. The opening quatrain of "Non pur quell'una bella ignuda mano" says "not just that one beautiful naked hand" but her other hand, her arms, serene eyes, starry brows, angelic mouth, rosy lips, pearly teeth, and sun-conquering forehead and hair all ensnare him because they are "oneste forme," or "virtuous forms." In the next sonnet, "Mia ventura et Amor m'avean sì adorno / d'un bello aurato et serico trapunto," the poet tells of his joy at having briefly possessed the glove: "My fortune and Love had so adorned me / with a beautiful embroidery of gold and silk"; but the day he lost it is now remembered with anger, sorrow, shame, scorn, and especially regret:

> che la mia nobil preda non più stretta
> tenni al bisogno et non fui più costante
> contra lo sforzo sol d'un angioletta,
>
> o, fuggendo, ale non giunsi a le piante
> per far almen di quella man vendetta
> che de li occhi mi trae lagrime tante.

(201, ll. 9–14)

[that I did not grasp my booty more tightly when I needed to, and was not more firm against the force of a mere angel; or, in fleeing, did not add wings to my feet and at least get revenge on that hand which draws no many tears from my eyes.].

It is important to observe that in Petrarch the hand may be treated separately as beautiful and blessed, as a "virtuous form" that joins other parts of Laura's body in both painfully ensnaring and awesomely inspiring the poet. Although he calls it a *bella ignuda mano,* fusing its contrary effects and his conflicting reactions, later poets would sometimes separate the *bella mano* and the *ignuda mano* motifs, thus shattering the tense unity of the original. Still other Petrarchists who ignore the glove and focus on the hand treat it either as a powerful though static aesthetic object or as an active agent of dynamic amatory gestures. For some, the hand of the lady becomes a surrogate for her body in its beauty, grace, and chaste virtue. For others, it is a symbol of her death-dealing cruelty. When the glove is focused upon, the psychological implications of the motif, and especially its latent eroticism, are increasingly and blatantly exploited. In all of this, naturally, abundant *maniera,* both mannered and mannerist, can be observed.

Petrarchism officially began, along with other manifestations of a surging vernacular literature, in the latter half of the fifteenth century. During its last three decades, several printed editions of the *Rime* appeared, along with the annotations that signal a classical text. By the turn of the century the first Italian Petrarchists were already publishing volumes of imitations in a style that unmistakably marks them as the first mannered Petrarchists. Prominent among these was Cariteo, or Chariteo, actually Benedetto Gareth (ca. 1450–1514), who penned the following typical example of that first wave of imitation:

> Mentre quella sottile e bianco mano
> bella, schietta, soave, dolce, amena
> degna, di gloriosa e chiara palma,
> si spoglia il guanto e poi passa pian piano
> per l'aurea testa, angelica e serena,
> io mi veggio spogliar di vita e d'alma.
> Poi quando si riveste il bel candore,
> sento spezzarmi in mille parti il core.[4]

[While that slender and white hand, beautiful, neat, gentle, sweet, pleasing, worthy of glorious and illustrious fame, despoils itself of its glove and then slowly makes its way through angelic and serenely golden tresses, I feel myself divested of life and soul. Then when the beautiful whiteness reclothes itself, I feel my heart break into a thousand pieces.]

The ingredients of a sterile Petrarchism are all present here in a poem that has no saving *maniera* and is instead merely *manierato*. Note the piling up of adjectives in the second line; the Petrarchan diction (from *sottile* to *candore*) and metaphors drawn from his favorite areas of experience; the echoing of Petrarch's psychic conflict and its expression in dualisms and oppositions; the dramatic contrast of inexpressible joy turned suddenly into overwhelming grief when the hand gloves itself again. The one fresh human touch Cariteo could have exploited, the ordinary and "realistic" gesture of running the hand through the hair, succumbs to the lure of a voyaging metaphor, not to mention alliterative onomatopoeia. Equally ominous is the hyperbole of the last line, an example of the literalization and materialization of Petrarch's amatory scenario that came to be a prominent feature of mannered Petrarchism. In brief, this technique consists of treating Petrarchan figurative expression as a literal or material base for further metaphorization, as we shall see. Less ominous than this literalization of Petrarch's metaphoric universe, but equally noteworthy because of its influence, is Cariteo's way of steering the whole poem toward its punch-line ending. Clearly, this poem exists in an autonomous and self-referential aesthetic world we now label Petrarchist, its chief inhabitants being poems by the master and his disciples. It asks to be read and judged according to the criterion of imitation it assumes; it makes no other claims.

In the sixteenth century, which witnessed a flood of Petrarchist poems on the motif of hand and glove, there were alternatives established and available to those poets who did not wish to risk the clever flashiness of the Caritean style.[5] One could, like Lodovico Ariosto (1474–1533), aim at a more frank and eclectic manner that combined the erotic plots of Latin elegy with the refined language of Petrarch's *Rime* to suggest the joyous impact of real, or allegedly real, passion, as in his *capitolo* 8:

> O mente ancor di non sognar incerta,
> quando abbracciar da la mia dea mi vidi,
> e fu la mia con la bocca sua inserta!
>
> O benedetta man, ch'indi mi guidi;
> o cheti passi, che m'andate inanti;
> o camera, che poi così m'affidi!
>
> (ll. 13–18)[6]

[O mind still uncertain whether it was dreaming or not, when I saw myself embraced by my goddess, my mouth enclosed with hers! O blessed hand that led me thence, O quiet footsteps that go before me, O chamber that then enfolds me!]

Another alternative was to aim at *maniera* in the sense of stylistic grace, clarity, facility, smoothness, and unruffled metaphoric surface, achieved by following Petrarch's *Rime* as a classical model to be imitated exclusively on its terms, in the way Pietro Bembo (1470–1547) and his classicist-minded followers did. Here is a sample:

> Io, che già vago e sciolto avea pensato
>   Viver quest'anni, e sì di ghiaccio armarme
>   Che fiamma non potesse omai scaldarme,
>   Avampo tutto e son preso e legato

Giva solo per via, quando da lato
    Donna scese dal ciel vidi passarme,
    E per mirarla, a piè mi cadder l'arme,
    Che tenendo, sarei forse campato.

Nacque ne l'alma insieme un fero ardore,
    Che la consuma, e bella mano avinse
    Catene al collo adamantine e salde.

Tal per te sono, e non men pento, Amore,
    Pur che tu lei, che sì m'accese e strinse,
    Qualche poco, Signor, leghi e riscalde.[7]

[I, who once thought to live these years pleasantly and free, and had so
armed myself with ice that no flame could now burn me, am now
aflame, seized and bound. I was going my way alone when I saw
passing to my side a woman descended from heaven, and in staring at
her let fall at my feet the armor with which I might have lived, had I
held on to it. There arose in my soul at the same time a savage desire
that consumes it, and a beautiful hand tied strong adamantine chains
about my neck. Thus am I, because of you, Love, and I do not regret
it, provided that you, Lord, bind and heat a bit that one who has so
inflamed and constricted me.]

This exercise in Petrarch's *maniera,* with its stylistic purity and thematic
conservatism, is perhaps best described by its own phrase "qualche poco";
yet it has the appeal of the virtues mentioned above, especially clarity and
grace. It wisely resists the temptation to exploit the standard figures of ice
and fire and the imagery of *la bella mano* chaining the poet-lover. It is
nevertheless a pallid version of the *innamoramento,* safe but uninspiring.
Whatever the poet's own feelings were, and even assuming that his inten-
tion was mainly to echo Petrarch rather than filter his own experience
through the master's, the poem's ultimate value is the pleasure of recogni-
tion and the comfort of familiarity it affords the reader who knows the
source by heart. The more scholarly minded reader of the time may even
have rejoiced at the act of linguistic preservation the poem also represents.
But it probably does not succeed any better than the mannered poem of
Cariteo in bringing Petrarchism to poetic life. The poet Tasso sensed the
problem of graceful clarity as a limited goal when he remarked that a
contemporary poet, Giambattista Pigna (1530–75), was sometimes "oscu-
retto," a little obscure, whereas Petrarch "è sempre chiaro," is always
clear. But Pigna's style is "ad arte e graziosamente oscuro," and his artfully

graceful obscurity does not arise out of poor expression but "profound thought"; furthermore, it adds "un non so che di maestà" ("a certain majesty") to his style.[8] In penning his own versions of the hand-and-glove theme, however, Tasso himself was not entirely successful in achieving an artful grace arising out of profound thought:

> Lasciar nel ghiaccio o ne l'ardore il guanto
> Amor più non solea,
> da poi che preso e 'n suo poter m'avea
> nel laccio d'oro ond'io mi glorio e vanto.
>
> Mentr'io n'andava ancor libero e scarco
> il candor m'abbagliò di bianca neve,
> sì che non rimirai la rete e i nodi;
> poi che fui colto e di spedito e leve
> tornai grave e impedito e caddi al varco,
> coperse il mio diletto e 'n feri modi
> sdegnò la bella man preghiere e lodi.
> Ahi, crudel mano, ahi, fera invida spoglia,
> chi fia che la raccoglia,
> né sdegni i baci e l'amoroso pianto?

(p. 222)

[Love was no longer wont to leave off her glove in heat or cold after she had seized and held me in her power with the golden snare that is my glory and pride. While I was going about free and unburdened, its glow dazzled me with snowy white so that I did not discern the net and the knot; then, when I was caught, and turned from being nimble and buoyant to being lumpish and plodding, and fell at the threshold, the beautiful hand covered my delight and in savage fashion disdained prayer and praise. Alas, cruel hand, alas, savage spoil, who can gather it in, not scorning kisses and amorous plaint?]

As the poet himself acknowledged, and the reader has guessed, the poem is a recycling of Petrarch's veil poem discussed above, with the glove substituting like an interchangeable piece for the other precious item of the beloved's clothing. Tasso attains some variety by enjambment and displacement of syntax, and by the device of compressed metaphor, or letting attributes and associations stand for things with which they can be connected in the amatory psychology of the Petrarchist lyric, a kind of metonymic code: heat and cold (summer and winter), Love (the beloved herself), golden snare (welcome entanglement or, often, her blond tresses);

net and knots (amorous bondage); captivity, wounds, spoils, spurned pleas (hunting and warfare assimilated to the *innamoramento* and its effects). While these may briefly give the reader pause, they certainly do not make the poem "oscuretto"; rather, its shorthand imagery creates at most some temporary murkiness. Here is a better sample of Tasso's skill:

> Non è questa la mano
> che tante e sèi mortali
> avventò nel mio co fiammelle e strali?
> Ecco che pur si trova
> fra le mie man ristretta,
> né forza od arte per fuggir le giova,
> né tien face o saetta
> che da me la difenda.
> Giusto è ben ch'io ne prenda,
> Amor, qualche vendetta,
> e se piaghe mi diè baci le renda.

(p. 245)

[Is this not the hand that hurled into my heart so many and such mortal little flames and darts? Behold how now it finds itself tightly squeezed within my hands, nor can any force or art help it to flee, and it has neither torch nor arrows to defend itself against me. It is only fair then, Love, that I take some revenge on it, and if it dealt me wounds I will give it back kisses.]

The key to the appeal of this poem is the social setting: the poet-lover finds himself dancing with his beloved and actually grasping tightly that *bella mano*! The amazed question at the beginning does more than gloat over the turned tables, for it poses the typically mannerist juxtaposition of the rival claims of art and reality. A realist writing in another time and place might argue from the social actuality of the scene that the amatory myth of the *bella mano* should be dismissed, along with the many poems that embody it. Thinking, too, of the first meeting of Romeo and Juliet on a similar occasion and the apparent normalcy of their physical greeting, such a critic might point to the gap between poetry and social experience, or to how the pernicious influence of idealistic literature on manners could produce the kind of paralysis of feeling that Suckling laments in the couplet quoted earlier.

Having risked the deflation of a potent erotic and poetic symbol, however, Tasso is not prepared to take the next fatal step to acknowledging that the beloved's awesome hand could actually be touched quite often on social occasions—especially as Petrarch's amatory scenario no longer unfolded in woods and streams but had retreated to the indoors of Renaissance palazzi. Instead, after having briefly and precariously exposed the convention to dissolution, he pulls back and retreats into Petrarchism by concluding with a witty inversion: he will forgive the beloved's cruelty and treat her with the mercy he hopes she may now at last be persuaded to show him, a new era of courtship inaugurated by promising kisses, perhaps. If not, he will release and continue to address her hand and glove, because he still desires her and, in any event, there is no other script to follow than the Petrarchist one, which insists that beautiful hands are fecund symbols that have a rich metaphoric life of their own in autonomous love poems.[9]

As before, we shall let Marino conclude this brief survey of the Italians with a remarkable poem that vividly illustrates the transition from mannerist to baroque hand-and-glove poems:

> Gli occhi di foco e 'l sen di ghiaccio armata,
> Omicidia amorosa il cor m'aperse,
> E de l'aperto core in odorata
> Spoglia l'arida ancor pelle converse.
>
> De la candida poi neve animata,
> Che vestita n'avea parte scoverse;
> Ma 'l caro oggetto, al vago sguardo ingrata,
> Tra 'l guanto e 'l manto avaramente offerse.
>
> Deh come avien che la man bella e cruda,
> Che del mio sangue tinta, Amor, mi stendi,
> Se m'apri tante piaghe, e me si chiuda?
>
> Ahi, bella mia, in quante guise offendi!
> Mi spogli il cor, ne vuoi mostrati ignuda,
> Ed a prezzo di morte i baci vendi!
>
> (*Poesie varie,* p. 80)

[Her eyes armed with fire and her breast with ice, the amorous homicide tore open my heart, and converted the still dry skin of the opened heart into a scented spoil. Then, of the glowing animate snow, which she had clothed, she revealed a part; but the precious object, unkind to the hungry gaze, displayed itself stingily between glove and cloak. Say, how is it that the lovely and cruel hand, stained by my blood, that you offer me, Love, opens such wounds in me yet closes itself off from me? Alas, my beautiful one, in how many ways you

offend! You despoil my heart, yet do not wish to show yourself naked,
and you sell kisses at the price of death!]

The ingredients of this bold attempt to inject new life into our theme are
typically baroque: rhetorical stridency, physical realism, violent contrast,
sensuousness (here expressed as sensuality also), and dynamic, dramatic
gesture. Scorning contemplation of a static, frozen object, Marino converts
the traditionally marmoreal hand into the murderous weapon of a mad-
dened homicide. Paradoxically, the very blood-stained hand that rips open
his chest so brutally is also capable of a reticent gesture of frustrating
concealment. This makes no more sense than the contradiction involved in
arousing desire and not satisfying it, which is what the poem is about. Far
from being concerned with mannerist aesthetic dilemmas and subtleties,
Marino tries to reinvigorate the tired tradition by making explicit and
validating what had always been its underlying physical passion. His de-
mand for nudity forces the convention to make sense, whereas the mannerist
alternative is to write poems about other poems, or concerns itself with how
to write poems on a conventional theme.

As our representative poems have shown, Petrarch and his Italian follow-
ers produced a provocative and varied body of poems on the theme of hand
and glove. While the sonnet form predominates among them, there are also
many other brief forms such as madrigals, *ballate,* and epigrams, as well as
longer *canzoni* that are devoted entirely or in part to exploring and exploit-
ing the theme. Most of these poems are mannered, a few are what I would
call mannerist, and some others, like the works of Tasso and Marino, are
also either proto-baroque or fully in the baroque style that was to dominate
the seventeenth century. It should be understood that in a poet like Marino,
and in several other European lyricists of the late Renaissance, the mannerist
mode of exploiting this and other amatory themes remains an option,
though the baroque style may prevail in, and therefore seem to characterize,
their total output.[10] Failure to recognize this mannerist survival is one
reason why such authors, as we have seen, have been claimed for both
mannerism and the baroque by some modern critics.

In addition to this body of poems, the Italian Petrarchists, again follow-
ing Petrarch's example in the *Rime,* also offered their European colleagues
the model of a cluster of poems on hand and glove as a brief sequence within
a *canzoniere,* or the pattern of a group of poems on the beloved's anatomical
parts in which the hand receives its due attention. There is also the indi-
vidual poem that constitutes an anatomical catalogue, with the hand allot-
ted a brief descriptive phrase, for which there was ample classical and
medieval precedent. A fifteenth-century example is Giusto de' Conti's col-

lection of poems appropriately entitled *La bella mano*. Another, from the next century, is Olimpo da Sassoferrato's series of *strombotti,* or epigrammatic octaves, in praise of his lady "incominciando al capo per insino alli piedi" (beginning with her head and continuing all the way to her feet).[11] It has been suggested that this latter series may have influenced in part the vogue for *blasons du corps feminin* inaugurated in France by Clément Marot (ca. 1496—1544) when in 1535 he sent back from exile in Ferrara his celebrated *Blason du beau tetin*.[12] But the descriptive genre of the anatomical *blason,* with its exclusive focus upon the separate parts of the female body, and written in a variety of serious, playful, and satiric moods drawing upon classical and medieval antecedents, is often different in form, purpose, and tone from Petrarchist *bella mano* poems.[13] There is no question, nevertheless, that the Petrarchist predilection for our theme dovetailed with the French phenomenon, and that the ensuing poetic tournament was penetrated by and, in turn, infiltrated European lyric poetry. This development, as we shall see, is especially noticeable in those poems that take up the motif of the beloved's anatomical parts as synecdoches of or surrogates for her beauty and character and their effects on the poet-lover. The repertory included, of course, such attendant actions as glances, smiles, and sighs, as well as personal or social gestures.

With specific regard to such actions and gestures, we should also note here two other, and related, aspects of sixteenth-century Italian Petrarchism and its European diffusion. First are the prose treatises and dialogues that deal exclusively with the beauty, breeding, and comportment of women, from both a laudatory and a satiric stance. These can be distinguished from the better-known works, such as Bembo's *Asolani* (named for the setting of the dialogues at Asolo and published in 1501), and Castiglione's *Il cortegiano* or *The Courtier* (published in 1528) that do not dwell upon bodily members or concern themselves with anatomical detail. Nor do they inquire into or prescribe the minutiae of personal and social behavior. In Bembo and Castiglione, Petrarchism blends with Neoplatonism and other sources of amatory and aesthetic theory in general discussions of female beauty and comportment as they inspire love or contribute to the cultivated social ambience of the *palazzo*.

Of those works that do focus more narrowly on the beauty, appearance, and actions of women, three deserve our attention. The first is by Agnolo Firenzuola (1493—1543), who completed his two dialogues *Delle bellezze delle donne* (On the Beauties of Women) in 1541.[14] His spokesman, Celso, quoting Petrarch and Ficino as well as Plato and Cicero, chats a good deal about bodily beauty as the product of harmony and proportion among the limbs. Thus, the finger of a hand can be "schietto e bianco" (trim and white) and thereby have its own appropriate beauty but not the "generale bellezza" of the philosophers, which is "una unione di diversi" (a union of diverse beauties). Furthermore, the hand and other "membra inferiori" do not share with the *bel viso* the power of its beauty to propel the beholder up the Platonic *scala amoris,* or ladder of love; but they do contribute to the beauty of the total body, "così vestite e coperte come ignude; e talor meglio, perciocché col vestirle garbatamente le s'empiono di maggior vaghezza" (as well dressed and covered as naked; and sometimes better, for by being dressed in a pleasing fashion they exude greater loveliness, p. 537). From the point of view of mannerism, it is interesting also that Celso praises one lady for "la maniera" (p. 575), and that after giving ideal measurements for the body and the head says there are others, rarely found in nature, that can be left to the painters, "i quali con una pennellata più e una meno le possono allungare e accortare come torna lor bene" (who with a stroke of the brush can lengthen or shorten these as seems good to them, p. 553). And finally, when pressed at the very end of the discourse by his audience of four ladies to say something more specific about the ideal hand, Celso responds as follows:

> La mano . . . si desidera pur bianca, e nella parte di sopra massimamente; ma grande, e un poco pienotta, con la palma un poco incavata, e ombreggiata di rose; le linee chiare, rare, ben distinti, ben segnate, non intrigate, non attraversate; i monticelli, e di Giove e di Venere e di Mercurio, ben distinte, ma non troppo alti; la linea particolare dimostratrice dell'ingegno, fonda e chiara, e da nessuna altra ricisa; quello scavo che è tra l'indice e 'l dito grosso, sia ben assettato, senza crespe, e di vivo colore. Le dita son belle quando son lunghe, schiette, dilicate e che un pochetto si vadano assotigliando verso la cima, ma sì poco, che appena si veggia sensibilmente. L'unghie hanno da esser chiare, e come balasci legati in rose incarnate, con la foglia del fior di melagrana; non lunghe, non tonde, né in tutto quadre, ma con un bell'atto, e con poco poco di curvatura; scalze, nette, ben tenute, sì che da basso appaia sempre quello archetto bianco, e di sopra avanzi della polpa del dito quanto la costola di un picciol coltello, senza che pur un minimo sospetto appaia d'orlo nero in sulle fine loro: e tutta la mano insieme ricerca una soave morbidezza, come se tocassimo fine seta, o sottilissima bambaggia. (pp. 594–95)

> [The hand . . . one desires of course that it be white, and especially the upper part; but large, and not too plump, with the palm a bit

concave and tinted with roses; its lines should be clear, uncommon, quite distinct, well marked, not intersecting, not criss-crossed; the little mountains, both of Jove and Venus as well as Mercury should be distinct but not too raised; the particular line that represents the intellect should be deep and clear, and intersected by no other; that hollow between the index finger and the thumb should be well compacted, without folds, and of vivid color. The fingers are beautiful when they are long, trim, and delicate, and when they taper just a bit toward the tips, but so little that one barely discerns it. The fingernails should be clear, and like rubies bound by fleshly roses, like the leaf of the pomegranate flower; not long, not round, nor entirely square, but with a beautiful design, and with very very little curvature; unmarred, neat, and well set, so that below there always appears that white little arch, and above there protrudes as much of the flesh of the finger as the spine of a little knife, without of course even a minimal hint of a black border at their end: and the whole hand together should as a result have a smooth softness, as though we were touching fine silk, or the most fine-spun cotton.]

Another such work, though far less learned and philosophical, is Alessandro Piccolomini's *Dialogo della bella creanza delle donne* (Dialogue on Beautiful Breeding in Women), published in 1540, in which the bawd Rafaella instructs a naive young wife, Margarita, in worldliness. At one point she asks her how she takes care of her hands, "Imperoché la bellezza de le mani è molto stimata in una giovine" (Because the beauty of the hands is highly prized in a young woman, p. 26). Later, she adds that if such a young woman has *belle mani,* she should seize "ogni occasione, che lei si porga, di mostrarle, come può accadere nel cavarsi e mettersi i guanti" (every occasion that presents itself to her to display them, as can happen when taking off and putting on gloves, p. 32).

If this example seems ironically anti-Petrarchistic, there is solemn seriousness in Federico da Udine's *Il libro della bella donna* (The Book of the Beautiful Lady), divided into three books and published in 1554.[15] At one point in Book 2, we are given a description of ideal hands that joins Firenzuola's in creating an iconology for lyric poets and for painters and sculptors, with frequent supporting citations from Petrarch himself and from contemporary Petrarchists, as well as classical authorities who confirm the ideal. From these "sacred" texts, the author prescribes the following by now familiar attributes: the hands must be ivory white, of course, but also "sottili" (thin or slender), and "lunghe" (long); they must have a marvelous "candore" (white glow), and be "tenerelle" (delicate) and "polite" (neat), as

well as "grassette" (a little plump) so that veins do not show too promi-
nently; and finally, "colorite e rosate alquanto" (a bit tinted and with a rosy
hue), and, inevitably, must have fingernails like oriental pearls
(pp. 250–51).

This prescription for a beautiful hand drawn from Petrarch and his
followers should alert us to the literary context of visual mannerism, and in
particular the representation of hands in mannerist portraits and history
painting. When we compare the hands of Raphael's *Donna velata* and
Bronzino's *Laura Battiferri* we note a startling difference. The Raphael
hands are idealized but appear natural, and in any event do not draw
attention to themselves. In contrast, the Bronzino hands, like the sitter's *bel
viso*, are distractingly ambiguous in appearance, being neither still nor
active, neither flesh nor stone, but a flattering visual paradox, a painted
oxymoron of the Petrarchist variety, an animate ivory. They also have the
other qualities—long, thin, tapered, delicate, tinted, and unveined—
listed above as requisite for the hands of *la bella donna*. Unlike the Raphael
hands, too, they are posed in a seemingly awkward fashion, the fingers of
the left hand pointing to the Petrarch poems or, more likely, merely
holding open the book in a way that seems to be anatomically difficult—a
visual equivalent to Tasso's "oscuretto" cited above. In a turn away from
natural appearance and toward abstraction, the left hand seems indeed to be
"posed," its fingers arranged to make an aesthetically appealing pattern or
design. It is understandable that some modern students of mannerism
should see such hands as expressions at least of nervous tension, if not as
symbols of psychic strain. While not ruling out such interpretations, the
Petrarchist context does suggest that an aesthetic canon that enjoyed wide
social acceptance is the underlying assumption.[16] Putting aside such mat-
ters as the psychic states of painter and sitter, and such questions as why the
painter, his sitter, and their audience would prefer to have such states
depicted in a portrait, we must assume that, like the poems in the book
Laura is holding, the hands are to be interpreted as laudatory indications of
her physical and intellectual worth.

Even a cursory glance at contrasting depictions of hands by High Re-
naissance and baroque painters and sculptor would enable an observer to
generalize about their relationship to mannerist hands. In High Renaissance
art the hand, whether in repose or in movement, is usually integrated into
the harmonious representation of the whole, even when it draws some
attention to itself because of a prominent gesture or the bravura skill of the
artist in depicting anatomical detail. Baroque hands, if one may so label
them, generally adhere to the High Renaissance manner, although with a
new emphasis on lifelike appearance and on rhetorical gesture—a most

celebrated example being the languid left hand of Teresa in Bernini's sculpture of the saint in ecstasy, found in Rome's S. Maria della Vittoria. Although that languid hand has its subtle meaning also, if we compare it to a mannerist depiction or sculpting of a hand, even a gesticulatng one, the Bernini version, despite the state of consciousness of Teresa, seems infinitely more "real" to the viewer. Obviously, mannerist artists, like Petrarchist poets, were not interested in or did not choose to represent such reality.

In his *Self-Portrait* and in other paintings such as the famous *Madonna of the Long Neck,* Parmigianino depicts hands that range somewhere between those of Raphael and Bronzino but closer to the latter in their appearance and pose. There would seem to be more emphasis on soft flesh than hard ivory, less strain in the arrangement of fingers. Nevertheless, from the literary and cultural contexts we have been analyzing, it would seem that the modern poet has perhaps mistaken the emphasis of Parmigianino's hand, magnified and thrust out at us in the *Self-Portrait*. Whereas Ashberry wonders whether it is "shield or greeting" or "the shield of a greeting" (p. 82), I would suggest that the hand of the painter has, rather, been put on display, is flaunted like a visual metaphor, as a surrogate for his idealized artistic self. That it is his own *bella mano* and not that of a Petrarchan mistress is just another of the witty inversions that underlie this strangely beautiful painting.

The literary motif of hand-and-glove may also provide a context for another fascinating and somewhat baffling Parmigianino work, his *Portrait of a Young Woman* (1535–37), traditionally titled with the name of a celebrated Roman courtesan named Antea or assumed to be the artist's mistress. She was in fact neither, but what interests us is her gloved right hand contrasted to the ungloved, typically mannerist left hand with which she fingers the chain around her neck. She is holding the other glove in her right hand, which seems to be supporting the head of a weasel or sable fur piece that is disturbingly lifelike. Because of the startling anatomical distortion of the woman's right shoulder and arm, the viewer's attention is drawn to the animal, which seems to slither down to her gloved hand in order to munch on the chain that is entwined about her fingers and also serves as its leash. The smaller chain echoes the larger one she is wearing on her breast and into which she has inserted the index finger of her ungloved left hand—either pulling it taut or being supported by it. Pope-Hennessy says there is a gold sheath on the snout of the animal, which seems to emphasize its ornamental nature, but he also points out that the weasel was a symbol of propriety (pp. 205–06). Freedberg emphasizes the erotic ideal: "Antea is the human, individual, feminine counterpart of Francesco's ideal conception of the male. In a realm where idea and matter perfectly coincide . . . Antea would be the woman of whom Francesco could have been the lover. Her portrait certainly has been painted *con amore*" (p. 120).

I would add that since the painter could not depict the gesture of donning or removing a glove without awkwardness, he chose instead to paint a visual paradox, to contrast gloved and ungloved hand, in a Petrarchan key, as an alternative way of affirming the amatory feeling which Freedberg detects. That contrast, which echoes the other ambiguities in the image, affirms the coincidence of real and ideal, passion and restraint, creative fantasy and artful control, that is its governing theme. It may be significant in this regard that the motif of gloved and ungloved hand occurs again in another famous painting by Parmigianino, the *Portrait of Gian Galeazzo Sanvitale, Count of Fontanellato,* also in Naples.

These Italian visual and literary representations of *la bella mano* and its accompanying *caro guanto* were welcomed everywhere in Europe that Petrarchism inspired imitation. The range and variety of such imitation is fairly overwhelming, but we can discern its main currents by making some divisions and establishing some working categories. Mannered and mannerist poems were written on the hand alone, or on the hand and glove, or on the glove alone. These run the gamut, too, from mere translation to fresh adaptation. The hand and glove are either praised or damned, with a good many ironic variations on these fundamental attitudes in between. The hand may be briefly cited as part of a catalogue of the beloved's beauties and virtues, or it may be sharply focused upon and metaphorically magnified. The hand may be a static object of contemplation or an active agent whose gesture is described and interpreted by its admirer and victim. The glove, in addition to sharing the adoration and opprobrium heaped upon the hand it covers and uncovers, arouses its own either subtly or unabashedly erotic responses.

In the category of translation, a version by Sir Thomas Wyatt (1503–42) of the archetypal hand poem by Petrarch can serve as our example, especially since it is also an adaptation of the complex sonnet original to a simpler stanzaic form:

> O goodely hand,
> Wherin doth stand
> My hert distrast in payne,
> Faire hand, Alas,
> In little spas
> My liff that doeth restrayne.
>
> O fyngers slight,
> Departed right,

So long, so small, so rownd,
Goodely bygone,
And yet alone
Most cruell in my wound.

With Lilis whight
And Roses bright
Doth stryve thy colour faire;
Nature did lend
Eche fyngers ende
A perle for to repayre.

Consent at last,
Syns that thou hast
My hert in thy demayne,
For seruice trew
On me to rew,
And reche me love againe.

And if not so,
Then with more woo
Enforce thiself to strayne
This simple hert,
That suffereth smart
And rid it owte of payne.[17]

Brief expressions of praise and blame, usually found in poems that catalogue the beloved's physical characteristics or expand upon a few of them, are found everywhere in European lyrics of the sixteenth and seventeenth centuries. Thus Maurice Scève (ca. 1510—ca.62) can extol "mains celestement blanches" in one poem, Philippe Desportes (1546—1606) can address a "guerrière main, de ma prise embellie" in another; or, pondering the paradoxical fusion of angel and warrior, Desportes can also invoke "une main trop belle et trop cruelle."[18] As for lengthier treatments, there is a *blason* by Claude Chappuys (1500—75) beginning "O doulce main, main belle, main polie," which can be juxtaposed to the *contre-blason* of Charles de la Huetterie (published in 1536), "O malle main, meschante et malheureuse."[19] Joachim du Bellay (1525—60) praises his beloved's hand for its learned inspiration:

La docte main, dont Minerve eust appris,
Main, dont l'yvoire en cinq perles allonge,
C'est, ô mon coeur! la lyme qui te ronge
Et le rabot qui polit mes ecris.[20]

Il Parmigianino, *La Bella* (Antea). Naples, Galleria Nazionale di Capodimonte.

[That learned hand, from which Minerva could have learned, that hand, whose ivory extends into five pearls, is, O my heart, the file that rasps you and the plane that smoothes my writings.]

Hugues Salel (1504—53) tells his pen that it cannot really describe his beloved's hand at all:

> Plume, vous travaillez en vain
> En voulant comparer la main
> De ma dame à mortelle chose,
> Soit lis, ivoire ou blanche rose,
> Pour ce que, quand Amour prétend
> De rendre l'oeil humain content,
> Ne peut montrer objet plus digne,
> O main jolie, o main divine.[21]

[Pen, you struggle in vain in wishing to compare the hand of my lady to a mortal thing, be it lilies, ivory, or white rose; for when Love proposes to content the human eye, he can show no more worthy object, O pretty hand, O divine hand.]

Pierre de Ronsard (1524–85), in his *Elégie à Marie Stuart* (1567), recalls the famous queen in mourning (wearing a billowing veil!), and praises her hands for *not* being bejewelled:

> Et vostre main, des plus belles la belle,
> N'a rien sinon sa blancheur naturelle,
> Et vos longs doigts, cinq rameaux inégaux,
> Ne sont pompeux de bagues ny d'anneaux.[22]

[And your hand, the most beautiful of the beautiful, has only its natural whiteness; and your long fingers, five branches unalike, are not lavished with bands or rings.]

Herbert of Cherbury (1583—1648), in his "A Description," begins to catalogue the lady's beauties and then comes to the hand, which he burdens with a startling biblical conceit:

> Here take her by the Hand, my Muse,
> With that sweet Foe, to make my Truce,
> To compact Manna, best compar'd,
> Whose dewy inside's not full hard.[23]

No wonder Aurelian Townsend (1583?—1651?), with a perhaps unsuspected ironic reference, can complain in his "Come Not to Me for Scarfs" of the inferiority of courtly to country love as follows:

> Att court new Fashions are not strange,
>   But heere wee ever keepe our old;
> There love (they say) consists in change,
> Heer, after one, all ours are told.
>   The first is last,
>   Because wee cast
> One hand can but another hold;
> But they have loves, wee understand,
> For every finger of the hand.[24]

Cherbury and Townsend have taken us into the seventeenth century, of course, reminding us that it was a time when German lyric poetry burst into creativity, with frequent recapitulation of Renaissance themes. Thus we are not surprised to hear Christian Hofmann von Hofmannswaldau (1617–69) praise his lady in the old-fashioned way with a catalogue that includes "zwey hande, derer grimm mich in den bann gethan" (two hands whose anger can excommunicate me); but then he strikes a familiar baroque note of poignant transitoriness in another poem, admonishing the hand that time will soon rob it of its powers, "die werden zeitlich weichen." In a similar mood, Martin Opitz (1597–1639), warning his mistress that there is not world enough and time, cruelly says, "Die hand als schnee verfallen, / Und du wirst alt" (Your snowy hands will decay, and you grow old).[25]

For the motif of the hand "in action," making a gesture or engaged in some activity, we turn first to the following mannered madrigal by the Spanish poet Gutierre de Cetina (ca. 1516–ca.55), which departs from the premise that the *bella mano* covers the beloved's eyes, thus playing the usual role of the *caro guanto* in its own case:

> Cubrir los bellos ojos
> con la mano que ya me tienne muerto
> cautela fué por cierto,
> que ansi doblar pensastes mis enojos.
>   Pero de tal cautela
> harto mayor ha sido el bien que el daño,
> que el resplandor extraño
> del sol se puede ver mientras se cela.
>   Así que, aunque pensastes
> cubrir vuestra beldad, única, immensa,

> yo os perdono la ofensa,
> pues, cubiertos, mejor verlos dejastes.[26]

[To cover your beautiful eyes with the hand that already has caused my death was certainly crafty, for you thought thus to double my sufferings. But far greater has been the good than the evil of this ploy, for the rare brilliance of the sun can be seen while it hides itself. So that, although you thought to cover your beauty, unique and immense, I pardon you the offense, for by covering them you have let them be seen better.]

A similar screening gesture is recalled by Ronsard in the sonnet to Hélène beginning "L'autre jour que j'estois sur le haut d'un degré" (The other day when I was at the top of a stair, *Oeuvres completes,* 1:219–20). In the octave of the sonnet, the poet describes in conventional fashion the devastating effect on him of his lady's glance as she was passing by. But despite this premise, with the real social setting and the natural encounter of poet and beloved that prove so effective in other poems of this series, the best Ronsard can manage here is mannered praise of her hand in the sestet:

> Lors si ta belle main passant ne m'eust fait signe,
> Main blanche, qui se vante estre fille d'un Cygne,
> Je fusse mort, Hélène, aux rayons de tes yeux.
> Mais ton signe retint l'ame presque ravie,
> Ton oeil se contenta d'estre victorieux,
> Ta main se resjouyt de me donner la vie.

[Then if your beautiful hand had not greeted me, that white hand, which can boast of being the daughter of a swan, I would have been dead, Helen, of the beams from your eyes. But your gesture kept my soul all but ravished, your eye was content in its victory, your hand rejoiced in granting me my life.]

If the previous poem shows that great poets can be mannered as well as mannerist on occasion, the following one by a very minor figure, Gabriel de Trellon (?– 1611), entitled "La Belle Main," proves the contrary for their lesser brethren. It is, in my view, an instructive example of a mannerist poem written in the active mode of hand depiction:

> Voyci la belle main et blanche et potelée,
> Qui prend tout, qui tien tout, qui sçait tout attirer
> Aux beaux rhets qu'elle tend: car qui pouroit tirer
> D'un filet si charmeur son ame ensorcelee?

Voyci la belle main, dont la corde est filée
Du petit arc d'Amour, main pour nous martirer
Qui luy bande son arc quand il veut nous tirer,
Et par qui de ses traits la poincte est afilée.

On dict qu'Amour estant par tout victorieux
Veut faire un feu de joye, et ceignant glorieux
Son chef de vieux Lauriers, de ses conquestes fresches

Doit dresser un Buscher qu'on n'ait encores veu:
C'est un monceau de coeurs traversé de ses flesches:
Et ceste belle main y doit mettre le feu.[27]

[Behold the beautiful hand, white and plump, that takes all, holds all, and knows how to snare all in the beautiful nets she spreads: for who would want to extricate his bewitched soul from such a charming net? Behold the beautiful hand by which the string of the little bow of love is spun, hand that martyrs us by drawing his bow when he wishes to shoot at us, and by whom the points of his arrows are sharpened. It is said that Love, being everywhere victorious, determined to make a bonfire, and, wreathing his head in venerable laurel, to erect a pyre of his fresh conquests such as had never been seen before: it is a pile of hearts pierced by his arrows, and this beautiful hand will light the fire.]

One notices here the isolation of the disembodied hand from all personal and social contexts. It has become pure symbol engaged in the various symbolic acts of spreading nets, spinning and drawing bow strings, sharpening arrows, and firing a holocaust of pierced hearts. In this surreal world, inhabited only by images and ideas that refer to previous poems, ironic inversion is the norm. The poet praises the lady's hand by depicting her awesome power as a surrogate for, and chief assistant to, the cruel god of love himself. All of Love's usual activities and effects are transferred to the *bella mano,* which has become his emblem. This compacting of amatory psychology into disembodied hands and gestures, with the accompanying familiar props (nets, bows, arrows, fire, pierced hearts), is typical of mannerist sensibility straining after fresh but recognizable and therefore necessarily recondite versions of standard motifs.

It is this emblematic notion of the hand, I think, that accounts for Nicholas Hilliard's otherwise puzzling *Portrait of a Youth,* a miniature that shows a lover clasping a woman's hand emerging from a cloud above.[28] This image and its elusive motto "Attici amoris ergo" may have a more precise context than ours, but I would suggest that it is a *bella mano* rescuing a

Nicholas Hilliard, *Portrait of a Youth*. London, Victoria and Albert Museum.

poet-lover from above, a symbol of amatory salvation by means of a valid instrument of the beloved's grace. As such, it is the familiar opposite of Gabriel de Trellon's motif of the hand as *cruelle*. If, too, as the motto hints, there is a Neoplatonic element involved, we must also remember that Petrarch had followed Dante in depicting the dead beloved as drawing him to Heaven, and subsequently the Petrarchists had described the *bella mano* as heavenly, celestial, and blessed in its capacity as symbol of the lady's power to confer spiritual regeneration as well as erotic suffering and bliss on her worshipers.

Our next example of mannerist description, this time in the static mode, comes from the second book of the *Arcadia* of Sir Philip Sidney (1554–86), where Zelmane sings of "each part" of Philoclea's beauty, including her hand:

> Now course doth lead me to her hand,
> Of my first love the fatal band;
> Where whiteness doth forever sit:
> Nature herself enamell'd it.
> For there with strange compact doth lie
> Warm snow, moist pearl, soft ivory.
> There fall those sapphire-coloured brooks,
> Which conduit-like with curious crooks,
> Sweet islands make in that sweet land.
> As for the fingers of the hand,
> The bloody shafts of Cupid's war,
> With amatists they headed are.[29]

This strange combination of imagery and meaning is the product of the conversion of the lady's hand into a miraculous landscape and its location in a poetic world where art has defeated nature by forcing her to become an artist herself. Like a goldsmith, nature has "enamell'd" the hand contrary to her norms, for she has allowed warm and cold, moist and dry, soft and hard to mingle artfully, the way a mannerist artist does when he gives the hand an ambiguous appearance. Strictly speaking, as we have seen, the veins ought not to be so prominent, and Sidney has undoubtedly been lured by the topographical conceit into emphasizing their appearance. But then, the brooks are extraordinary themselves in being sapphire-colored and in the decorative curves they follow as they define islands of flesh. Similarly "bloody," the fingernails have a contrasting purple tint and are also jewel-like, and therefore equally precious. In sum, though an abstruse and gro-

tesque problem, this hand is, in the mannerist sense, an aesthetic triumph
and therefore the most appropriate possible compliment to its possessor.

Interestingly enough, immediately after this description a dog steals
Philoclea's glove, "whose fine proportion showed well what a dainty guest
was wont there to be lodged" (p. 191), and takes it to its master, Am-
phialus, along with a book of four or five leaves of paper also belonging to
her. When Amphialus agrees to return the papers but expresses a desire to
keep her glove, the jealous Zelmane (or Pyrocles) engages him in a duel and
wounds him. This episode of chivalric Petrarchism makes clear how the
hand-and-glove motif had penetrated narrative as well as lyric forms, and
also how crucial to the glove theme is the traditional motif asserting that
whatever comes into contact with the lady is envied by the lover, who
wishes to take its place.

Whereas Amphialus preferred the glove to the book belonging to
Philoclea, Edmund Spenser (1552—59) was content, in the very first poem
of his *Amoretti,* indeed in its opening lines, to envy his own book in the
hands of his beloved:

> Happy ye leaves! when as those lilly hands,
> Which hold my life in their dead doing might,
> Shall handle you, and hold in loves soft bands,
> Lyke captives trembling at the victor's sight.[30]

Although Spenser is not usually discussed in the context of mannerism, and
need not be, we should remember that, as Mario Praz pointed out some
time ago, the basic conceit of this poem came from the mannered Petrarch-
ist Tebaldeo.[31] And the reader may recall, too, that Andrea del Sarto,
Bronzino, and other painters had popularized the portrait motif of a lady
reading a volume of Petrarch's love poems. If nothing else, there is a
mannerist context for Spenser's initial and governing sonnet of the
sequence.

The glove motif also attracted Maurice Scève, who penned this strange
version:

> Vous, Gantz heureux, fortunée prison
> De liberté vouluntairement serve,
> Celez le mal avec la guerison,
> Comme vostre umbre en soy tousjours conserve
> Et froit, et chault, selon que se reserve
> Le libre vueil de necessaire aisance.
>   Mais, tout ansi qu'à son obeissance

Dedens vous entre, et sort sa blanche main,
Je sortiray de l'obscure nuisance,
Où me tient clos cest enfant inhumain.

(no. 169, p. 131)[32]

[You happy gloves, fortunate prison of liberty and in voluntary serf-
dom, you hide the malady with the cure, as your darkness always
preserves within itself both cold and heat, according as (her) free will
reserves for itself a necessary freedom. But in the same way as at her
behest her white hand enters and exits from you, I exit from the dark
suffering within which this inhuman child has enclosed me.]

This treatment is typical of mannerist poems by Scève, who is wont to focus
sharply upon traditional images and motifs and coax them into becoming
surreal verbal emblems of paradoxical psychic states, parallel to the visual
emblems that appeared in his *Délie*. The totally abstract context, the image
of the glove and its enclosing darkness, the repeated contrast between
freedom and confinement, the sudden appearances of the hand—like
epiphanies—all convey vividly the emotional flutterings and the fluctua-
tions of mood in an amatory experience overwhelmed by successive waves of
desire, frustration, and despair. In the best mannerist fashion, the poet has
gazed penetratingly at a conventional image and exploited its resonances in
a way that could produce a merely clever redeployment of the norms, but
instead, because of the sheer intensity of the imaginative pursuit, results in
a reaching out to experiential thought and feeling. Not even the trite
reference to Cupid (the "inhuman child" of the last line) can entirely
disperse the effect created by the poet's earlier licensing of his sensibility.
Indeed, one explanation of the unsatisfactory ending might well be that in
this poem Scève's art has turned in on itself completely; and having arrived
at a near hallucinatory core, it must return to the surface, and the safety, of
a cliché.

In contrast, there is the more conventional wit of Desportes, who strug-
gles to work one more variation on the glove theme by introducing a
religious conceit and accomplishes at least a considerable degree of *maniera*:

Je la doy bien hair ceste main ennemie
Qui decocha sur moy tant de traits rigoreux,
Et du sang de ma playe encor tout chaloureux,
M'escrivit dans le coeur le nom de Parthenie.

Toutesfois je l'adore, et la peine infinie
N'en sçauroit retirer mon oeil trop desireux;

Peussé-je luy donner cent baisers amoureux,
Pour vanger mon outrage et la rendre punie!

Ce bel amas de neige excessif en froideur
Pourroit en le preseant refraichir mon ardeur,
Si le secours d'un mal se prend de son contraire.

Mais puis qu'un si grand prix à ma foy n'est promis,
Au moins baisons son gand. Il est toujours permis
De baiser le Dessus d'un sacré reliquaire.[33]

[I should certainly hate this enemy hand that lets fly so many harsh arrows at me, and with the still hot blood of my wound inscribes in my heart the name of Parthenie. Nevertheless, I adore it, and the infinite pain is not enough to remove from it my too desiring eyes; would that I could confer a hundred loving kisses there, to avenge my insult, and punish it! This beautiful mass of snow, excessively cold, could, if it were pressed, cool my ardor. But since so great a reward for my faith is not permitted, at least let us kiss her glove. It is always licit to kiss the cover of a sacred reliquary.]

This poem was to be duly echoed by Henry Constable (1562–1613) in the couplet of his sonnet entitled "To his Ladies hand upon occasion of her glove which in her absence he kissed":

And I thy glove kisse as a thing devine
Thy arrowes quiver and thy reliques shrine.[34]

It is also worth noting that Constable has another poem, "To his Mistrisse upon occasion of a Petrarch he gave her, shewing her the reason why the Italian Commenters dissent so much in the exposition thereof" (p. 133), the reason for the dissent being, of course, that Petrarch had foretold the existence of Constable's mistress, and therefore anyone who had not seen her would not understand! Among his sonnets there is also one, "To Mr. Hilliard upon occasion of a picture he made of my Ladie Rich" (p. 158), which says that "no man knew aright / To give to stones and pearles true die and light / Till first youre art with orient nature strive" (ll. 6–8), a typical mannerist statement about vying with nature. Finally, this same poet has a poem, "Of his Ladies vayle wherewith she covered her" (p. 132), which nods in muddled fashion in the direction of the *bel velo* theme discussed in the previous essay.

Barnabe Barnes (1569–1609), in sonnet 63 of his *Parthenophil and Parthenophe,* echoes a familiar wish with regard to the *bella mano* but makes an extension to other parts of the lady's anatomy and other ornamental objects bedecking it that will have a future:

> Would I were chang'd to my mistresse gloves,
> That those white lovely fingers I might hide,
> That I might kiss those hands, which mine hart loves
> Or else that cheane of pearle, her neckes vain pride, . . .[35]

But for genuine rehabilitation of such, by now tired, motifs as opposed to Scève's rare kind of intensification, one must look mainly to the poets of the seventeenth century, who tried to invent new or fresh approaches to the Petrarchan scenario by challenging its theology, extending its thematic range, and including realistic subjects and settings hitherto regarded as lying outside its domain. The following poem by Richard Lovelace (1618–57), deservedly famous, startles us because of its witty conceits and eroticism, but especially with its underlying extended metaphor drawn from the economic and social experience of owning, renting, and farming property and the attendant class structure:

Ellinda's Glove

> Thou snowy farm with thy five tenements!
>   Tell thy white mistress here was one
>   That call'd to pay his daily rents;
> But she a-gathering flow'rs and hearts is gone,
> And thou left void to rude possession.
>
> But grieve not, pretty ermine cabinet,
>   Thy alabaster lady will come home;
>   If not, what tenant can there fit
> The slender turnings of thy narrow room,
> But must ejected be by his own doom?
>
> Then give me leave to leave my rent with thee:
>   Five kisses, one unto a place;
>   For though the lute's too high for me,
> Yet servants knowing miniken nor base
> Are still allow'd to fiddle with the case.[36]

In an even more daring poem, "Her Muff," Lovelace imagines the ten fingers as white nuns who are doing disciplinary penance by wearing coarse smocks, that is, the hairy fur muff (ll. 8–10). In the closing lines, the poet makes brutally explicit the erotic implications that had always hovered about the *caro guanto* theme:

> But I, in my invention tough
> Rate not this outward bliss enough,
> But still contemplate must the hidden muff.[37]

Seeking fresh invention, the poets of the sixteenth century had not been as "tough" as Lovelace in that their exploitation of motifs related to the hand tended to focus on the hand itself and its fingers, its conventional appearance or gestures, or on such normal accoutrements as gloves and rings. Both Serafino and Scève, for example, had written about the ring circumscribing the finger of the *bella mano,* but neither of these two extraordinarily witty poets, manipulating with entirely different results the shorter, often epigrammatic forms of the *dizain* and the *strombotto,* had looked very far beyond the conventional thematic borders.[38] In the case of Scève, a far greater poet and infinitely more imaginative and intelligent than the Italian court entertainer, we have seen that his penetrating poetic eye looks inward rather than outward, that he prefers to concentrate on the hand and its associations rather than, like Desportes, to bring in clever analogies that have an immediate appeal in their surprisingly partial correspondence but no lasting resonance or insight. Obviously there is a principle here that may be useful for distinguishing mannered from mannerist poems, and mannerist from proto-baroque thematic exploration.

The sixteenth-century poets also initiated but did not fully exploit the motif of the hand actively engaged in some domestic or social activity. One particularly interesting example is the fair but cruel seamstress, the beloved's fingers engaged in embroidery. Here is Wyatt's version, the better of two he wrote on this motif:

> Who hath herd of suche crueltye before?
> That when my plaint remembred her my woo
> That caused it, she cruell more and more
> Wisshed eche stitche, as she did sit and soo,
> Had prykt myn hert, for to encrese my sore;
> And, as I thinck, she thought it had been so;
> For as she thought this is his hert in dede,
> She pricked herd and made her self to blede.[39]

In canto 24 of the *Orlando furioso,* the poet Ariosto narrates the pathetic death of Zerbino and, in a passage for which he has been criticized (ottava 66), draws the following brilliant but brief analogy in describing a stream of red blood against the gleaming armor of the wounded warrior:

> Così talora un bel purpureo nastro
> ho veduto partir tela d'argento

> da quella bianca mano più ch'alabastro,
> da cui partir il cor spesso mi sento.[40]

[thus have I seen a silver cloth divided with a beautiful purple strip by that hand whiter than alabaster which has often made me feel my heart divided.]

At the other extreme is Marino's hectic baroque version of the motif:

> È strale, è stral, non ago
> quel ch'opra in suo lavoro,
> nova Aracne d'amor, colei ch'adoro;
> onde, mentre il bel lino orna e trapunge,
> di mille punte il cor mi passa e punge.
> Misero! e quel sì vago
> sanguigno fil che tira,
> tronca, annoda, assotiglia, attorce e gira
> la bella man gradita,
> è il fil de la mia vita.
>
> (*Poesie varie*, p. 70)

[A dart, a dart, not a needle, she uses in her labor, new Arachne of love, she whom I adore; so that while she embroiders and adorns the lovely cloth, she pierces and stabs my heart with a thousand points. Wretched! And that so lovely sanguine thread which the beautiful and pleasing hand draws, cuts, ties, thins, twists, and turns is the thread of my life.]

The Wyatt, Ariosto, and Marino versions of the cruel seamstress may be contrasted to this justly famous Góngoresque treatment of the related motif of the ring on the finger of a proud beauty:

> Prisión del nácar era articulado
> de mi firmeza un émulo luciente
> un dïamante ingenïosamente
> en oro también él aprisionado.
>
> Clori, pues que su debo apremïado
> de metal aun precioso no consiente,
> gallarda un día, sobre impacíente,
> lo redimió del vínculo dorado.
>
> Mas ay, que insidïoso latón breve
> en los cristales de su bella mano
> sacrílego divina sangre bebe:

> púrpura ilustró menos indïano
> marfil; invidïosa, sobre nieve
> claveles deshojó la Aurora en vano.[41]

[A diamond was a fetter for the jointed mother-of-pearl (a lucent competitor of my constancy), and itself also ingeniously fettered in gold. Clori, then, who will not have her finger constrained by metal, no matter how precious, one day gracefully and also impatiently redeemed it from the golden chain. But alas, for an insidious bit of brass sacrilegiously drinks divine blood from the crystals of her lovely hand: purple on Indian ivory shone less brightly; in envy, Aurora scattered carnations on the snow, in vain.]

The occasion is trivial enough, simply the removal of a ring from a finger, and the accident that occurs would not ordinarily be quite so momentous. But from Petrarchan ideology and mannerist poetics Góngora has drawn the notion of focusing upon a finger that is a synecdoche for the beautiful hand that is, in turn, a surrogate for its beauteous owner. The theme of the ring confining a finger, a scaled-down version of the glove enveloping a hand, is merged here with the related motif of the cruel seamstress who pricks her own finger and thus causes it to bleed. But the meaning of the poem remains difficult to grasp at first because of its dislocated syntax, its puzzling designation of objects by figurative substitutions (jointed mother-of-pearl for finger, metal for ring, prison and fetter for the diamond in the ring and the ring on the finger, drinking blood from crystals for pricking the finger), and its compressed expression and condensed similes in the closing tercet. The vivid contrasts of the last two images—white and red being the traditionally extolled colors of love—and especially the spectacular gesture of Aurora are very much in the baroque style; but it is noteworthy that they represent an extension outward of analogy into nature and mythology, prompted by the resultant color rather than the action of the hand itself. When the poet focuses on the pricked finger, he proposes the contracted and gratuitous image of a bold bit of metal sacrilegiously drinking blood from the crystal (glass) that is her flesh, not as a similitude but as an event. Although this conceit is obviously intended to flatter, it is also grotesquely inappropriate and has no meaningful reverberations within the poem. The persistence of such mannered conceits into the seventeenth century, and the mixture of mannerist and baroque features in this poem, should alert us, not only to the dangers of categorizing and labeling poets and their works, but also of adducing certain individual poems as clinching evidence.

Obviously, the poet who wished to give new life to this theme and was prepared to extend its range and widen its context, rather than to probe it ever more relentlessly, could create a poem like "Celia bleeding, to the Surgeon" by Thomas Carew (1594/5–1640), with which I shall conclude this essay:

> Fond man, that canst beleeve her blood
>   Will from those purple chanels flow;
> Or that the pure untainted flood,
>   Can any foule distemper know;
> Or that thy weake steele can incize
> Thy Crystall case, wherein it lyes.
>
> Know; her quick blood, proud of his seat,
>   Runs dauncing through her azure veines;
> Whose harmony no cold, nor heat
>   Disturbs, whose hue no tincture staines;
> And the hard rock wherein it dwells,
> The keenest darts of Love repels.
>
> But thou reply'st, behold she bleeds;
>   Foole, thou'rt deceived; and dost not know
> The mystique knot whence this proceeds,
>   How Lovers in each other grow;
> Thou struckst her arme, but 'twas my heart
> Shed all the blood, felt all the smart.[42]

The poem, while recalling both Sidney's landscape and Wyatt's needle, as well as Góngora's brass sliver, nevertheless takes its departure from a quite different premise. The setting is not only realistic but ordinary, for we are told that a surgeon is preparing to bleed the lady "for real" and in the presence of the poet. The surgeon-outsider, not conversant with Celia and the Petrarchan scenario, actually believes that his instrument can penetrate her flesh ("the Crystall case" and "hard rock"), though insiders—namely, frustrated lovers—know that it has repelled "the keenest darts of love" in the past. When Celia is in fact made to bleed, as announced by the triumphant outsider, here poet-lover responds by acclaiming with desperate bravura a miracle of Petrarchan theology that he asserts transcends mere physical reality. He thus avoids having to acknowledge the truth that Celia can be penetrated and can bleed, and thereby averts the threat to the fragile ideals of love poetry from skeptical outsiders who dwell in the so-called real world. Recognizing, too, that his own realistic premise has perhaps also threatened the convention, Carew asserts the existence of a mystic knot that outsiders would not be able to see or understand, and that allows him also to conclude his poem by safely incorporating his own innovative but risky motif into the orthodox amatory tradition.

We might now be reminded of Donne's flea and that poet's invocation of the baroque poetic world of material reality leavened by marvels and wonders, the transcendence of normal barriers, metamorphosis and interpenetration among beings of nature and the various realms of human experience. Instead of the double vision of mannerism, with one eye on the object and another on previous poems about that object, we have the unitary aesthetic assumption of a mystic knot that can be intuited, if not untied, by the *ingegno* of the poet. Whereas the mannerist love poems we have been analyzing tend to begin with conventional themes and then proceed to exploit them, only occasionally having realistic reverberations, this poem by Carew and other baroque love poems tend to begin with ordinary situations which they then link up, surprisingly if not startlingly, with Petrarchan orthodoxy, thanks to the power of unconfined wit. Of course, these last are unproved generalizations, and I hope to support them in detail in a future study of the baroque love lyric. Suffice it here to say that, as I have suggested several times and will argue at greater length in the Postlude, one helpful way of defining literary mannerism is not only to measure its suspected lyric creations against the more solidly established and clearly understood norms of Petrarch's *Rime,* but also to juxtapose those creations with models of the baroque style.

5

Postlude: Three Versions
of the Pastoral Invitation to Love

Although art historians may disagree to some extent about the origins, nature, and diffusion of the Italian baroque style in the visual arts, there would appear to be a consensus that it was, at least in part, due to a reaction against mannerism. According to this view, toward the end of the sixteenth century the naturalism of Caravaggio and the return to High Renaissance classicism in the works of the Carracci pronounced the doom of mannerism and heralded the later age of Bernini, Rubens, and Poussin. Then, for a goodly portion of the seventeenth century, the full baroque style prevailed in Italy and many parts of Europe, with various modulations and adaptations of its aesthetic tenets, including French classicism and its impact. As John R. Martin has pointed out, however: "The shift from Mannerism to Baroque was not sudden or abrupt but was complicated by considerable overlapping. Though the earliest manifestations of Baroque art appeared well before the year 1600, Mannerism was still a living force in many European centres during the first decades of the seventeenth century."[1] Martin finds it more profitable, therefore, to define *baroque* in contrast to *mannerism* not by chronology but by the juxtaposition of allegedly representative works. One such contrast he draws is between Rubens's *Descent from the Cross* of 1611–12 and Salviati's *Deposition* of 1547–48, concluding that in the Salviati "Mannerist refinement and artifice prevail over nature and feeling," thereby indicating one reason for the reaction against mannerism (p. 21). Later Martin wrote of the sophistication, the artificiality, and the "abstract and precious tendencies" of late mannerism (p. 54). Hence it would seem that while juxtapositions of mannerist and baroque works are useful for delineating the nature of both, the point of view of the critic, as here, can hardly avoid giving the impression that the "defeated" style got what it deserved! Or, put another way, mannerism is identical with the overly refined *maniera* and the creatively arid *manierato* against which the baroque reacted in such a "healthy" fashion.

Titian, *Nymph and Shepherd*. Vienna, Kunsthistorisches Museum.

A literary historian testing the validity and value of the art historian's chronological scheme and comparative method for Renaissance literature has, of course, to avoid rigidly charting parallel chronological sequences of styles in the different arts, especially since, as I believe, literary mannerism does not seem to share with visual mannerism and baroque, or with literary baroque for that matter, a clear stylistic profile of its own. It is not so much an autonomous style as a mode or modulation of the Renaissance literary style that predominated in Italy and elsewhere in the sixteenth century. Nevertheless, given the homogeneity of much of Renaissance culture, it would be surprising if there were not an analogous, if not a parallel, development of literary and visual styles and modes. As for the comparative method, it has long been a technique of literary analysis to juxtapose poems in different styles or from different eras in order to illuminate them, and this technique presents few problems for the critic of mannerism as long as the analysis is not coerced by the visual parallels that may be invoked. Thus, in the course of this study I have occasionally juxtaposed allegedly mannerist and arguably baroque poems as an additional way of defining literary mannerism, although my emphasis has been upon comparison with the Petrarchan norm.

The juxtaposition of mannerist and baroque poems, then, can be effective, provided that one recognizes the dangers just noted and also, as pointed out earlier, that such interpretive activity inevitably makes its way along a circular path, so that at best one can only gather insights en route rather than arrive at a final destination. One must avoid, too, assumptions that the baroque rescued us from mannerism, or that the mannerist mode was either a trivialization or a fascinating adaptation of Renaissance lyric style. But in order to determine whether, given these restrictions, the method of juxtaposition can still be a valuable means of clarification, one must put it to a test. To that end I have reserved this final chapter for a brief trial exercise that will also serve as a postlude to my study of literary mannerism. In addition, I have shifted the focus away from Petrarchism to pastoralism in order to broaden the scope of the inquiry and also thereby to encourage others to extend their investigations of these matters into other Renaissance literary genres and modes. In the brief analysis that follows, then, I juxtapose three pastoral poems, two of which are quite famous but all three of which are representative enough to provide us with significant evidence for our inquiry.

In the anthology *Englands Helicon,* first published in 1600 as a pioneering collection of pastoral lyric, appeared a pair of poems, one by Marlowe, the other by "Ignoto" (probably, though not certainly, Ralegh), on the theme of the pastoral invitation to love.[2] The Marlowe poem had appeared a year earlier in *The Passionate Pilgrime* in a four-stanza version that Fredson Bowers argues is the original, and it is certainly the case that the six-stanza version of *Englands Helicon* is a problem, what with its two concluding stanzas and the awkward repetition of *delight* in the last one, not to mention other, less crucial textual details.[3] Also, in the second edition of his *The Compleat Angler* (1655) Izaak Walton inserted an additional stanza to make a seven-stanza version, further complicating an already complex textual tradition. The reply by "Ignoto" (attributed to Ralegh by Walton) has an equally slippery textual history, beginning with *The Passionate Pilgrime*, where only its first stanza appears with Marlowe's four.[4] In *Englands Helicon*, in both editions of Walton's work, and in manuscript sources, the poem is given along with Marlowe's in either an equal or unequal number of stanzas, but usually paired. Thus, although Bowers suggests that it may not have been the original intention to have the Invitation and the Reply formally symmetrical as well as paired, the evidence of *Englands Helicon*, Walton's editions, and other sources where they are both given does indicate a desire for symmetry as well as juxtaposition—even, I might add, at the expense of the integrity of the individual poems, their stanzaic order, and their thematic development.

For the approach I wish to take, the muddled textual tradition of these poems is not as significant as the urge to symmetry and pairing in their presentation and publication; and the questions raised by their editors in search of authentic versions even if they could finally be answered, would not be as crucial to my concerns as the antithetical nature of the arguments presented by the two poems, which are their unshakable thematic core. But the reader should be aware of these textual uncertainties, as I have tried to be. It will be helpful also to know that the inspiration for Marlowe's poem was, in all probability, the myth of Polyphemus and Galatea, known to the Renaissance from such classical works as Theocritus, *Idylls* (ll) and Ovid, *Metamorphoses* (13), where the ugly herdsman Polyphemus attempts through song to persuade the sea-nymph Galatea to join and love him. As is well known, Marlowe's adaptation inspired countless imitations of his own poem and evoked many replies in his day, long afterward, and even into our own time, in what is surely one of the most enduring of Renaissance literary traditions.[5]

Although both poems are familiar in their *Englands Helicon* versions through frequent anthologizing, I quote them here in order to place their details before the reader's eye:

> The passionate Sheepheard to his love
>
> Come live with mee, and be my love,
> And we will all the pleasures prove,
> That vallies, groves, hills and fieldes,

That vallies, groves, hills and fieldes,
Woods, or steepie mountaine yeeldes.

And we will sit upon the Rocks,
Seeing the Sheepheardes feede theyr flocks,
By shallow Rivers, to whose falls,
Melodious byrds sing Madrigalls.

And I will make thee beds of Roses,
And a thousand fragrant poesies,
A cap of flowers, and a kirtle,
Imbroydred all with leaves of Mirtle.

A gowne made of the finest wooll,
Which from our pretty Lambes we pull,
Fayre lined slippers for the cold:
With buckles of the purest gold.

A belt of straw, and Ivie buds,
With Corall clasps and Amber studs,
And if these pleasures may thee move,
Come live with mee, and be my love.

The Sheepheards Swaines shall daunce & sing,
For thy delight each May-morning,
If these delights thy minde may move;
Then live with mee, and be my love.

(p. 192)

No reader, to my knowledge, has ever claimed that this is a baffling poem or dismissed it as merely a charming trifle. If one had to "locate" it, he would surely place it well above the "average" Elizabethan song but certainly not in the vicinity of, say, Donne's "Air and Angels." And yet it has its puzzling paradoxes, for its shepherd is no shepherd, his love is not what she appears to be (and certainly not the nymph Ralegh or "Ignoto" says she is), and the invitation is both more and less than it seems. The implication of the second and last stanzas that the passionate shepherd and his beloved will sit and observe other (real?) shepherds and their servants gives away his identity as still another of those Renaissance lovers or poet-lovers who are visitors to rather than natives of the green world. The other activities promised, including entertainment by song and dance and the creation of the most luxurious and ornamented clothing nature can offer is another indication that here is no shepherd but in fact a poet-lover urging his equally sophisticated (and urbanized?) love to cast aside the restraints associated with civilization and enjoy the freedom and delight of a still possible golden age—except, of course, that she would not be expected to live in truly primitive fashion! In brief, she is being asked to join him at play, to take on the role of a shepherdess who will be adored by him and worshiped by the other inhabitants of the pastoral world.

If the genuineness of the invitation is suspect for these reasons, and taking into account still other considerations—such as the failure to be precise about sleeping arrangements, even though we are told that not only many days and nights but whole seasons and years will pass—the reader can only conclude that the poem is in fact what we suspected from the first, an attempt at seduction. And the question of its effectiveness as such is therefore crucial, as we shall see. Finally, if we are to understand with Ralegh that Marlowe's persona addresses his invitation to a "nymph," we have the additional ironies evoked by the deliberately ambiguous usage of that term by Renaissance poets.

As W. W. Greg pointed out some time ago, Renaissance pastoral poets, following Boccaccio's practice, often referred to their heroines or their beloveds as nymphs out of motives of flattery—and, I would add, wish fulfillment.[6] But as a painting like Titian's *Nymph and Shepherd* and countless poems like Petrarch's "Non al suo amante più Diana piacque" (discussed above, p. 106) prove, both painters and poets knew perfectly well that nymphs in classical mythology were daimons associated with natural places or forces; hence they were painted or described as nearly or totally nude, like some of their sister deities of greater importance. They could be wooed by clothed poets or shepherds, real or temporary, as well as by other deities, and they themselves sometimes aggressively wooed illustrious or attractive mortals, as we know from such obvious examples as Echo, Calypso, and the nymph of the spring Pegae, who dragged Hylas down into a watery life with her. To call a beloved a nymph, then, was, as Marlowe and Ralegh were well aware, an obvious ploy, but also one rich in ironic resonances and possibilities, as when Marlowe's poet-lover goes into such detail about elegant natural clothing, undoubtedly to reassure his sophisticated beloved, when we know that his ultimate purpose was not to dress her as a shepherdess but to undress her, to have her be *his* nymph. Like his predecessor Polyphemus wooing Galatea, he must also be aware that his task is complicated by his own ineptitude and the fact that, at the very moment he sings to her, she may be happily entertaining one of her own kind, her Acis. Indeed, if we recall a more recent painting, Manet's updating of the *fête champêtre* theme in his *Luncheon on the Grass*, we realize that the paradox involved in the idea of a nude nymph juxtaposed with a clothed mortal, the singer and the inspiration or object of his song, still has its appeal, even if in the Manet it is cast in the typically twentieth-century mode of parody.

We turn next to Ralegh's companion poem, which, if Marlowe's is an invitation to love, might be tersely characterized as a declination of love:

> The Nimphs reply to the Sheepheard
>
> If all the world and love were young,
> And truth in every Sheepheards tongue,
> These pretty pleasures might me move,
> To live with thee, and be thy love.
>
> Time drives the flocks from field to fold,
> When Rivers rage, and Rocks grow cold,
> And *Philomell* becommeth dombe,
> The rest complaines of cares to come.
>
> The flowers doe fade, & wanton fieldes,
> The wayward winter reckoning yeeldes,
> A honny tongue, a hart of gall,
> Is fancies spring, but sorrowes fall.
>
> Thy gownes, thy shooes, thy beds of Roses,
> Thy cap, thy kirtle, and thy poesies,
> Soone breake, soone wither, soone forgotten:
> In follie ripe, in reason rotten.
>
> Thy belt of straw and Ivie buddes,
> Thy Coral claspes and Amber studdes,
> All these in mee no meanes can move,
> To come to thee, and be thy love.
>
> But could youth last, and love still breede,
> Had joyes no date, nor age no neede,
> Then these delights my minde might move,
> To live with thee, and be thy love.

Ralegh's nymph has not simply declined the invitation of Marlowe's shepherd; in doing so she has also rejected the literary nature and basis of that invitation. Not only is she *not* a nymph (who would hardly be so humanly concerned with mortality), she is a thoughtful mortal woman who insists that her *mind* has not been moved by the shepherd's tongue, or his poetry, to become his ideal shepherdess. Her grim discourse on time, change, and death invalidates the pastoral ideal, scorns the notion that a golden age of gentle primitivism can be recreated, and raises serious doubts about the power of poetry to transcend mutability and decay, especially since it so often, as in this instance, lies about the true nature of things. Even Marlowe's admission of change in his reference to the passing of the seasons and the need for wool gown and lined slippers against the winter cold is overwhelmed by Ralegh's litany of decadence and disintegration. In sum, Marlowe's shepherd has provided no convincing assurance that he can extricate his lady from the relentless cycle of the natural year and deliver her into a sempiternal spring, or rescue her from the ultimate decay of the world by immortalizing her. If we had *his* response, it would probably express considerable bewilderment that his intention had been taken so ponderously, and considerable disappointment that so promising a ploy had failed.

The Ralegh poem, then, can be read both as a reply to Marlowe's in the sense of offering a necessarily complementary philosophical view, and also as a rebuke in that its palpable attempt at seduction is so transparent and thus ineffective. For our purposes, too, it is desirable to see it and Marlowe's as essentially one poem. To the question of which view is right, a typical Renaissance answer might be: both. In the Renaissance view, opposites can sometimes be harmonized or transcended, particularly if one can break through to another dimension of thought or existence; but more often than not one must accept a paradoxical coexistence of alternatives. Marlowe's shepherd is surely not very practical-minded, whereas Ralegh's nymph espouses a paralyzing realism. Poetry, too, both lies and tells a special kind of truth. In any event, this necessary balance of opposites, whether epistemologically or rhetorically intended, occurs everywhere in Renaissance culture—indeed, to the extent that it is virtually its signature. In literature it ranges from the antithesis within a single line of poetry to the alignment of phrases and clauses in a Ciceronian period, and from the employment of contrasting plots and ideas in individual plays and poems to the pairing of separate works espousing opposing concepts, as in our example.

In the visual arts, as is equally well known, the opposition also occurs as an equilibrium of forces within the painted or sculpted human figure; and in the composition or design of ensembles, similar attention is paid to contrasting figural poses and gestures in pictures and to contrasting spaces, forms, and light in structures. Even in paintings that involve the symmetrical arrangement of figures flanking a sacred personage, as in Raphael's *Marriage of the Virgin* or Andrea del Sarto's *Madonna of the Harpies* and scores of *sacre conversazioni,* the figures are given poses and gestures that attain variety through complementarity of movement. These also join contrasts of color and light to form a network of *contrapposti*. In this connection, the art

historian David Summers has recently affirmed the common rhetorical basis
of such composition in the sister arts:

> The word *contrapposto,* now exclusively used for a figural composition
> in which the weight of the body is shifted to one leg with a consequent
> adjustment of the other parts of the body, is taken from the Latin
> *contrapositum,* in turn translated from the Greek *antithesis,* a rhetorical
> figure in which opposites were set directly against one another. In the
> Renaissance, *contrapposto* had a wider meaning than it has now, and
> could refer to any opposition—chiaroscuro, for example, or the jux-
> tapositions of old and young, male or female. Antithesis was a major
> means of elocution and a major means of pictorial composition from
> Alberti onward, and, once again, was defined with special care by
> Leonardo. The pattern for *contrapposto* composition was thus rhetorical;
> the setting of visual contrasts created vividness just as the setting of
> opposites in rhetoric or poetry created a memorable and convincing
> vividness.[7]

In sum, Marlowe's poem demanded its complement for more reasons than
the simple one of poetic challenge, and Ralegh's reply is not so much a sour,
late Renaissance expression of despair as its necessary *contrapposto*. Those
who replied later, including John Donne, Robert Herrick, and Charles
Cotton, did not limit themselves, however, to replicating or answering
Marlowe; for as we shall see, they considered the two poems as one.

John Donne's "The Bait" is in several ways a mannerist response to the
Marlowe-Ralegh invitation and declination:

> Come live with mee, and bee my love,
> And we will some new pleasures prove
> Of golden sands, and christall brookes,
> With silken lines, and silver hookes.
>
> There will the river whispering runne
> Warm'd by thine eyes, more then the Sunne.
> And there the'inamor'd fish will stay,
> Begging themselves they may betray.
>
> When thou wilt swimme in that live bath,
> Each fish, which every channell hath,
> Will amorously to thee swimme,
> Gladder to catch thee, then thou him.

> If thou, to be so seene, beest loath,
> By sunne, or Moone, thou darknest both,
> And if my selfe have leave to see,
> I need not their light, having thee.
>
> Let others freeze with angling reeds,
> And cut their legges, with shells and weeds,
> Or treacherously poore fish beset,
> With strangling snare, or windowie net:
>
> Let coarse bold hands, from slimy nest
> The bedded fish in banks out-wrest,
> Or curious traitors, sleave-silke flies
> Bewitch poore fishes wandring eyes.
>
> For thee, thou needst no such deceit,
> For thou thy selfe art thine owne bait,
> That fish, that is not catch'd thereby,
> Alas, is wiser farre then I.[8]

At first glance Donne's poem affirms its status as a participant in a poetic tournament. It dutifully echoes Marlowe's opening line, follows the formal model of the octosyllabic stanzas and their rhyme scheme, and adds only one more to the total of six employed by Marlowe and Ralegh in the versions of their poems printed in *Englands Helicon*. That there are longer versions Donne could easily have known should discourage speculation of the kind once proposed by an overly eager student of mine who thought the seven stanzas represented Donne's deliberate attempt to "elongate" his poem, a typical mannerist device!

In its title and very first stanza, "The Bait" makes us aware that the Marlowe-Ralegh poem has evoked a complex and richly ironic response. The title, for example, refers not only to the real bait used by real fishermen in the fifth and sixth stanzas but also to the beloved herself *and* the poem addressed to her. In the first stanza, inspired perhaps by another anonymous invitation poem in *Englands Helicon* that includes among the promised delights the prospect of fishes offering themselves to the lady's hands (p. 194), Donne transposes the setting wholly from celebratory public pastoral to private and quasi-mythical piscatorial. The resulting "new" pleasures proffered emphasize an isolated, almost surreal setting and implements made of precious metals, minerals, and cloth, either natural (sands, brooks) or manufactured (lines, hooks), but in either case contributing with their luxuriance to the sense of a completely poetized or "artificial" world.

The hyperbole of the second stanza, asserting confidently that the be-loved's beauty will utterly dominate nature, both transposes Marlowe's flattery upward and checkmates Ralegh's realism. From being merely the center of crowded attention she is in Marlowe's setting, the lady in Donne's vision is upgraded to the status of a real nymph or goddess who can command nature. Thus she dominates its agents, illumines its surfaces, and is at home in its depths and recesses—and is therefore immune to its cyclical changes and ultimate decay. This familiar conceit is reinforced by the third and fourth stanzas, in which the motif of the solitary nymph bathing is evoked along with assurances to a shy bather that her glow will "darken" normal light. This should mean that no one can observe her bathing. But the poet-lover, if he has leave—that is, if unlike Actaeon he is allowed to get close enough to her "site"—will be able to do without the light of the darkened sun and moon and see her by her own glow. Unlike other, distant observers, he will "have" her light—or, more precisely, her. The passionate fisherman would then be as fortunate as the amorous fish who "naturally" steer toward and stay within her "sight."

The realistic depiction of actual fishing that is given in the fifth and sixth stanzas might strike the reader as a gratuitous passage of bravura display, which in part it surely is, as we shall see. But it also represents the necessary antithesis to the idealization of the first stanzas. Donne is almost flaunting his realism, making it vividly known that he is thoroughly aware of what fishing is really like, and more important, that he can render it effectively if he pleases. The final stanza, however, reminds us that such reality is fraught with deceit: catching fish is physically ugly and painful, certainly not the piscatorial idyll which poetry can make it out to be. And what is more, real fishing is morally suspect. How much more aesthetically and morally gratifying it is to attract the fish with one's awesome beauty and, without culpability, cause them to choose their own fate! What fish, or lover, could resist such a bait? And what lady, or reader, would not agree that the poet, albeit with an urbanely deceptive argument, has made an impressive case for accepting his invitation?

That impressive case is, in fact, Donne's answer to the dilemma posed by the Marlowe-Ralegh pair of poems. The way to overcome the nymph's reluctance to heed the shepherd's pleas is to appeal more artfully and therefore more powerfully to her vanity, her integrity, and her thoughtful mind. One does this in several ways: by means of the transposition and intensification of praise, by acknowledging reality and representing it yet showing it to be inferior to the poetic world the poet is able to conjure up with his art, and by guaranteeing to the beloved total command over both nature and her humble lover—and total privacy should she decide to reward her poet-fisherman (or amorous fish) with proximity. If one objects that the reluctant beloved would hardly be content to have all this said in a poem that publicizes a private invitation, the answer would be that such awesome beauty as she possesses would make itself known in any event. And if there is a real concern on her part with transience and decay, what better hedge against disintegration and oblivion than a memorable poem, especially one that will "snare" future generations of readers as she has snared the poet-lover and as it has "baited" her?

Lest it be thought that Donne's poem, as a typical exercise of his "metaphysical" wit, needs no mannerist label, I would point out how much it is a transaction between itself and previous poems, how fully it is set in and crucially assumes an autonomous and enclosed aesthetic world, and how thoroughly absorbed it is in the problem of how to write a poem on a conventional theme or within a tradition. I would note, too, that along with other successful works in the mannerist mode it does not remain entirely entrapped within its self-sufficient poetic universe, for both its analysis of the artifices of persuasion and its artful juxtaposition of the "deceits" of poetry and truth take us outside the poem to ponder such matters in the wider context of the ambiguous nature of art and its relationship to a slippery reality.

Its artful juxtaposition suggests, also, an interesting analogy with visual mannerism. In his *Il Manierismo: bilancio critico del problema stilistico e culturale,* Georg Weise, as we have noted, discusses with copious illustration the formal vocabulary used by mannerist painters in their stylization of the human figure. He emphasizes in particular the posing of contrasting figures twisting in opposite directions, and the resultant linear antithesis of abstract or decorative curves (pp. 60–66). For Weise, this denotes a preference for the "artificial" over the "natural" posing of the human figure, and therefore, in my terms, a tendency to be more mannered that mannerist. In Donne's poem there is also an artful juxtaposition, as we have seen, of real and ideal fishing that may seem to have similarly artificial or purely decorative motives, since it is artifice that is made to triumph. But because of the complexity of his intention, and the sequential nature of a poem as contrasted to the spatial concentration of a painting, Donne is able both to utilize the "abstract" artfulness of the contrast and to exploit its "realistic" content in the effective presentation of his theme. Again, what might have been merely an exercise in *maniera,* or worse, *manierato,* is thus given a meaningful complexity that is typically mannerist or, perhaps more important, extraordinarily appealing in its total impact, satisfying both "eye" and mind.

Finally, there is another link with visual mannerism, admittedly more tenuous, that nevertheless deserves at least a mention. In Izaac Walton's *The Compleat Angler,* where "The Bait" is quoted, one of his interlocutors, Venator, or Hunter, says that Donne made the poem "to shew the world that he could make soft and smooth Verses, when he thought smoothness worth his labour."[9] Although Walton is echoing here a familiar theme in contemporary criticism of Donne's style, the remark does bear some relationship to the issue of *maniera* raised in Italian literary and art circles. In those terms, Donne can be said to have aimed, at least in part, at the unruffled elegance of *maniera* but, as I have argued, also intended and achieved something more that justifies the inclusion of his poem among mannerist works.

We need not tarry over Herrick's "Live, live with me, and thou shalt see," which is addressed to Phillis and was published in *Hesperides* (1648).[10] It is written in octosyllabic couplets that total fifty-six lines, exactly twice the number of Donne's poem, and therein may lie one explanation of its disappointing failure to leaven our convention. Another may be that it is content to reword Marlowe's invitation at greater length and in greater detail drawn from the Herrick repertoire of country rituals, festivals, and "sweets" that delight eye, ear, and palate. Indeed, far from exploring or exploiting the ironies and the paradoxes of his predecessors, Herrick strikes a parodic note when he mischievously undercuts them by paring their complexities down to simple declarative statement. Thus, he says that Phillis shall have "a Bag and Bottle" impressive enough so that they assure "The Wearer's no meane Shepheardesse," (l. 24). Of the "Sheep-hook" he will send her he says, "This, this alluring Hook might be Lesse for to catch a sheep, then me" (ll. 44—46). Near the end of the poem, enumerating the clothing accessories she will wear and their "winning colors," he says "they shall move / Others to Lust, but me to Love." Elsewhere, in a poem apart from our tradition, he had stressed with Cavalier accent that "Clothes do but cheat and cousen us" and that his heart and eye would be won "with flesh, not Drapery" (p. 208). And surely Phillis would have preferred the frank poet of these verses to the one who protests so much and so flatly. Perhaps the poem can best be summed up as *manierato,* but in this instance we have self-parody, Herrick exploiting and succumbing too quickly to his own *maniera* by persuading Phillis to come to his own ready-made "Country." It is thus just another in a series of such invitations he had already issued.

Much more interesting, though by a lesser poet, is "An Invitation to Phillis" by Charles Cotton the Younger (1630–87). It is the longest invitation yet (eighty-two lines), but its baroque opulence of image and theme offers so illuminating a contrast to its predecessors, especially to Donne's poem, and it is relatively so little known, that it is worth quoting here in full:

An Invitation to Phillis

Come live with mee and be my Love
And thou shalt all the pleasures proove
The mountaines' towring tops can show,
Inhabiting the vales below.
From a brave height my starre shall shine
T'illuminate the desart Clime.
Thy Summer's Bower shall overlooke,
The subtill windings of the Brooke
For thy delight which onely springs,
And cutts her way with Turtle's Wings.
The Pavement of thy Roomes shall shine,
With the Bruis'd treasures of the Mine,
And not a Tale of Love, but shall
In Mineture adorne thy wall.
Thy Closett shall Queenes Casketts mock
With rustick jewell of the Rock,
And thyne own light shall make a Gemme,
As bright of these, as Queenes of them.
From this thy Spheare, thou shalt behould
Thy Snowy Ewes troope o'er the mold,
Who yearely pay my Love a peece
Of Tender Lamb, and Silver Fleece.
And when Sols Rayes shall all combine
Thyne to out burne, though not out shine,
Then at the foote of som Greene Hill,
Where Crystall Dove runns murmuring still,
Weele Angle for the bright eyd Fish,
To make my Love a dainty Dish;
Or, in a Cave, by Nature made,

Fly to the Covert of the Shade,
Where all the Pleasures wee will Proove,
Taught by the little God of Love.

And when bright Phebus scorching beames,
Shall cease to Guild the Silver Streames,
Then in the could Armes of the Flood
Wee'le bathing coole the factious blood,
Thy beautious Limbs the Brooke shall grace,
Like the reflex of Cynthia's face,
Whilst all the wondring fry do Greete
The welcom Light, adore thy feet,
Supposeing Venus to be come
To send a kisse to Thetis home.
And following night shall trifled bee,
Sweete; as thou know'st, I promis'd thee;
Thus shall the Summers dayes, and Nights,
Be dedicated to thy delights.
Then live with mee, and be my Love
And all these Pleasures shalt thou proove.

But when the sapless Season brings
Cold Winter on her shivering wings,
Freezing the Rivers Liquid Face,
Into a Crystall Lookeing-Glass,
And that the Trees theire Naked bones
Together knock, like Skeletons,
Then with softest, whitest Locks,
Spun with the tribute of thy flocks,
We will orecast thy whiter Skin,
Winter without, a Springe within.
Att the first peepe of day Ile rise,
To make the sullen Hare thy prise
And thou with open Armes shalt com
To bidd thy Hunter welcom home.
The Partridge, Plover, and the Poote
Ile with the subtle Mallard shoote;
The Fellfare, and the greedy Thrush
Shall drop from every Hawthorne Bush,
And the slow Heron downe shall fall,
To feede my Fayrest Fayre withall,

> The Fether'd People of the Ayre,
> Shall fall to be my Phyllis' Fare,
> Noe storme shall touch thee, Tempest move;
> Then live with mee, and be my Love.
>
> But from her cloister when I bring,
> My Phyllis to restore the Springe,
> The Ruffling Boreas shall withdraw,
> The Snow shall melt, the Ice shall thaw;
> The Ague-ish Plants Fresh Leaves shall shew,
> The Earth put on her verdant hue,
> And Thou (Fair Phillis) shalt be seene
> Mine, and the Summers beautious Queene.
> These, and more Pleasures shalt thou proove;
> Then Live with mee, and be my Love.[11]

The key to Cotton's version may well be the word *all* in the second line. The comprehensiveness of his vision, and the inclusiveness of his verbal recording of it, as promised by *all,* was in fact his unique contribution to the tradition and an answer to Donne's *new*. By then, that tradition had established a required sequence of invitation, a catalogue of pleasures, and the repeated, clinching invitation, the first and last usually being perfunctory echoes of Marlowe's corresponding lines. Unlike his predecessors, Cotton expands the middle section; and although, like Donne, he uses it to incorporate by juxtaposition Ralegh's opposing realism, he does so with greater sweep and in greater detail. But he does not cancel it out; instead, he dissolves Ralegh's and other antithetical arguments in the continuum of the natural cycle. The strategy requires that neither nature nor art be seen in isolation or in disassociation from each other. In Cotton's baroque vision—ranging from great heights to deep depths, from far distance to close-up, from seclusion within to sudden emergence without—the cycles and attendant activities of the seasons comprehend the general category as well as the concrete material instance. Change and disintegration are metamorphosis and transformation. There are no divisions, oppositions, or tensions that do not melt into the orderly process that is *all*. Thus it is not necessary to take refuge in art, to rely less on abstractions from matter than did previous poems, to form in the mind an inner design for a fresh creation. Nor must one shun art for physical nature. In his own poem Cotton does gaze steadily at the natural world, but he peers at it through a literary screen that does not filter out and soften its material surfaces, blur its physical processes, or mitigate its sometimes burdensome effects on human life. Here the focus has shifted from the nymph and passion to topography, and the poet seems at times to be more the owner of a large estate showing around a prospective buyer than a smitten lover aching to possess his beloved; nor does he exhibit anything like Marvell's skill at managing swift and spectacular changes of scenery. Still, as is suggested by his intermittent transformation of Phillis into a natural force and his occasional reduction of his traditional role as passionate shepherd to eloquent nature guide, there is a bursting capacity for change in, and a fluid linkage among art, nature, and human experience, that allows for precisely such a variety and transformation of roles.

The power that makes it possible to apprehend and record the fluid barriers, the metamorphoses, and the cyclical transformations—the constant scene changes—that characterize the vast spectacle of a universe in orderly disorder is, of course, human wit. But if there is an unresolved tension in this poem it is not between the wit and literary sophistication of its author and his genuine experience of country life on the family estate at Beresford Hall, including those activities of shepherds, hunters, and fishermen alluded to in the poem. Perhaps because its author lacked talent and inspiration or was trapped in the eclectic fusion of his predecessors' poems, and perhaps reflecting, too, the general literary situation of its age, the poem hesitates at times not between world views but between styles, not between nature and art but between kinds of wit.[12] Chronologically, Cotton was the heir of the Metaphysical and Cavalier poets, several of whom were friends of his father, and was memorialized by his friend Izaak Walton, for whose *The Compleat Angler* he wrote a supplement. At the same time, he was a contemporary of John Dryden and lived well into the Restoration. His was not the problem of the frustrated realist who wishes to transcribe material nature ever more faithfully, or that of the visionary romantic who struggles to render its spiritual impact, but the dilemma of the baroque classicist steering a course between witty exploration of the odd corners the sensibility might seek out and the equally witty notation of the congruences of more normal experience. Thus, the poem is addressed to Herrick's Phillis but recalls Donne and Marvell in "coole the factious blood" and "the Bruis'd treasures of the Mine;" and evokes Carew and Lovelace in "Freezing the Rivers Liquid Face, / Into a Crystall Lookeing-Glass" and "the Trees theire Naked bones / Together knock, like Skeletons." Another direction is taken, however, with figures such as "Snowy Ewes," "Silver Streams," and "Fether'd People of the Ayre" toward the generalized image and the decorous epithet.

In contrast to Donne's mannerist version of our theme, where art triumphs, Cotton's poem, in typical baroque fashion, compels art to acknowledge the spectacular fullness and transformative richness of nature as its source and inspiration, its ally, and in a sense its mirror image. The cycle of the seasons determines the division of the poem: spring (ll. 1–32), summer (ll. 33–48), winter (ll. 49–72), spring again (ll. 73–82). We begin on a mountain top overlooking a valley, from which Phillis will shine like a star. Her cavernlike bower will be paved with precious metals but also surrounded by the "rustic jewelry" of rock formations. Just as her home will be a rustic cave that is nevertheless adorned by depictions of tales of love, so the natural light sparkling from metal and crystal will vie with and be ruled by her own. The decorated bower contrasts with a "natural" cave they will seek out after fishing, so that the queen of this pastoral world, Phillis, and her humble but eloquent shepherd can become ordinary rustic lovers enjoying *all* of Cupid's pleasures.

To this point there is nothing Phillis cannot be or have, thanks to a profligate nature and her shepherd guide to its treasures. Even the coming of oppressive summer heat signals and ushers in still another pleasure, bathing, and allows Phillis to play her traditional role as nymph enchanting the waters and their creatures, who assume in this case that Venus herself has arrived.

The onslaught of winter, however, recalls the antithetical theme of death and disintegration proposed by Ralegh's nymph, and Cotton does not flinch from its effects. He does redeem them, however, for the frozen face of a river is a mirror in which another face can see itself. And the cold that causes tree branches to knock against each other like skeletons also makes it necessary to wear the beautifully soft and white fleece that preserves the waiting spring within. There is plenty and variety in the winter food available to the hunter and a domestic coziness in the ritual of sallying forth to and returning from the hunt to be welcomed by Phillis with open arms. Thus Phillis cannot be discomfited by nature in its harsh mood because its balancing compensations have been pointed out, and staged, by her shepherd.

This domestic scene is transformed again, however, with the return of spring. Phillis, taking the familiar generative footsteps outside of her bower, where she has been cloistered all winter like a holy nun, reanimates dead nature and brings back the green world, over which she now presides again as queen. What *more* pleasures she could experience, having already been and savored *all,* is puzzling until one realizes that the shepherd, or poet-lover, is setting no limits either on nature's or on his own capacity for endless inventiveness and surprise.

It may be overstatement, even in this final paragraph of my study, where I might expect to be somewhat indulged, to label Cotton's conclusion a typical baroque response to the mannerist creative dilemma, especially since it may be fairly charged that he wills rather than demonstrates the fecundity he promises. But his failings as a poet do not invalidate his argument for our purposes, so that Phillis, leaving her art-filled and artfully created cloister to restore the spring, may stand as an emblem of the baroque poet's reluctance to inhabit imaginatively any isolated realms, or to have his sensibility hemmed in or hedged about by borders or boundaries. Similarly, Donne's denigration of real fishing and his preference for weaving elaborate verbal snares may stand as typical of the attitude that governs poems in the mannerist mode, which insist that whatever else art may be, it is first of all art, even at the risk of being *manierato*. And although it may create and inhabit its own world of imaginative works and its first allegiance must be to itself, art, even thus defined as autonomous and self-referential, is also a part of experience, if only as a negative exemplum. As we have also seen, however, an intense preoccupation with aesthetic goals can produce a satisfying *maniera,* the exquisite refinement of the supremely sure and polished work, and, less often, a work of art that may have *maniera* but also something more that makes it at least more interesting if not a better work of its mannerist kind. That something more, a stimulating or disturbing complexity of form and content, comes about when inner design unexpectedly comments on itself or other realities, when it suddenly illuminates with its deployed artificial light those odd corners of being where mimetic natural light has not penetrated.

Notes

Chapter 1

1 "Art and Scholarship," *Meditations on a Hobby Horse* (London and New York: Phaidon, 1971 [1963]), p. 110. As indicated in my preface, the discussion that follows will refer briefly to items listed in the Selected Bibliography on the term and concept of mannerism. I have paid special attention to updating my essay in *The Meaning of Mannerism* (1972) to include significant materials published since then through 1983. I have found especially helpful the bibliographical items assembled by Branimir Anzulovic (1974), Milton Kirchman (1979), Richard Studing and Elizabeth Kruz (1979), Francesco Bonavita (1980), and Esther Nyholm (1977−82).

2 I am aware that *baroque* has also been traced to the name of a tricky type of syllogism, but apart from its being a less glamorous example for my argument than a pearl, the flawed syllogism serves equally well to illustrate the neoclassicist idea that "baroque" art is both superficial and false. See René Wellek, *Concepts of Criticism* (New Haven: Yale University Press, 1963), pp. 115−16; Erich Hubala, *Baroque and Rococo Art* (New York: Universe Books, 1976), p. 5, adds the verb *baroquer,* which he says was the French cabinet-maker's term for turning and curving.

3 In his article on the "double origins" of the concept of mannerism (Strudi Vasariani, 1952), pp. 181−85, Georg Weise gives examples of *manière* in French and Italian courtly literature, including a *canzone a ballo* by Lorenzo de' Medici (1449−92) in which behavioral *maniera* is recommended; it may be read in *Opere,* ed. Attilio Simioni (Bari: Laterza, 1914), 2:299–301. The *canzone,* beginning "Io vi vo' donne, insegnare" has the lines "Se tu vai, stai, o siedi / fa d'aver sempre maniera" (If you go, stay, or sit / make sure you always do so with manner, p. 301).

4 Ed. Bruno Maier (Turin: UTET, 1964), p. 148. All future citations of Castiglione will be from this edition.

5 On the intellectual stature and social status of the artist, see the excerpts from sixteenth-century sources edited by Paola Barocchi in the second volume of her *Scritti d'arte del Cinquecento* (1973), pp. 1265−1521, and Castiglione, *Il cortegiano,* bk. 1, pp. 172−73; also, Anthony Blunt, *Artistic Theory in Italy* (1962 [1940]), pp. 48−57; Rensselaer W. Lee, *Ut Pictura Poesis* (1967 [1940]), pp. 41−49; the first chapter of Rudolf and Margot Wittkower's *Born under Saturn* (1969 [1963]), pp. 1−16; Milton Kirchman, *Mannerism and Imagination* (1979), pp. 206−32; Arnold Hauser, *The Social History of Art* (1957 [1951]), 2:52−84; Andrew Martindale's *The Rise of the Artist in the Middle Ages and Early Renaissance* (New York: McGraw Hill, 1972) gives the background.

6 The text of Vasari used throughout is *Le vite dei più eccellenti pittori, scultori e architetti,* ed. Licia and Carlo L. Ragghianti in four volumes (1971−78), cited hereafter by volume and page number. There is no critical edition of the *Lives* in English, but several nearly complete translations of the 1568 edition are available, though outdated. These include the translations by Margaret E. Foster (1850); and Gaston du C. de Vere (1912−15), the standard version; and, less reliable, by A. B. Hinds (1900; rpt. 1963 in Everyman's Library). There is a brief selection by George Bull in the Penguin Classics series (1965). Also available in English is *Vasari on Technique, Being the Introduction to the Three Arts of Design,* trans. L. S. Maclehose with commentary by G. B. Brown (1907; rpt. Dover Books, 1960). Vasari gives his own artistic autobiog-

raphy at the conclusion of his *Vite* (4:984– 1032). The best introduction to Vasari's life and works in English is now T. S. R. Boase, *Giorgio Vasari: The Man and the Book* (1979).

In his introduction to the *Lives,* p. 10, C. L. Ragghianti speculates that Vasari dropped *artefici* from an early version of his title because it suggested a "limited" significance vis-à-vis men of letters. That he continued to use it in the text, however, must mean that the alternatives, like *artista,* were not as yet widely used and acceptable. On the whole Vasari does not, however, push the implied *argumentum ex universo,* according to which God is the Supreme Artist *(artifex)* and the individual artist a "creator" *(artefice)* whose activity imitates or parallels His. It is also significant that the "letterato" Benedetto Varchi, in his lecture on Michelangelo's sonnet beginning "Non ha l'ottimo artista," cites Dante's use of *artista* as a justification for preferring this Tuscan word to the Latinate *artefice* and the plebeian *artigiano (Scritti d'arte,* ed. Barocchi, 2:1326– 27). See also Kirchman, *Mannerism and Imagination,* pp. 225– 26, and Leatrice Mendelsohn-Martone, *Benedetto Varchi's "Due Lezzioni"; "Paragoni" and Cinquecento Art Theory* (1982), 2:229– 38. For other aspects of Vasari's theory, see also the essays by Guglielmo de Angelis d'Ossat, Eugenio Garin, and Giuliano Tanturli in *Il Vasari storiografo e artista* (1976), pp. 773– 82, 259– 66, 275– 98; Vincenzo de Ruvo, "La concezione estetica di Giorgio Vasari," in *Studi Vasariani* (1952), pp. 47– 56; Maurice Pourier, "The Role of the Concept of *Disegno* in Mid-Sixteenth-Century Florence," in *The Age of Vasari,* exhibition catalogue (Princeton, N.J.: Princeton University Press, 1970), pp. 53–66.

7 The Berni quotation ("Ei dice cose, e voi dite parole") is from his "Capitolo a fra Bastian dal Piombo" (1534) in *Rime,* ed. Giorgio Barberi-Squarotti (Turin: Einaudi Editore, 1969), p. 179, l. 31; the well-known Sidney phrases are from his *Astrophel and Stella,* sonnets 15, 74, cited from *The Anchor Anthology of Sixteenth-Century Verse,* ed. Richard S. Sylvester (Garden City, N.Y.: Anchor Books, 1974), pp. 425, 459.

8 For the literary sources of the theory of imitation, see the treatises, ed. Bernard Weinberg, in *Trattati di poetica e retorica del Cinquecento* (vols. 1– 4, 1970– 74; and translated excerpts in Allan H. Gilbert, ed., *Literary Criticism: Plato to Dryden* (1962 [1940]), pp. 213– 533; some useful secondary treatments include: "Imitation," *Encylopedia of Poetry and Poetics,* ed. Alex Preminger, with Frank J. Warnke and O. B. Hardison (Princeton, N.J.: Princeton University Press, 1965), pp. 378– 81; Ferruccio Ulivi, *L'imitazione nella poetica del Rinascimento* (1959); Bernard Weinberg, *A History of Literary Criticism in the Italian Renaissance* (1961), pp. 349– 423; Baxter Hathaway, *Marvels and Commonplaces* (1968), pp. 88– 132, and *The Age of Criticism* (1962), pp. 3– 125; Harry Berger, Jr., "The Renaissance Imagination: Second World and Green World" (1965), pp. 36– 78; Harold S. Wilson, "Some Meanings of 'Nature' in Renaissance Literary Theory" (1941), pp. 430– 48; more recently, the articles by George W. Pigman III, "Versions of Imitation in the Renaissance" (1980), pp. 1– 32, and "Imitation and the Renaissance Sense of the Past" (1979), pp. 155– 77; Thomas M. Greene's *The Light in Troy* (1982) is one of the best books ever written on the general subject.

For *imitatio* in art theory, there are the texts assembled by Barocchi in *Scritti d'arte,* 2:1529– 1607, and *Trattati d'arte del Cinquecento fra Manierismo e Controriforma,* 3 vols., 1960– 62; Eugenio Battisti's "Il concetto d'imitazione nel Cinquecento" (1960), pp. 175– 215; Lee, *Ut Pictura Poesis,* pp. 9– 16; Kirchman, *Mannerism and Imagination,* pp. 183– 205.

On the relations between literary and art theory there does not as yet exist a study that deals with the subject thoroughly, but there are valuable suggestions in Robert J.

Clements, "The Identity of Literary and Artistic Theory in the Renaissance" (1969), pp. 1–26; also, Carlo Ossola's *Autunno del Rinascimento: Idea del Tempiro dell'arte nell'ultimo Cinquencento* (1970), while primarily concerned with treaties on art, includes Tasso and some other literary figures and sources in its analysis.

9 On Vasari's theory, see above, note 6, and Anthony Blunt, *Artistic Theory in Italy* (1962 [1940]), pp. 86–102; Boase, *Giorgio Vasari*, pp. 43–148; Kirchman, *Mannerism and Imagination*, pp. 99–232 passim; Esther Nyholm, *Arte e teoria del manerismo*, (1977), 1:181–98.

10 In discussing "mannerist" critics like G. B. Armenini, Blunt points out that their "confidence in the absolute rightness of their particular style, and the undue importance which they attribute to it as an end in itself . . . justify the name of Mannerists, as opposed to Stylists, for the painters and theorists . . . and brings us to the more obvious translation *manner* as the closer approximation to the meaning of *maniera*" (pp. 156–57). Pending universal acceptance of such a distinction, however, this writer prefers to translate *maniera* by either "style" or "manner" or both, to indicate the differing degrees of specific or abstract reference they suggest, among other criteria, historical and semantic. See also, Riccardo Scrivano, *Il manierismo nella letteratura del cinquecento* (1959), pp. 44–45.

11 Pliny's anecdotes in his *Natural History* about Zeuxis include the report that he painted grapes in so lifelike a fashion that birds pecked at them, and that he based his painting of Venus or Helen for the Temple of the Crotonians on the individual beautiful features of five different young girls who modeled for him in the nude (35. 64–66). Also, that Apelles did a painting of a horse that was so realistic it caused some real horses instantly to neigh (35. 95). See *The Elder Pliny's Chapters on the History of Art*, ed. Eugénie Sellers, trans. K. Jex-Blake (1896) (Chicago: Chicago University Press, 1968), or the Loeb Library edition of the *Natural History*, vol. 9, trans. H. Rackham (London-Cambridge, 1952), pp. 308–11, 330–31.

12 In his life of Mantegna (2:479), Vasari refers to the "subtle investigations" and "great study" this artist and his contemporaries devoted to imitating "the true properties of natural things."

13 Erwin Panofsky has traced the history of this notion from Plato to Bellori in his now classic *Idea, A Concept in Art Theory* (1968 [1924]), with special attention to mannerism on pp. 71–79. Sidney's "fore-conceit" occurs in his *Apology for Poetry*, ed. Forrest G. Robinson (Indianapolis and New York: Library of Liberal Arts, 1970), p. 16; Lucy Gent, *Picture and Poetry* (1981), makes the connections with art theory. See also Kirchman, *Mannerism and Imagination*, pp. 172–82.

14 In his life of Leonardo da Vinci (2:597–619), Vasari has the artist discoursing on the *idea* to the duke of Milan in order to explain why "elevated geniuses" may be working most (inner activity) when apparently working least (with their hands). Leonardo was attempting to justify his delays in finishing *The Last Supper* (p. 607).

15 Vitruvius was the Roman author of the only extant treatise on architecture (ca. 40 B.C.) that survived from antiquity and was quite influential in the Renaissance; Pliny's *Natural History* (A.D. 70) contained much attractive lore about ancient art and artists, as we have seen; Lucian (A.D. 120–200) included several influential descriptions of works and legends about artists such as Apelles in his satiric writings; the elder Philostratus (fl. ca. A.D. 210) and his followers of the same name described real and imaginary paintings in their *Imagines;* Cennino Cennini composed a *Libro dell'arte* (ca. 1390) invaluable for its technical details; Lorenzo Ghiberti's *Commentarii* (ca. 1450) includes information about himself and the art of his time; Alberti's three treatises on painting, sculpture, and architecture, written from 1436 to 1472, served

as basic texts for subsequent writers on these arts; Leonardo wrote notes for a treatise on the art of painting and other unpublished miscellaneous comments that apparently circulated in manuscript. Vasari also knew other writings, including chronicles, treatises, brief lives, letters, *paragoni* or contests of the arts; not all of these have survived or, like some of the writings and sayings of Leonardo and Michelangelo, have survived only in fragments or through hearsay.

16 Vasari's contemporary sources included Baldassare Castiglione's *Cortegiano* (1528), Paolo Giovio's *Lives* (1546, 1551), Giambattista Gelli's *Lives* (1549), and possibly the pioneering critical treatises of Marco Girolamo Vida (1527), Gian Giorgio Trissino (1529), Bernardino Daniello (1536), Cinthio Giraldi (1541–49), Bernardo Segni (1549: an Italian translation of the *Poetics* of Aristotle); and certainly the critical writings of Pietro Bembo, Giovanni della Casa, Benedetto Varchi, and Pietro Aretino. He was part of a literary circle that included Paolo Giovio, Annibale Caro, Anton Francesco Doni, Vincenzo Borghini, and Pier Francesco Giambullari. Also, Vasari was educated and well read in humanist literature generally, both the classics and the moderns from Dante to Ariosto (see Ragghianti, Introduzione, pp. 9–59).

17 On contemporary literary debates, see Weinberg's *History*, 2:819–1112; Hathaway, *Marvels and Commonplaces*, pp. 31–38, and *The Age of Criticism*, passim; Greene, *The Light in Troy*, pp. 171–96; Robert L. Montgomery, *The Reader's Eye: Studies in Didactic Theory from Dante to Tasso* (1979), pp. 117–68.

18 In the introduction to his translation of selected *Lives* in the Penguin Classics series, pp. 9–13, George Bull echoes the conventional view of Vasari's cautious management of his affairs as less than admirable.

19 "Non basta agl'artefici, come molti dicono, fatto ch'egli hanno l'opere, scusarsi con dire: elle sono misurate a punto dall'antico e sono cavate da' buoni maestri, atteso che il buon giudicio e l'occhio più giuoca in tutte le cose, che non fa la misura de le seste" (Life of Cronaca the architect, 2:831: "It is not enough for artists to excuse themselves, as many do, after finishing their works, by saying: they are proportioned exactly according to the antique, and drawn from the best masters. For good judgment and the eye count more in everything than does the measurement of the compasses"). See Robert Klein, "Judgment and Taste in Cinquecento Art Theory," in *Form and Meaning* (1981 [1961]), pp. 161–69, and David Summers, *Michelangelo and the Language of Art* (1981), pp. 332–46, 352–63, 368–79.

20 In a celebrated letter to Castiglione on the "Galatea" fresco in the Farnesina, Raphael says, "To paint a beauty I need to see many beauties, but since there is a dearth of beautiful women, I use a certain idea which comes into my mind" (Blunt, *Artistic Theory*, p. 64); in his *Idea*, Erwin Panofsky says that Raphael's "idea" meant a mental image of a beauty surpassing nature, whereas Vasari's "idea" meant any image conceived in the artist's mind—namely, a conceit, notion, invention, or theme (pp. 59–68).

21 Blunt, *Artistic Theory*, p. 154, says that Raffaello Borghini, in his *Il Riposo* (1584), appears to be the first critic to say that a painter has or lacks *maniera*, without qualification, meaning Vasari's *gran' maniera*. But clearly, in a passage like this, Vasari all but says the same thing.

22 As Vasari makes clear in the previous quoted passage and elsewhere, *disegno* can also mean merely drawing or draughtsmanship (see, for example, his life of Correggio, 2:635).

23 *Disegno* had for Vasari and others the added advantage of providing a common basis for the different arts, hence avoiding the *paragone*, or contest of the arts, and especially painting versus sculpture, which had persisted as both a genuine rivalry and a literary exercise since the early Renaissance and had been given fresh impetus by the arguments

of Leonardo, who favored painting. There are English excerpts from Leonardo's writings on the subject along with other relevant comments by Varchi, Cellini, Bronzino, and Michelangelo in Robert Klein and Henri Zerner, *Italian Art, 1500–1600* (1966), pp. 4–16, and Elizabeth G. Holt, *A Documentary History of Art* (1981–82 [1947]), 1:275–79, 2:15–16, 35–37. For the Italian sources, see Barocchi's *Trattati d'arte,* 1:3–82, and *Scritti d'arte,* 1:465–711. On the history and significance of the *paragone* there is a comprehensive study by Leatrice Mendelsohn-Martone (see above, n. 6); also, Erwin Panofsky's *Galileo as a Critic of the Arts* (1954) discusses the contribution of the famous astronomer to the debate, and Summers, *Michelangelo and the Language of Art,* pp. 269–78, analyzes Michelangelo's response to the inquiry sent out by Benedetto Varchi in 1546 asking the views of several contemporary artists on the matter. In the above cited pages of the *Trattati d'arte,* Barocchi gives both Varchi's lecture on the theme and the epistolary replies, all published in 1547.

24 On the concept of *grazia,* derived in all probability from classical *venustas* via Castiglione's discussion of *sprezzatura,* or nonchalance, see Blunt, *Artistic Theory,* p. 97, who also argues earlier (pp. 93 ff.) that Vasari opposes *grazia,* based on instinctive judgment, to beauty, based on rules. See also Barocchi, *Scritti d'arte,* 2:1613–1711; Samuel H. Monk, "A Grace beyond the Reach of Art" (1944), pp. 131–50; Edward Williamson, "The Concept of Grace in the Work of Raphael and Castiglione" (1947), pp. 316–24; Wayne A. Rebhorn, *Courtly Performances: Masking and Festivity in Castiglione's "Courtier"* (1977), pp. 44–47; Edoardo Saccone, "*Grazia, Sprezzatura,* and *Affetazione* in Castiglione's *Book of the Courtier*" (1979), pp. 34–54.

25 Vasari says that if Correggio had been able to see antique works and the good modern ones, he would have been an even greater artist (2:634). But contrast this to the treatment of Raphael and Michelangelo below, n. 27, and that treatment with the discussion of the relationship between Bronzino and his master Pontormo (4:427–28).

26 This passage should be confronted with the excerpt from Cicero's *Orator* quoted and discussed by Panofsky, *Idea,* pp. 11–18.

27 Writing of Raphael and Michelangelo (2:801–03), Vasari praises the former for abandoning his attempt to imitate the latter's manner, especially his treatment of the nude, against his natural bent. In effect, Raphael left to Michelangelo those areas of art he excelled in and turned to others in which he himself had a chance to excel, and did.

28 On the arrival in Florence of engravings by Dürer and Schongauer "di maniera tedesca," see also 2:390, 3:123 ("Life of Andrea del Sarto"). See also the *vita* of Salviati (4:645–81), where that artist's temper and censuriousness are emphasized, adding to the suggestion given by the *vite* of Rosso and Pontormo that the competitive spirit of the art world might also provoke or foster neurotic behavior.

29 In his life of Alberti (2:167–76) Vasari insists on the value of both *teorica* and *pratica* (p. 167), especially when the *teorica* comes from learned artists themselves ("dotti artefici"). One might suspect that this was an ideal due more to Renaissance habits of balancing opposites and seeking means than to real belief in the possibility of very often reconciling such conflicting emphases in an artist's training and temperament. In any event, the tension between *teorica* and *practica* is a fundamental problem for Vasari and his contemporaries.

30 In his life of Andrea Verrocchio (2:465–66), Vasari tells the anecdote of how this artist, near death, requested that a poorly made crucifix brought before him be replaced by one from the hand of Donatello, lest he die in despair from gazing upon a wretched work of art!

31 Lodovico Dolce, *Dialogo della pittura intitolato l'Aretino* (1557), in Barocchi, *Trattati d'arte,* 1:143–206. See also Mark W. Roskill, *Dolce's "Aretino" and Venetian Art Theory of the Cinquecento* (1968), which includes the text, a translation, and copious

notes. The motif of effortlessness as a desirable stylistic trait that is also "natural" as opposed to "forced," emphatically endorsed here, recurs in Vasari, as we have seen: an especially interesting example is his argument that Taddeo Zuccaro's great facility of manner was assisted by nature (4:773–74). Vasari would not, of course, endorse the implied preference of Dolce for Raphael over his hero Michelangelo.

32 On the European diffusion of mannerism in the visual arts, see Franzsepp Würtenberger, *Mannerism: The European Style of the Sixteenth Century* (1964), and the catalogue of the Council of Europe Exhibition, *Die Triomf van het Manierisme* (1955). There are good introductions to European visual mannerism in English by Alastair Smart (1971–72) and R. E. Wolf and Ronald Millen (1968). For full references to these and other visual materials see the Selected Bibliography.

33 The standard work on the academies is Nikolaus Pevsner's *Academies of Art Past and Present* (1940). See also R. S. Samuels, "Benedetto Varchi, the *Accademia degli Infiammati*, and the Origins of the Italian Academic Movement" (1976), pp. 599–633, for the literary parallel; also, Marco Rosci, "Manierismo e accademismo nel pensiero critico del Cinquecento" (1956), pp. 57–81.

34 The Decree of the Council, the Veronese trial document, and other related materials excerpted and translated into English may be read in Holt, *A Documentary History of Art*, 2:62–70, and in Klein and Zerner, *Italian Art, 1500–1600*, pp. 119–33.

35 The classic study by Emile Mâle, *L'Art religieux après le Concile de Trente* (1932) concerns itself with religious art; for the secular, see Blunt, *Artistic Theory*, pp. 103–36; Lee, *Ut Pictura Poesis*, pp. 32–41; Kirchman, *Mannerism and Imagination*, pp. 154–71. In her *Trattati d'arte* and *Scritti d'arte* collections, Barocchi has edited some treatises on the decorum of sacred art: see especially the selections from the writings of Giovanni Andrea Gilio, Gabrielle Paleotti, and Carlo Borromeo in *Trattati*, vols. 2, 3, and in the *Scritti d'arte* the excerpts in vol. 1, pt. 4, pp. 235–462. Bartolomeo Ammannati's moving letters in which he repents having sculpted the nude are excerpted in English in *Artists on Art*, ed. Robert Goldwater and Marco Treves (1972 [1945]), pp. 99–101.

36 The traditional historiography would be typified by Burkhardt, Symonds, and De Sanctis. A more balanced and transitional view can be found in, for example, Robert S. Lopez's *The Three Ages of the Italian Renaissance* (1970), pp. 54–74; for the fully revisionist view, see Eric Cochrane's introduction and contribution to *The Late Italian Renaissance* (1970), pp. 7–20, 43–73. A fair Catholic point of view is offered by M. R. O'Connell in his *The Counter-Reformation, 1560–1610* (1974).

37 Though not listed because of its relative unimportance, Anton Francesco Doni's set of dialogues entitled *Disegno* (1549) should be mentioned here for its title and the fact that its interlocutors include Nature and Art. Of the treatises mentioned, those by Pino, Danti, and Comanini are given in full by Barocchi in her *Trattati d'arte* (1:95–139, 209–69; 3:239–79) and generous selections from these and the others under appropriate topics in the three volumes of her *Scritti d'arte*. There are also individual modern editions or reprints with commentary of virtually all of them, as listed in the appended bibliography below. There are excerpts in English in Klein and Zerner, *Italian Art, 1500–1600*, from Pino (pp. 14–16; 58–60), Aretino's letters (pp. 53–58), Danti (pp. 100–05); 182–83), Lomazzo (pp. 111–16), Borghini (pp. 153–55), Zuccaro (pp. 168–73). Holt, *A Documentary History of Art*, vol. 2, has excerpts from Lomazzo (pp. 74–86) and Zuccaro (pp. 87–92); Goldwater and Treves, *Artists on Art*, give Armenini (pp. 108–11), Lomazzo (pp. 111–13), and Zuccaro (pp. 114–16). George Bull has translated a selection of Aretino's letters for Penguin series (1976), and there are complete English translations of Dolce by Mark W. Roskill (1968), of Armenini by Edward J. Olszewski (1977), of Lomazzo

by Richard Haydocke (1598). As indicated earlier, the texts have been discussed by Blunt, Panofsky, Lee, Ossola, Kirchman, Nyholm and Summers, among others already mentioned, but there is now a bulky list of studies of these materials, in English and other languages, dating from the early histories and analyses by Schlosser (1924) and Venturi (1936) and continuing to the recent survey by Esther Nyholm (1982), from which I give a selection in the Selected Bibliography.

38 These are conveniently assembled in English translation in *Michelangelo: A Self-Portrait*, ed. and trans. Robert J. Clements (1963), and studied in the same author's *Michelangelo's Theory of Art* (1961), which should now be supplemented by David Summers's exhaustive study of these matters in his *Michelangelo and the Language of Art* (1981). Both Clements (completely) and Summers (with reservations) accept the authenticity of Francisco de Hollanda's controversial *Dialogos em Roma*, which record conversations held in 1536 in which Michelangelo was uncharacteristically clear and prolix in setting forth his views; but writers of dialogues often presented the ideas of their interlocutors in adaptation, and, as Summers shows, most of the opinions expressed by Michelangelo in De Hollanda's writings are also found in other sources.

39 See above, notes 8 and 17, for references to texts and commentary.

40 *A History of Literary Criticism in the Renaissance* (New York: Harcourt, Brace & World, 1963 [1899]), p. 3.

41 The quotation is from the translation by Kathrin Simon published with an introduction by Peter Murray (Ithaca, N.Y.: Cornell University Press, 1967). Graf's comment is in his "Il fenomeno del Secentismo," *Nuova Antologia* 119 (1905): 358. I am indebted to Antonio Illiano for reminding me of this reference in a splendid review he published of *The Meaning of Mannerism* in *Comparative Literature Studies* 12 (1975): 159–64.

42 Panofsky, *Idea*, pp. 154–77; in his *Studies in Seicento Art and Theory* (1947), p. 3, Denis Mahon points out that in the seicento the prevailing artistic language was the baroque, whereas the predominant trend in art theory was toward the classic—in part, I would add, because mannerism gave outraged classicist theory a suitable target and thereby eased the contradiction, contemporary baroque being more "classical" than earlier mannerism, as in Baldinucci's treatment of Bernini (Holt, *A Documentary History of Art*, 2:106–23). Bellori, on the other hand, praised the Carracci as saving art from both the mannerists *and* Caravaggio's naturalism (Panofsky, *Idea*, pp. 175–77); on the critical rejection of *maniera*, see also John Shearman's "Maniera as an Aesthetic Ideal," in *Studies in Western Art* (1963), pp. 200–21 (also available in *Renaissance Art*, ed. Creighton Gilbert [1970], pp. 181–221) where he surveys the hostile reactions in detail; in his later study, *Mannerism* (1967), Shearman alludes to and summarizes but does not republish all of his earlier material. In his "Cinquecento Mannerism and the Uses of Petrarch" (1971), Aldo Scaglione points out that the use of *manierista* as an interdisciplinary term goes back to Martello's *Commentario* of 1710, where it is used in a treatment of parallel visual and literary effects (p. 149).

43 According to De Sanctis (1870), "l'Ariosto . . . non ha maniera, perché è tutto obbliato e calato nelle cose, e non ha un guardare suo proprio e personale. . . . Perciò il suo ingegno è trasmutabile in tutte guise, non secondo il suo umore, ma secondo la varia natura delle cose." Quoted in Aldo Borlenghi, ed., *Ariosto* (Palermo: Palumbo, [1961]), p. 166.

44 Cf. Ernst Cassirer's remark, "For art, especially plastic art, is now no longer derived from pleasure in the imitation of the varied multiplicity of sensible things. It has found a different and a purely spiritual goal. It expresses within its own sphere what characterizes and distinguishes mankind as a whole. Beauty becomes, to express it in Kantian terms, the symbol of immortality; for in the capacity of man to produce from

himself a world of forms, there is expressed his innate freedom . . . art is for him not a particular realm of human activity, but the expression and revelation of the primary creative nature of man." From his essay on Pico della Mirandola, in *Renaissance Essays,* ed. Paul O. Kristeller and Philip P. Wiener (New York and Evanston: Harper & Row, 1968), p. 47.

45 The essay is conveniently reprinted in *Readings in Art History,* vol. 2 (1969), ed. Harold Spencer, pp. 119–48, which I use here. The Wittkower article appeared in *Art Bulletin* 16 (1934): 123–216, and, like Pevsner's study, strongly influenced Sypher and other critics of mannersm as a crisis style.

46 Note the following titles: Klaus-Peter Lange, *Theoreticker des literarischen Manierismus* (1968), which deals with Tesauro and Pellegrini, the baroque theorists; Erich Burck, *Von römischen Manierismus* (1971), which deals with "classical" mannerism; Christiane Wanke, *Seneca, Lucan, Corneille: Studien zum Manierismus der römischen Kaiserzeit und der französischen Klassik* (1964), which deals with perennial mannerism; and R. G. Warnock and Roland Falter, "The German Pattern Poem: A Study in Mannerism of the Seventeenth Century," in *Festschrift für Detlev W. Schumann* (1970), pp. 40–73, which assumes that pattern poems are to be identified with literary mannerism; Gerd Henniger's comparative anthology, *Beispiele manieristischer Lyrik* (1970), includes poets generally treated elsewhere as baroque and argues for a link between mannerism and modern romanticism. On the other hand, Hugo Friedrich's *Epochen der Italienischen Lyrik* (1964), has a section on "Manierismus" (pp. 593–616) and, like the studies of Georg Weise, applies Curtius's figurative rhetoric to a specific historical era.

47 The subtitle of Hocke's 1959 work, *Manierismus in der Literatur,* is "Sprach-Alchemie und esoterische Kombinationkunst"; his earlier (1957) *Die Welt als Labyrinth* bears the subtitle "Manier und Manie in der europäische Kunst" and posits five mannerist periods: Alexandrian, Silver Latin, Late Medieval, Italian Renaissance, Romanticism.

48 By a curious historical transformation of metaphor, Vasari's *sforzato,* or strain, which concerned him as a problematic feature of the treatment of nature by Pontormo, has become the modern "strain," with all of its psychological associations (3:887).

49 In my "The Mannered and the Mannerist in Late Renaissance Literature," published in *The Meaning of Mannerism,* pp. 6–24. I have been properly punished by painful observation that the term has had some vogue, and by the frequent spectacle since 1972 of my students raising their hands and asking, "is this an example of *Angst-*Mannerism, Professor?"

50 The motif of crisis, and of intellectual cross-currents and popular undercurrents, was not, of course, restricted to discussions of mannerism, though it appears in several of them. The cultural conflicts and cross-currents of the era have been explored by historians and critics such as Hiram Haydn (*The Counter-Renaissance,* 1951), Eugenio Battisti (*L'antirinascimento,* 1962), André Chastel (*The Crisis of the Renaissance, 1520–1600*); see also the studies of R. S. Lopez and Eric Cochrane, cited above, n. 36 (both 1970), and Helmut G. Koenigsberger, "Decadence or Shift? Changes in the Civilization of Italy and Europe in the Sixteenth and Seventeenth Centuries," in *Estates and Revolutions: Essays in Early Modern European History* (1971), pp. 278–97.

51 I am indebted in these pages, and elsewhere as well, to the discussion of the Congress by Henri Zerner in his "Observations on the Use of the Concept of Mannerism," in *The Meaning of Mannerism,* pp. 105–19.

52 Gombrich's earlier essay, "The Renaissance Conception of Artistic Progress and Its Consequences," as well as the presentation at the Twentieth Congress, "Mannerism: The Historiographic Background," are conveniently available in his *Norm and Form* (1971 [1966]), pp. 1–10, 99–106.

53 See above, note 42; for a critique of Shearman's views, consult Zerner's essay, referred

to above in note 51.

54 In his *Rinascimento e barocco* (1960), p. 225, Eugenio Battisti remarked that, in general, mannerism seemed to him to be characterized by a "mancanza di corraggio" (curiously echoed in the title of Kenneth Clark's Bickley Lecture, *A Failure of Nerve: Italian Painting 1520–1535,* published in 1967, though Clark was not precisely echoing Battisti's negative appraisal of mannerism).

55 For example, see Edward E. Lowinsky, "Music in Renaissance Culture," in *Renaissance Essays* (see above n. 44): "Not only does the range of texts set to music broaden immensely, they reveal with a new degree of sharpness the changes in the mental climate of the age. The restlessness and disenchantment of the late Renaissance are mirrored vividly in the texts of a Stoic and even cynical nature" (p. 352).

56 *Renaissance Quarterly* 29 (1976): 107–10. The year before, Henri Zerner had published his *The School of Fontainebleau: Etchings and Engravings* (1969), an example of the focus on texts I mentioned above as being essential to study of mannerism and typical of activity in art history in the decade of the sixties.

57 Contrast this to an earlier view of Meyer Shapiro, "Leonardo and Freud," in *Renaissance Essays,* pp. 330–31: "Whether smoothly harmonized or left in an unresolved state of torturous involvement, these opposed movements within the idealized individual are a characteristic of High and Late Renaissance art: in the first case, they form a classical canon in which the body is stable, though active, and relaxed, though confined; in the other case, they anticipate the Mannerist style of the mid-sixteenth century, where the classical form appears strained or affected, the result of an effort that deforms and depresses the individual, who is increasingly an introverted or tragic figure."

58 In addition to the ideas quoted, there is also Freedberg's tackling of the terminology problem: "Within the term 'Mannerism' I include not only the phenomena of the Maniera proper (or 'high Maniera') of the mid-century, but those in the decades that precede and follow which are visibly more related to it than to the classical style of the High Renaissance or to the nascent Baroque. It seems proper also to include within the generic term. . . . even the so-called anti-classical aspects of this phase in Florence. . . . a hallmark of the first maturing of the new style is the concession of a major role to the quality of *grazia,* and a stress upon the function of the work of art as ornament. . . . Artists . . . who employ basic principles of the Maniera, but who do not share the high Maniera's restrictive conception of the function of a work of art, may more properly be defined Mannerist rather than 'Maniera' painters" (pp. 683–84, n. 3).

59 Studing and Kruz list nearly thirty different exhibitions and related publications, mostly from the decades of the sixties and seventies, with Fontainebleau the most popular subject. From their list and my own research I am aware of the following American doctoral dissertations: David L. Wagner, "Mannerism as a Concept of Historical Periodization" (University of Michigan, 1960); Jewell K. Vroonland, "Mannerism and Shakespeare's Problem Plays" (Kansas State University, 1969); Peter T. Schwenger, "Andrew Marvell and the Aesthetics of Mannerism" (Yale University, 1971); Branimir Anzulovic, "Mannerism in Literature: The Adventures of a Concept" (Indiana University, 1972); and Francesco Bonavita, "The Concept of Mannerism in *Cinquecento* Literature" (City University of New York, 1980).

60 There were other published books and articles in the early years of the decade that, while not directly concerned with the issue of mannerism, offered related and relevant scholarly and critical materials; see, for example: R. V. Young's *Richard Crashaw and the Spanish Golden Age* (1982), David Quint's *Origin and Originality in Renaissance Literature: Versions of the Source* (1983), and Margaret Ferguson's *Trials of Desire* (1983), all published by Yale University Press.

Chapter 2

1 Throughout, I use and quote the edition of the *Vita* by Guido Davico Bonino (Turin: Giulio Rinaudi Editore, 1973). This essay began its life in 1970 as a lecture, never published, given to the Renaissance Seminar at Columbia University. In the meantime, several publications have appeared which, I am pleased to note, express views that parallel some of my own early speculations, and to which I am indebted for additional details of interpretation. These include: Dino S. Cervigni, *The "Vita" of Benvenuto Cellini: Literary Tradition and Genre* (Ravenna: Longo Editore, 1979); Jonathan Goldberg, "Cellini's *Vita* and the Conventions of Early Autobiography," *Modern Language Notes* 89 (1974): 71–83; and Marziano Guglielminetti, *La "vita" di Benvenuto Cellini* (Turin: Giappichelli, 1974). Much of the recent bibliography on Cellini is preoccupied with autobiography, but the following can serve as useful introductions to his life and works as well as to his literary mannerism (for his visual artistry, see below, n. 2): Enrico Carrara, "Manierismo letterario in Benvenuto Cellini," *Studi romanzi* 19 (1928): 171–200; Bruno Maier, "Benvenuto Cellini," *Letteratura italiana, I minori* (Milan: Marzorati, 1961), 2:1133–55, his introduction to the 1968 edition of the *Vita* (Milan: Rizzoli), pp. 9–10, 16–17, and his study *Umanità e stile di Benvenuto Cellini* (Milan: Trevisini, 1952). See also, Ettore Bonora, "Benvenuto Cellini scrittore," *Storia della letteratura italiana* (Milan: Garzanti, 1966), 4:449–58, 688–90; Nino Borsellino, "Benvenuto Cellini," *La letteratura italiana: storia e testi* (Bari: Laterza, 1973), 5:652–76; *Benvenuto Cellini artista e scrittore* (Rome: Accademia Nazionale dei Lincei, 1972). In his "Manierismo e accademismo nel pensiero critico del cinquecento" (*Acme* 9 [1956]:68), Marco Rosci says: "Il Cellini è tipico esempio di amore 'manieristico' di artista e di tecnico per la propria arte e per la materia da essa trattata" (Cellini is a typical example of the "Mannerist" love of the artist and artisan for his own art and the materials it treats), an attitude which, as I will argue, is a key also to his literary mannerism. On this issue, see also Mario Pomilio, "Gusto episodico e coscienza letteraria nella *Vita* di Benvenuto Cellini," *Convivium* 20 (1951): 667–725. For an opposing view, there is Paul F. Grendler's *Critics of the Italian World, 1530–1560: Anton Francesco Doni, Nicolò Franco and Ortensio Lando* (Madison: University of Wisconsin Press, 1969), p. 8: "Few literary rules and conventions bound authors. Probably the best known book to come from this period, Benvenuto Cellini's *Autobiography* (composed 1558), was written by an itinerant artist who ignored all literary conventions, including veracity."

2 For Cellini's visual artistry, including his mannerist credentials, see: Charles Avery, *Florentine Renaissance Sculpture* (New York: Harper & Row, 1970), pp. 203–10; John Pope-Hennessy, *Italian High Renaissance and Baroque Sculpture*, 3 vols. (London: Phaidon, 1963), esp. 2:69–72, 3:44–47, 94–95, 99–100; Detlef Heikamp, *Benvenuto Cellini* (Milan: Fabbri, 1966), pp. 2, 3–4; the studies by Cesare Brandi, "Il Cellini scultore," and Bruno Bearzi, "Benvenuto Cellini ed il Perseo," in *Benvenuto Cellini artista e scrittore*, pp. 9–16, 45–56; see also Rudolf Wittkower and Margot Wittkower, *Born under Saturn* (New York: W. W. Norton, 1963), pp. 187–90; Cellini's works, as we have seen, are also taken up in many of the studies of mannerism mentioned in chapter 1 above, and listed in the Selected Bibliography.

3 The attitude to Cellini's "primitivism" and Varchi's nonintervention has been thoroughly analyzed by Maria Luisa Altieri Biagi, "La *Vita* del Cellini. Temi, termini, sintagmi," in *Benvenuto Cellini artista e scrittore*, pp. 61–163. The history of Cellini criticism was surveyed by Bruno Maier in "Svolgimento storico della critica su Benvenuto Cellini" (pts. 1 and 2) in *Annali triestini* 20–21 (1950–51): 173–202, 105–106, and in "Cellini e la critica contemporanea," *Ausonia* 7 (1952): 34–38.

4 I quote from the edition of the treatise in *Opere,* ed. Carlo Cordié (Milan-Naples:

Riccardo Ricciardi, 1960), p. 1026.

5 Cellini wrote his autobiography intermittently between 1558 and 1566, when he broke off. The latest reference he makes to himself involves the purchase of a farm in December of 1566, but the last detailed events he narrates belong to the year 1562. Since he died in 1571, we have no autobiographical account of the last years when he wrote his other works, perhaps because his relations with his patron had soured and he did not wish to record those later activities or because he lacked the will, out of boredom or illness, to continue.

6 See, for example, Castiglione, *Il cortegiano,* ed. Bruno Maier (Turin: UTET, 1964), book 2, sec. 13, p. 209.

7 Among Cellini's minor writings is a brief discourse, "Sopra la differenza nata tra gli scultori e' pittori circa il luogo destro stato dato alla pittura nelle essequie del gran Michelangelo Buonarroti" (On the difference existing between sculptors and painters in reference to why painting was given a place on the right in the obsequies of the great Michelangelo Buonarroti), in *Opere,* pp. 1113–14. On his contribution to the debate inaugurated by Varchi, and on the genre of the *paragone,* see above, chapter 1, note 23.

8 ". . . con gran passione, e non senza lacrime, io gli stracciai e gitta'gli al fuoco con salda intenzione di non mai più scrivergli" (and with great passion, and not without tears, I tore them up and threw them into the fire with the solid intention of never writing them again), *Opere,* p. 1026.

9 See R. R. Bolgar, "Hero or Anti-Hero? The Genesis and Development of the *Miles Christianus,*" in *Concepts of the Hero in the Middle Ages and the Renaissance,* ed. Norman T. Burns and Christopher Reagan (Albany: SUNY Press, 1975), pp. 120–46.

10 For example, of the Perseus statue Pope-Hennessy says that there "*maniera* reigns supreme" and that "the whole scheme has been frozen and rationalized" (*Italian High Renaissance and Baroque Sculpture,* p. 47); Avery says: "The final version has the elegant, effortless poise that was the hallmark of Mannerist art: no suggestion of the struggle, no flicker of movement is allowed to disturb the serenity of the graceful pose. Crude reality, physical force and overwrought emotions did not appeal to Cellini, an artist who knew very well the type of patron for whom he was working, men who sought personal aggrandizement through the virtuosity of the artistic performance which they sponsored rather than through the grandeur or nobility of the ideas which the works incorporated" (*Florentine Renaissance Sculpture,* pp. 206–07).

11 For example, *Vita,* pp. 57, 94, 432.

12 *Vita,* pp. 356–57: "Quando questa opera io posi agli occhi del Re, messe una voce di stupore, e non si poteva saziare di guardarla" (When I placed this work before the eyes of the king, he burst out in amazement, and could not get enough of looking at it).

13 See, for example, *Vita,* p. 358, where he refers callously to his first child, a girl, and her mother, his model, and pp. 410–11, where he grieves intensely over the death of a son, but says he accepted the loss and in his usual fashion made a virtue of necessity.

14 See, for example, *Vita,* pp. 416–17, the scene in which Bandinello calls Cellini a sodomite and is answered by an ironic wish that humble Benvenuto could indulge such a marvelous taste, given its frequency among gods, emperors, and kings. The reply caused the tense audience, including an angry duke, to break into laughter, thus defusing an awkward situation.

15 *Vita,* p. 158, the stabbing of Pompeo, and p. 341, the maiming with his dagger of two Parisians who had brought suit against him.

16 In the *Vita,* p. 366, Benvenuto has King Francis say: "Però è da fare un gran conto di Benvenuto, che non tanto che l'opere sue restino al paragone dell'antiche, ancora quelle superano" (Therefore we must highly value Benvenuto, for not only do his works equal those of the ancients, they surpass them).

17 A bit later on, Benvenuto refers to the unfolding spectacle of the great Sack of Rome

going on below before his eyes, but refuses to report it in detail: "Per tanto io non mi voglio mettere a descrivere tal cosa; solo seguiterò descrivere questa mia vita che io ho cominciato, e le cose che in essa a punto si appartengano" (But I do not wish to begin describing such a thing; I will continue to describe only this life of mine that I have started, and those matters that are precisely a part of it, p. 79). Thus does Cellini reject history except insofar as it touches upon his own story—namely, at the moment, his martial exploits.

18 *Vita,* p. 312. But Cellini turns back from the planned visit to the Holy Sepulchre when he is offered new terms by King Francis equal to those given Leonardo da Vinci!

19 *Vita,* pp. 382–83: "E queste mie cose io non le scrivo per boria mondana, ma solo per ringraziare Idio, che m'ha campato da tanti gran travagli" (And I write these things of mine not out of worldly arrogance but only to thank God, who has rescued me from so many great trials).

20. On the creation of the Perseus statue and critical opinion of its aesthetic merits, see above, notes 2, 10.

Chapter 3

1 "Costume," *A Concise Encyclopaedia of the Italian Renaissance,* ed. J. R. Hale (New York and Toronto: Oxford University Press, 1981), p. 102.

2 From the immense bibliography now accumulated on Petrarch and Petrarchism, I would recommend the following few among those many that are relevant, directly or indirectly, to the issue of mannerism: Leonard Forster, *The Icy Fire: Five Studies in European Petrarchism* (Cambridge: Cambridge University Press, 1969); Luzius Keller, ed., *Ubersetzung und Nachahmung im europaïschen Petrarkismus: Studien und Texte* (Stuttgart: Metzlersche Verlagsbuchhandlung, 1974); William J. Kennedy, "The Petrarchan Mode in Lyric Poetry," in *Rhetorical Norms in Renaissance Literature* (New Haven: Yale University Press, 1978), pp. 20–41; Mario Praz, "Petrarch in England," *The Flaming Heart* (New York: Doubleday Anchor Books, 1958), pp. 264–86; Stephen Minta, *Petrarch and Petrarchism: The English and French Traditions* (Manchester: Manchester University Press, 1980), and *Love Poetry in Sixteenth-Century France,* published by the same press in 1977; see also the studies already mentioned above in my first chapter by Greene (n. 8), Pigman (n. 8) and Scaglione (n. 42), and cited below in the notes to this chapter (especially 5, 6 and 10), and the following chapter, note 2.

3 Chicago and London: Chicago University Press, 1969, pp. 54–74.

4 I quote Dante from the edition of Charles Singleton (Princeton: Princeton University Press, 1970), 1:92; Boccaccio's remark is from his *Genealogia deorum gentilium,* vol. 14, ed. Pier Giorgio Ricci in the *Prose latine* (Milan-Naples: Riccardo Ricciardi, 1965), p. 942; Donne's phrase is from his *Devotions upon Emergent Occasions* (1624), ed. John Sparrow (Cambridge: Cambridge University Press, 1923), p. 113; Bunyan's admonition occurs at the conclusion to the first part of his *The Pilgrim's Progress,* ed. Roger Sharrock (Harmondsworth, Middlesex: Penguin Books, 1978), p. 207.

5 "The Fig Tree and the Laurel," *Diacritics* 5 (1975): 34–40. See also Guido Almanzi, "Petrarca o della insignificanza," *Paragone* 296 (1974): 68–73; Arnaud Tripet, "Pétrarque et le langage," in *Francis Petrarch, Six Centuries Later: A Symposium,* ed. Aldo Scaglione (Chapel Hill: University of North Carolina, 1975), pp. 223–35; Jill Tilden, "Conflict in Petrarch's *Canzoniere,*" in *Petrarca 1304–1374. Beiträge zu Werk und Wirkung,* ed. Fritz Schalk (Frankfurt am Main: Vittorio Klostermann, 1975), pp. 287–319; Richard Waswo, "The Petrarchan Tradition as a Dialectic of Limits," *Studies in Literary Imagination* 11 (1978): 1–16; and the essays by Amedeo Quondam mentioned above in chapter 1. Since my interest is not in the ultimate status and

meaning of Petrarch's text but in Petrarchism, that is, how he was read and understood by sixteenth-century readers, I do not pause here to discuss at length the issues raised by Freccero, Greene, and other recent critics. For my thematic purposes, what Petrarch "says" about Laura in the poems suffices.

6　I quote from the edition of the *Rime* (or *Canzoniere*) by Gianfranco Contini with notes by Daniele Ponchiroli (Turin: Giulio Einaudi, 1968), poem 77, p. 109. All future quotations of Petrarch will be from this text and are referred to by number and page. A convenient and excellent bilingual edition of the *Rime* is Robert Durling's *Petrarch's Lyric Poems* (Cambridge, Mass.: Harvard University Press, 1976). See also Contini's "Petrarca e le arti figurative," *Francesco Petrarca Citizen of the World,* ed. Aldo S. Bernardo (Padua: Editrice Antenore, and Albany: State University of New York Press, 1980), pp. 115–31. In the same volume there are also articles by Jean Seznec (pp. 133–50) and Denis Stevens (pp. 151–78) on Petrarch and Renaissance art and music.

7　I have corrected the twelfth line of this sonnet, which in my copy of Contini incorrectly repeats the ninth line here, from other authoritative editions.

8　See p. 482 of Cellini's *Vita* and the comment of the editor that she was "buona poetessa, e onesta donna," and who reminds us that in two sonnets Cellini compared her, inevitably, to Petrarch's chaste Laura. The poems, beginning "Con quel soave canto e dolce legno" and "Quella più ch'altra gloriosa e bella," are discussed by Bruno Maier in "Le rime di Benvenuto Cellini," *Annali triestini* 22 (1952): 307–58.

9　*The Portrait in the Renaissance,* A. W. Mellon Lectures in the Fine Arts, 1963, The National Gallery of Art, Washington, D.C., Bollingen Series XXXV, 12 (Princeton: Princeton University Press, 1979 [1963]), pp. 234–35. For the Bronzino portrait, see also Luisa Becherucci, *Manieristi toscani* (Bergamo: Istituto Italiano d'Arti Grafiche, 1944), pp. 50–51. Bronzino's own poems are edited by Giorgio Cerboni in Andrea Emiliani's *Il Bronzino* (Milan-Busto Arsizio: Bramante, 1960). For the portrait by Andrea del Sarto, see John Shearman, *Andrea del Sarto* (Oxford: Clarendon Press, 1965), 2:270–71; S. J. Freedberg, *Andrea del Sarto* (Cambridge, Mass.: Harvard University Press, 1963), 2:183–85; Raffaele Monti, *Andrea del Sarto* (Milan: Edizioni di Comunità, 1981 [1965]), p. 173.

10　Simone Turberville has translated excerpts from Girolamo Malipiero's *Il Petrarcha spirituale* (1536) in *Allegorica* 1 (1976): 126–65. This Minorite prefaced his "conversions" of the *Rime* with a dialogue in which the *cupiditas* of the poet and his unintentional evil influence are asserted and the "divinization" of his poems defended on the ground that Petrarch might thereby win salvation. There is no thorough account in English of the phenomenon of Petrarchism as a cultural force in sixteenth-century Italy, although it is touched upon by several of the writers on Petrarchism cited thus far. See also Luigi Baldacci, *Il Petrarchismo italiano nel Cinquecento* (Milan: Riccardo Ricciardi, 1957); Luigi Russo, *Il Petrarchismo italiano del '500* (Pisa: Libreria Goliardica, 1958); the anthology *Il Petrarchismo,* ed. Giacinto Spagnoletti (Milan: Garzanti, 1959); the still valuable essay by Arturo Graf, "Petrarchismo ed antipetrarchismo," in *Attraverso il Cinquecento* (Turin: Loescher, 1926), pp. 3–86; Donald L. Guss, *John Donne Petrarchist* (Detroit, Mich.: Wayne State University Press, 1966), and his "Petrarchism and the End of the Renaissance," in Scaglione, ed., *Francis Petrarch, Six Centuries Later,* pp. 384–401; E. H. Wilkins, "A General Survey of Renaissance Petrarchism," *Studies in the Life and Works of Petrarch* (Cambridge, Mass.: Harvard University Press, 1955), pp. 280–99; Elizabeth Cropper, "On Beautiful Women, Parmigianino, *Petrarchismo* and the Vernacular Style," *Art Bulletin* 58 (1976): 374–94.

11　Quoted and discussed by Ulrich Schulz-Buschaus, *Das Madrigal* (Bad Homburg vor der Höhe: Gehlen, 1969), pp. 214–15.

12 *Rime,* ed. Daniele Ponchiroli (Turin: Einaudi, 1967), pp. 64–65.

13 I am particularly indebted here to William J. Kennedy's essay on "The Petrarchan Mode in Lyric Poetry" (see above, n. 2) for his discussion of "rhetorical strategies of voice and address" as they reveal themselves in stylistic particulars.

14 Sir John Suckling's "Loving and Beloved," ll. 11–12, quoted from *Ben Jonson and the Cavalier Poets,* selected and edited by Hugh Maclean (New York: W. W. Norton, 1974), p. 253.

15 *Opere,* vol. 1, ed. Bruno Maier (Milan: Rizzoli, 1963), p. 746. In his note Maier says the "donne ferraresi" wore veils until 1576, when the custom ceased, apparently thanks to Marfisa's lead.

16 *Poesia del Quattrocento e del Cinquecento,* ed. Carlo Muscetta and Daniele Ponchiroli (Turin: UTET, 1959), p. 1477. The editors refer to Rota's "sensuale ricerca dell'effetto" (sensual striving after effect) as a proto-baroque quality. Another anthologist, Carlo Bo, says of this particular poem in his *Lirici del Cinquecento* (Milan: Garzanti, 1945) that it has a "dolce scansione e fuori di qualunque violenza risolutiva" (sweet scansion and an avoidance of any violent resolution whatsoever, p. 273).

17 Cf. *Rime* 279 (p. 353), 282–86 (pp. 356–60), 302 (p. 376), 328 (p. 407), 336 (p. 419), 342 (p. 425), 316 (p. 439), 359 (p. 442), and 362 (p. 451).

18 Giambattista Marino, *Poesie varie,* ed. Benedetto Croce (Bari: Laterza, 1913), p. 79. I also quote from this edition the lines from "La bella vedova" discussed below.

19 Pope-Hennessy, *The Portrait in the Renaissance,* p. 236. Interestingly, the widow sits at a table that has standing on it a reduction of Michelangelo's *Rachel* from the Julius tomb, and small figures from the Medici Chapel appear on the edge of the table, as they do on Cellini's *Saltcellar* (p. 235), i.e., more mannerist art about art.

20 I quote Surrey and, immediately after, Sidney, from *The Anchor Anthology of Sixteenth-Century Verse,* ed. Richard S. Sylvester (Garden City, N.Y.: Anchor Books, 1974), pp. 184–85 (Surrey) and 429–30 Sidney).

21 *Ben Jonson and the Cavalier Poets,* p. 217.

Chapter 4

1 *Self-Portrait in a Convex Mirror: Poems by John Ashbery* (New York: Penguin Books, 1982 [1975]), p. 68. Mary Ann Caws has meditated upon the Ashbery poem, Parmigianino's painting, and mannerist and surrealist hand gestures in her *The Eye in the Text,* pp. 51–52, 59–69. In the poem, Ashbery (p. 74) quotes S. J. Freedberg on the painting, particularly the argument that the surprise and tension lie in the concept rather than in the realization of the portrait. See Freedberg's *Parmigianino: His Work in Painting* (Cambridge, Mass.: Harvard University Press, 1950), pp. 104–06.

2 On the *bel piede,* see James Villas, "The Petrarchan Topos 'Bel Piede': Generative Footsteps," *Romance Notes* 11 (1969): 167–73, who takes up its European diffusion. On Petrarchan anatomy, see also Claude-Gilbert Dubois, *Le Maniérisme* (Paris: Presses Universitaires de France, 1979), pp. 16–18, who in speaking of "la manière et la main" refers to the Parmigianino *Madonna of the Long Neck* as "aussi une madame aux longues mains" (p. 17). Giovanni Pozzi, "Il ritratto della donna nella poesia d'inizio Cinquecento e la pittura di Giorgione," *Lettere italiane* 31 (1979): 3–30, takes up Petrarch's contribution to the formation of a canon of beauty, as does Elizabeth Cropper in the article "On Beautiful Women, Parmigianino, *Petrarchismo,*" mentioned above (chap. 3, n. 10). Both Pozzi and Cropper emphasize that Petrarch never described Laura's body in great detail, but the exception that is the subject of this chapter is, of course, her hand. Although my own narrower emphasis is on the *bella mano* as a

literary motif and on poetic texts, Cropper's important essay, which I regret having encountered only recently, offers valuable background and support for my argument insofar as it takes up the transmission of a concept of ideal feminine beauty from early Renaissance vernacular sources. These influenced Petrarch's interpreters, such as Bembo and Firenzuola, and the resulting canon in turn affected painters from Parmigianino to Poussin.

More recently, Bertrand Schmidt has also taken up the hand motif as part of his study of "La Métamorphose et les 'objets de madonna': Mellin de Saint-Gelais et les pétrarquistes de la fin du quattrocento," in *Poétiques de la métamorphose: de Pétrarque à John Donne,* ed. Guy Demerson (Saint-Etienne: Publications de l'Université de Saint-Etienne, 1981), pp. 81–94; see also Gordon Poole, "Il topos dell' 'effictio' e un sonetto del Petrarca," *Lettere italiane* 32 (1980): 3–20; and Nancy J. Vickers, "Remembering Dante: Petrarch's 'Chiare, fresche et dolci acque," *Modern Language Notes* 96 (1981): 1–11. M. B. Ogle's survey, "The White Hand as a Literary Conceit," *Sewanee Review* 20 (1912): 459–69, is still useful.

3 For example, the anonymous epigrams in *The Greek Anthology and Other Poems,* ed. Peter Jay (Harmondsworth, Middlesex: Penguin Books, 1981), p. 76, in which the poet says he wishes to be the wind touching the beloved's uncovered breasts, or a rose nestled there. There is also, of course, Catullus on Lesbia's sparrow (*Carmina* 2) and Ovid's wish to be the ring he sends to his mistress (*Amores* 2.15).

4 *Le rime di Benedetto Gareth detto il Chariteo,* ed. Erasmo Pèrcopo, 2 vols. (Naples: Accademia delle Scienze, 1892), 2:48. See also his series of poems on the lady's cloak, a variant of the *velo,* joined with hand and glove: sonnets 87–89, 2:109–11.

5 Since almost all of them wrote on our theme, and they are usually associated with Cariteo as mannered Petrarchists (and I shall be referring to only some of them later), I should note here the names of Serafino Aquilano (1466–1500), Antonio Tebaldeo (1456–1537), Panfilo Sasso (1455–1527), Baldassare Olimpo da Sassoferrato (1480–1540), and Marcello Filosseno (1450–1520), all of whom published or had their poems published in the first three decades of the century. Rota, whom we quoted in the previous chapter, is often bracketed with some other mid-to-later sixteenth-century poets as dissidents who returned to the more witty style of Cariteo, Serafino, and Tebaldeo in revolt against the classist-minded imitation of Petrarch associated with Pietro Bembo (1470–1547) and his followers. These anti-Bembists would include, among others, Angelo di Costanzo (1507–91) and Luigi Tansillo (1510–68), also Neapolitans or southerners in origin and ambience like Cariteo and Serafino, so there is a north–south tension here also. This historic scheme, best known to English readers from Mario Praz's "Petrarch in England," pp. 264–86, simplifies matters, in my view, by positing "flamboyant" revolt in cyclical alternation with classicist or purist reaction, whereas the concept of mannerism and the distinctions I have suggested allow us profitably to look at individual poems rather than to characterize vaguely the different poets and schools.

6 *Opere minori,* ed. Cesare Segre (Milan-Naples: Riccardo Ricciardi, 1954), pp. 181–83. The editor indicates the source as Propertius *Elegies* 2.15.

7 *Opere in volgare,* ed. Mario Marti (Florence: Sansoni, 1961), p. 455.

8 *Le considerazioni sopra tre canzoni di G. B. Pigna,* in Torquato Tasso, *Le prose diverse,* ed. Cesare Guasti (Florence: Le Monnier), 2:110. I owe this reference to C. P. Brand, *Torquato Tasso* (Cambridge, Mass.: Harvard University Press, 1965), pp. 142–43. In this same edition, immediately following, is Tasso's also relevant lecture on a sonnet by della Casa (pp. 115–34). At one point in this latter lecture, he refers to Casa's style with the phrase "quella maniera di stile" (pp. 117–18).

9 See also Tasso's "La man ch'avvolta entro odorate spoglie" (*Opere,* p. 671), which

anticipates Marino's poem cited below.

10 See my "Mannerist and Baroque Lyric Style in Marino and the Marinisti," *Forum Italicum* 7 (1973): 318–37.

11 Giusto dei Conti (1379–1449) composed his poems around 1440 to commemorate the death-dealing hand of a Bolognese beauty named Elisabetta. There is a modern edition by Leonardo Vitetti, 2 vols. (Lanciano: Carabba, 1918). Olimpo's strombotti were published in his *Libro d'amore chiamato gloria* (1520), recently edited by Franco Scatiglini (Ancona: L'Astrologi, 1974).

12 Leonard Forster, *The Icy Fire,* pp. 80–83 and p. 175, n. 2.

13 See the *blasons* in *Poètes du XVIe siècle,* ed. Albert-Marie Schmidt (Paris: Gallimard, 1953), pp. 291–364. On the *blason,* consult Annette and Edward Tomarken, "The Rise and Fall of the Sixteenth-Century French Blason," *Symposium* 29 (1975): 139–63, and D. B. Wilson, *Descriptive Poetry in France from Blason to Baroque* (New York: Barnes & Noble, 1967). Also, Alison Saunders, *The Sixteenth-Century "Blason poétique"* (Bern-Las Vegas: Peter Lang, 1981).

14 *Opere,* ed. Adriano Seroni (Florence: Sansoni, 1958), pp. 521–96.

15 This and the work by Federico da Udine discussed below may be read in *Trattati del Cinquecento sulla Donna,* ed. Giuseppe Zonta (Bari: Laterza, 1913), pp. 3–69; 223–308.

16 See above, note 2, and in particular the cited articles by Giovanni Pozzi and Elizabeth Cropper. Of the Bronzino portrait it could be said, to quote S. J. Freedberg's comment upon another painting by the artist, that "the semblance of statuary that has been given to the figure has made it seem asensuous; nevertheless, it conveys a quality of distilled and accentually displaced sensuality," and its commanding presence "does not result from the reproduction that may be in it of nature; the reality it conveys is that of its powerful reality of art" (*Circa 1600: A Revolution in Style in Italian Painting,* 1983, pp. 52–53).

17 *Collected Poems of Sir Thomas Wyatt,* ed. Kenneth Muir and Patricia Thomson (Liverpool: Liverpool University Press, 1969), pp. 65–66. See also in this edition, "Who hath herd of suche cruelty before?" (p. 32), discussed below, and two other poems: "What nedeth these thretning wordes and wasted wynde?" (p. 35), on the glove theme, and "She sat and sowde that hath done me the wrong" (p. 40), on the motif of the fair seamstress.

18 The Scève is from the *Délie, dizain* no. 367, "Assez plus long qu'un siècle Platonique," 1.8, in *Poètes du XVIe siècle,* p. 197. The Desportes quotations are from his "Beaux noeuds crespes et blonds, nonchalamment espars" and "Deux clairs soleils la nuict estincelans," in *Les Amours de Diane,* ed. Victor E. Graham (Geneva: Droz, 1959), 2:300, and "Deux clairs soleils la nuict estincelans" in *Les Amours d'Hyppolyte,* ed. Victor E. Graham (Geneva: Droz, 1960), p. 71. For the *Délie,* see also the edition by I. D. McFarlane (Cambridge: Cambridge University press, 1966), which has the original accompanying emblems, and, in the notes, details of Petrarchist sources.

19 The Chappuys *blason* is in *Poètes du XVIe siècle,* pp. 326–27; the Charles de la Huetterie poem is cited by D. B. Wilson, *Descriptive Poetry in France from Blason to Baroque,* p. 42.

20 *Poètes du XVIe siècle,* p. 417.

21 "De la main de Marguerite," in *Anthologie poétique française,* ed. Maurice Allem (Paris: Garnier-Flammarion, 1965), 1:196.

22 *Oeuvres complètes,* ed. Gustave Cohen (Paris: Gallimard, 1950), p. 294, vol. 2 ll. 13–16.

23 *English Seventeenth-Century Verse,* vol. 2, ed. Richard S. Sylvester (New York: W. W.

Norton, 1974 [1969]), p. 202, ll. 45–48.

24 Ibid., p. 249, ll. 101–09.

25 See Hoffmanswaldau's "Ein haar, so kühnlich trotz der Berenice spricht," and "Es wird der bleiche Tod mit seiner kalten Hand," in *The German Lyric of the Baroque in Translation,* ed. and trans. George C. Schoolfield (Chapel Hill: University of North Carolina Press, 1961), pp. 186–89. The Opitz poem, "Ach liebste, lass uns eilen," in *Baroque Poetry,* selected and translated by J. P. Hill and E. Caracciolo-Trejo (London: J. M. Dent, 1975), p. 152.

26 In *Renaissance and Baroque Poetry of Spain,* ed. and trans. Elias L. Rivers (New York: Charles Scribner's Sons, 1966), p. 83. An excellent prose rendering follows the text, but I have retranslated the poem, with its help, in order to attain a literalness consistent with my practice throughout this study.

27 In *La Poésie française et le maniérisme,* ed. Marcel Raymond (Geneva: Droz, 1971), p. 121.

28 Pope-Hennessy, *The Portrait in the Renaissance,* pp. 254–55, includes the portrait and refers thus to it and its puzzling inscription: "the exact context eludes us." The motto Attici amoris ergo (Because of Attic love) may refer to Neo-platonic love, which would explain the hand emerging from a cloud above and grasping or lifting the sitter's hand. Pope-Hennessy argues that in miniatures of this kind "the Petrarchan love sonnet for the first and only time found a visual equivalent" (p. 255). See also John Murdoch et al. *The English Miniature* (New Haven: Yale University Press, 1981), p. 42, and Erna Auerbach, *Nicholas Hilliard* (London: Routledge & Kegan Paul, 1961), pp. 100, 299. The miniature bears the date 1588 opposite the motto, both flanking the sitter.

29 *The Countess of Pembroke's Arcadia,* ed. Maurice Evans (Harmondsworth, Middlesex: Penguin Books, 1977), p. 291.

30 *The Complete Poetical Works of Spenser,* ed. R. E. Neil Dodge (Boston: Houghton Mifflin, 1936 [1908]), p. 717.

31 *The Flaming Heart,* p. 277. The Tebaldeo poem begins, "Beata carta ne la man raccolta."

32 Cf. also in the *Délie,* dizain no. 198, p. 141, another poem on the glove theme beginning, "Gant envieux, et non sans cause avare / De celle doulce, et molle neige blanche," which is not a mannerist poem, and not very interesting either.

33 *Diverses Amours,* ed. Victor E. Graham (Geneva: Droz, 1963), pp. 62–63. I owe this reference and the Constable imitation to Anne Lake Prescott's discussion in *French Poets and the English Renaissance* (New Haven: Yale University Press, 1978), p. 148.

34 *Poems,* ed. Joan Grundy (Liverpool: Liverpool University Press, 1960), p. 131.

35 Ed. Victor A. Doyno (Carbondale and Edwardsville: Southern Illinois University Press, 1971), p. 39, ll. 5–8.

36 *Minor Poets of the Seventeenth Century,* ed. R. G. Howarth (London: J. M. Dent & Sons, 1969 [1931]), p. 270.

37 Ibid., p. 316.

38 See, for example, in the *Délie,* nos. 347, and 349 (pp. 190–91). For Serafino, *Le rime di Serafino de' Ciminelli dall'Aquila,* ed. Mario Menghini (Bologna: Romangnoli-dall'Acqua, 1894), 1:89–116. Cf. also Scève and Serafino on the glove theme; the former's *dizains* and the latter's *strombotti* are cited in *Die Strombotti des Serafino dall'Aquila,* ed. Barbara Bauer-Formiconi (Munich: Wilhelm Fink, 1967), p. 318.

39 *Collected Poems,* p.32. See also p. 40, "She sat and sowde that hath done me the wrong." The editors mention the influence of Italian sources but cite no specific one for "Who hath herd" or "She sat and sowde." There is a vague similarity between the latter and Scève's "Ouvrant ma Dame au labeur trop ardente" (*Délie,* no. 332, p. 185).

40 Ed. Lanfranco Caretti (Milan-Naples: Riccardo Ricciardi, 1963 [1954]), p. 618.

41 *Obras completas* (Madrid: Aguilar, 1956), p. 516. See also his "En el cristal de tu divina mano" (p. 485).

42 *English Seventeenth-Century Verse,* 2:359.

Chapter 5

 1 *Baroque* (New York: Harper & Row, 1977), p. 12. See also S. J. Freedberg's *Circa 1600: A Revolution in Style in Italian Painting* (1983), which charts the change to baroque also by juxtaposition of paintings by mannerists and their successors.

 2 *Englands Helicon,* ed. Hugh Macdonald (London: Routledge and Kegan Paul, 1949), pp. 192–93.

 3 *The Complete Works of Christopher Marlowe,* ed. Fredson Bowers (Cambridge: Cambridge University Press, 1973), 2:519–33. The four-stanza and six-stanza versions are given on pp. 536–37.

 4 On the Ralegh poem, its versions and authorship, see *The Poems of Sir Walter Ralegh,* ed. Agnes Latham (Cambridge, Mass.: Harvard University Press, 1962), pp. 111–14. The text of the poem, which I quote below, is on pp. 16–17.

 5 For the sources and diffusion of the Marlowe poem, the essential study is still R. S. Forsythe's "The Passionate Shepherd and English Poetry," *PMLA* 40 (1925): 692–742. He does not, of course, include such modern parodies as those of C. Day Lewis (1935) and Ogden Nash (1931), both of which begin with Marlowe's first line.

 6 *Pastoral Poetry and Pastoral Drama* (New York: Russell & Russell, 1959 [1905]), p. 158, n. 1.

 7 *Michelangelo and the Language of Art,* p. 76.

 8 *The Elegies and the Songs and Sonets,* ed. Helen Gardner (Oxford: Clarendon Press, 1965), pp. 32–33. An interesting parallel to Donne's fishing poem is Scève's *dizain* no. 221, beginning "Sur le Printemps, que les Aloses montent," on a similar theme (*Poètes du XVIe siècle,* p. 148).

 9 Izaak Walton and Charles Cotton, *The Compleat Angler,* ed. John Buxton (Oxford-New York-Toronto-Melbourne: Oxford University Press, 1982), p. 167.

10 *The Complete Poetry of Robert Herrick,* ed. J. Max Patrick (New York: Anchor Books, 1963), pp. 256–57.

11 *Poems,* ed. John Buxton (London: Routledge & Kegan Paul, 1958), pp. 41–43.

12 By taking up Cotton with the Cavalier writers in the "social" mode as opposed to the Restoration writers in the "public" mode, Earl Miner makes a valid case from the perspective of his viewpoint on seventeenth-century literary developments. My reference to these matters is intended to suggest only that, from the perspective of a history of seventeenth-century style, Cotton's poem under discussion here seems at times to be transitionally polyphonic. For Miner's rehabilitative treatment of Cotton, see *The Cavalier Mode* (Princeton: Princeton University Press, 1971), passim.

Selected Bibliography on the Concepts and Controversy
Generated by Interpretations of Mannerism (Chapter 1)

Mannerism as Term and Concept

Antal, Friedrich. "The Problem of Mannerism in the Netherlands." In his *Classicism and Romanticism*, pp. 47– 106. New York: Harper & Row, 1973.

_____. "The Social Background of Italian Mannerism." In his *Classicism and Romanticism*, pp. 158– 61. New York: Harper & Row, 1973.

Anzulovic, Branimir. "Mannerism in Literature: A Review of Research," pp. 54– 64. *Yearbook of General and Comparative Literature*, 1974.

Artz, Frederick B. *From Renaissance to Romanticism: Trends in Style in Art, Literature and Music, 1300– 1830*. Chicago: University of Chicago Press, 1963.

Atti del congresso internazionale sul tema "Manierismo in arte e musica," Rome, 1973. Florence: Olschki, 1974.

Battisti, Eugenio. "Manierismo o antirinascimento." In his *L'antirinascimento*, pp. 19– 45. Milan: Feltrinelli, 1962.

_____. "Sfortune del manierismo." In his *Rinascimento e barocco*, pp. 216– 57. Turin: Einaudi, 1960.

_____. "Storia del concetto di manierismo in architettura." *International Center for the Study of Architecture* 9 (1967): 204– 10.

Becherucci, Luisa. See under "Mannerism." In *Encyclopedia of World Art*, 9;445– 78. New York: McGraw-Hill, 1964.

Benincasa, Carmine. *Sul manierismo come dentro a uno specchio*. Pollenza: Nuova Foglio, 1975.

Bialostocki, Jan. *The Art of the Renaissance in Eastern Europe*. Ithaca, N.Y.: Cornell University Press, 1976.

_____. "Der Manierismus zwischen Triumph und Dämmerung." In his *Stil und Ikonographie*, pp. 57– 76. Dresden: VEB Verlag der Kunst, 1966.

_____. "Two Types of International Mannerism: Italian and Northern." *Umeni* 18 (1970): 105– 09.

Boase, A. M. "The Definition of Mannerism." *Proceedings of the Third Congress of the International Comparative Literature Association*, pp. 43– 55. The Hague: Mouton, 1962.

Borgerhoff, E. B. O. "Mannerism and Baroque: A Simple Plea." *Comparative Literature* 5 (1953): 323– 31.

Bousquet, Jacques. *Mannerism: The Painting and Style of the Late Renaissance*. Translated by S. W. Taylor. New York: Braziller, 1964.

Brahmer, Mieczyslaw. "Le Maniérisme: Terme d'histoire littéraire." *Acta Litteraria Academiae Scientiarum Hungaricae*, 5:251– 57. Budapest: Akadémiai Kiadó, 1963.

Briganti, Giuliano. *Italian Mannerism*. Translated by Margaret Kunzle. Leipzig: VEB Edition, 1962.

_____. "Notizie sulla fortuna storica del manierismo." In his *Il Manierismo e Pellegrino Tibaldi*, pp. 39– 49. Rome: Cosmopolita, 1945.

Burgum, E. B. "Marxism and Mannerism: The Aesthetic of Arnold Hauser." *Science and Society* 32 (1968): 307—20.

Carozza, Davy A. "For a Definition of Mannerism: The Hatzfeldian Thesis." *Colloquia Germanica* 1 (1967): 66—77.

Caws, Mary Ann. *The Eye in the Text: Essays on Perception, Mannerist to Modern.* Princeton: Princeton University Press, 1981.

Chastel, André. *The Crisis of the Renaissance, 1520—1600.* Translated by Peter Price. New York: Skira, 1968.

_____. "What Is Mannerism?" *Art News* 64 (1965): 22—25.

Clark, Sir Kenneth. *A Failure of Nerve: Italian Painting 1520—1535.* Oxford: Clarendon Press, 1967.

Cochrane, Eric. *Florence in the Forgotten Centuries, 1527—1800.* Chicago: Chicago University Press, 1973.

_____, ed. *The Late Italian Renaissance, 1525—1633.* New York: Harper & Row, 1970.

Coletti, Luigi. "Intorno alla storia del concetto di manierismo." *Convivium* 17 (1949): 801—11.

Curtius, E. R. *European Literature and the Latin Middle Ages.* Translated by W. R. Trask. New York: Pantheon Books, 1953.

De Capua, Angelo G. "Baroque and Mannerism: Reassessment." *Colloquia Germanica* 1 (1967): 101—10.

Dresden, Sem. "La Notion de manière au XVIe siècle et dans la poétique moderne." *Revue de Littérature Comparée* 51 (1977): 134—41.

Dubois, Claude-Gilbert. *Le Manierisme.* Paris: Presses Universitaires de France, 1979.

Dumont, Catherine. "Le Maniérisme: Etat de la question." *Bibliothèque d'Humanisme et Renaissance* 28 (1966): 439—57.

Dvorák, Max. "El Greco and Mannerism." *Magazine of Art* 46 (1953): 14—23.

_____. *Geschichte der Italienischen Kunst im der Renaissance.* 2 vols. Munich: Piper, 1927—28.

_____. *Kunstgeschichte als Geistesgeschichte: Studien zur Abendländischen Kunstwentwicklung.* Munich: Piper, 1924.

Elliot, J. H. "The Mannerists." *Horizon* 15 (1973): 84—104.

Fasola, G. N. "Storiografia del manierismo." *Scritti in onore di Lionello Venturi*, 1:429—47. Rome: De Luca, 1956.

Freedberg, S. J. *Circa 1600: A Revolution in Style in Italian Painting.* Cambridge, Mass.: Harvard University Press, 1983.

_____. "Observations on the Painting of the Maniera." *Art Bulletin* 47 (1965): 187—97.

_____. *Painting in Italy, 1500—1600.* Baltimore: Penguin Books, 1971. Reprinted 1975.

Friedlaender, Walter. *Mannerism and Anti-Mannerism in Italian Painting.* New York: Columbia University Press, 1957.

Friedrich, Hugo. *Epochen der Italienischen Lyrik*, pp. 593—606. Frankfurt am Main: Klostermann, 1964.

_____. "Manierismus." In *Literatur II*, edited by Friedrich Wol-Helmut and Walter Killy, 2:353—58. Frankfurt am Main: Fischer, 1965.

Frey, Dagobert. *Manierismus als Europäische Stilerscheinung.* Stuttgart: Kohlhammer, 1964.

Fubini, Enrico. "Il manierismo come categoria storiografica." In *Atti del congresso internazionale sul tema "Manierismo in arte e musica,"* Rome, 1973, pp. 3—11. Florence: Olschki, 1974.

Gillespie, Gerald. "Renaissance, Mannerism, Baroque." In *German Baroque Literature: The*

European Perspective, edited by Gerhart Hoffmeister, pp. 3–24. New York: Frederick Ungar, 1983.

Goff, Penrith. "The Limits of Sypher's Theory of Style." *Colloquia Germanica* 1 (1967): 111–57.

Gombrich, E. H. "Mannerism: The Historiographic Background." In his *Norm and Form,* pp. 99–106. London: Phaidon, 1971.

——————. "The Renaissance Conception of Artistic Progress and Its Consequences." In his *Norm and Form,* pp. 1–10. London: Phaidon, 1971.

Grassi, Ernesto. "La mania ingenosa. Il significato filosofico del manierismo." In *L'umanesimo e "la Follia",* edited by Enrico Castelli, pp. 109–26. Rome: Edizioni Abete, 1971.

*Hartmann, Horst. "Barock oder Manierismus?" *Weimarer Beiträge* 7 (1961): 40–60.

Hatzfeld, Helmut. "Mannerism Is Not Baroque." *L'Espirit Créateur* 6 (1966): 225–33.

Hauser, Arnold. *The Crisis of the Renaissance and the Origin of Modern Art.* 2 vols. London: Routledge & Kegan Paul, 1965.

——————. *The Social History of Art.* Vol. 2. New York: Vintage Books, 1957.

Haydn, Hiram. *The Counter-Renaissance.* New York: Scribner's, 1950.

Hocke, G. R. "Aion e Chronos: L'espansione dell'imaginazione." In *Tiziano e il manierismo europeo,* edited by Rodolfo Palluchini, pp. 435–57. Florence: Olschki, 1978.

——————. *Manierismus in der Literatur.* Hamburg: Rowholt, 1959.

——————. *Die Welt als Labyrinth: Manier und Manie in der Europaische Kunst.* Hamburg: Rowholt, 1957.

Hoffmann, Hans. *Hochrenaissance, Manierismus, Fruehbarock.* Leipzig: Seemann, 1938.

*Klaniczay, Tibor. *Az Manierismus.* Budapest: Gondolat, 1975.

——————. "La Crise de la Renaissance et le maniérisme." *Acta Litteraria Academiae Scientiarum Hungaricae* 13 (1971): 269–314.

——————. "La lotta antiaristotelica dei teorici del manierismo." In *Tiziano e il manierismo europeo,* edited by Rodolfo Palluchini, pp. 367–87. Florence: Olschki, 1978.

——————. "La Naissance du maniérisme et du baroque au point de vue sociologique." *Renaissance, Maniérisme, Baroque.* Actes du XIe stage internationale de Tours, pp. 215–23. Paris: Vrin, 1972.

Koenigsberger, H. G. "Decadence or Shift? Changes in the Civilization of Italy and Europe in the Sixteenth and Seventeenth Centuries." In his *Estates and Revolutions: Essays in Early Modern European History,* pp. 278–97. Ithaca, N.Y.: Cornell University Press, 1971.

Lange, Klaus-Peter. *Theoretiker des Literarischen Manierismus.* Munich: Wilhelm Fink, 1968.

Lockwood, Lewis. "On 'Mannerism' and 'Renaissance' as Terms and Concepts in Music History." *Atti del congresso internazionale sul tema "Manierismo in arte e musica,"* Rome, 1973, pp. 85–96. Florence: Olschki, 1974.

Lopez, R. S. *The Three Ages of the Italian Renaissance.* Charlottesville: University of Virginia Press, 1970.

Lowinsky, Edward E. "The Problem of Mannerism in Music: An Attempt at a Definition." *Atti del congresso internazionale sul tema "Manierismo in arte e musica,"* Rome, 1973, pp. 131–218. Florence: Olschki, 1974.

*Macchioni Jodi, Rodolfo. *Barocco e manierismo nel gusto otto-novecentesco.* Bari: Adriatica Editrice, 1973.

Mahon, Denis. *Studies in Seicento Art and Theory.* London: Warburg Institute, 1947.

Manierismo, Barocco, Rococò: Concetti e termini. International Meeting, Rome, 1960. Problemi Attuali di Scienza e di Cultura, quaderno 52. Rome: Accademia Nazionale dei Lincei, 1962.

Martz, Louis L. "Marvell and Herrick: The Masks of Mannerism." In *Approaches to*

Marvell: The York Tercentenary Lectures, edited by C. A. Patrides, pp. 194–215. London: Routledge & Kegan Paul, 1978.

_____. *The Wit of Love.* Notre Dame, Ind.: University of Notre Dame Press, 1969.

Melchiori, Giorgio. *The Tightrope Walkers: Studies of Mannerism in Modern English Literature.* London: Routledge & Kegan Paul, 1956.

Miedema, Hessel. "On Mannerism and *maniera.*" *Semiolus* 10 (1978–79): 19–45.

Mirollo, James V. "The Mannered and the Mannerist in Late Renaissance Literature." In *The Meaning of Mannerism,* edited by Franklin W. Robinson and Stephen G. Nichols, Jr., pp. 7–24. Hanover, N.H.: University Press of New England, 1972.

Nicolich, Robert N. "The Baroque Dilemma: Some Recent French Mannerist and Baroque Criticism." *Oeuvres & Critiques* 1 (1976): 21–36.

Nyholm, Esther. *Arte e teoria del manierismo.* 2 vols. Odense, Denmark: Odense University Press, 1977–82.

Orozco Diaz, Emilio. *Manierismo y barroco* Salamanca: Anaya, 1970.

_____. *Manierismo y barroco.* Madrid: Ediciones Cátedra, 1975. A second edition of the above augmented by the essay that follows.

_____. "El retrato a lo divino, su influencia, y unas obras desconocidas de Resueño." *Goya* 120 (1974): 351–58.

Palisca, Claude. "Towards an Intrinsically Musical Definition of Mannerism in the Sixteenth Century." In *Atti del congresso internazionale sul tema "Manierismo in arte e musica,"* Rome, 1973, pp. 313–31. Florence: Olschki, 1974.

Palluchini, Rodolfo, ed. *Tiziano e il manierismo europeo.* Florence: Olschki, 1978.

Peckham, Morse. *Man's Rage for Chaos: Biology, Behavior, and the Arts.* New York: Schocken Books, 1967.

Pevsner, Nikolaus. "The Architecture of Mannerism." In *Readings in Art History,* edited by Harold Spencer, 2:119–48. New York: Scribner's, 1969.

Pinder, Wilhelm. "Zur Physiognomik des Manierismus." *Die Wissenschaft am Scheidewege,* pp. 148–56. Leipzig: Barth, 1932.

Praz, Mario. *Mnemosyne: The Parallel between Literature and the Visual Arts.* Princeton: Princeton University Press, 1970.

Quondam, Amedeo, and Giulio Ferroni, eds. *La "locuzione artificiosa": Teoria ed esperienza della lirica a Napoli nell'età del manierismo.* Rome: Bulzoni, 1973.

_____. *La parola nel laberinto: società e scrittura nel manierismo a Napoli.* Bari: Laterza, 1975.

_____, ed. *Problemi del manierismo.* Naples: Guida, 1975.

_____. "La trasgressione dal codice: Problemi del manierismo e proposte sul metodo." *Letteratura e critica. Studi in onore di Natalino Sapegno,* 2:417–44. Rome: Bulzoni, 1975.

Raimondi, Ezio. "Per la nozione di un manierismo letterario." In *Manierismo, Barocco, Rococò: Concetti e termini.* International meeting, Rome, 1960. Problemi Attuali di Scienza e di Cultura, quaderno 52, pp. 57–79. Rome: Accademia Nazionale dei Lincei, 1962.

Renaissance, Maniérisme, Baroque. Actes du XIᵉ stage internationale de Tours. Paris: Vrin, 1972.

Robinson, Franklin W., and Stephen G. Nichols, Jr., eds. *The Meaning of Mannerism.* Hanover, N.H.: University Press of New England, 1972.

Scrivano, Riccardo. "La discussione sul manierismo." In his *Cultura e letteratura nel Cinquecento,* pp. 231–84. Rome: Ateneo, 1966.

_____. "Retorica e manierismo." *Rassegna della letteratura italiana* 83 (1979): 40–58.

_____. "Gli studi di Georg Weise sul rinascimento e sul manierismo." In his *Cultura e letteratura nel Cinquecento,* pp. 287–313. Rome: Ateneo, 1966.

Sebba, Gregor. "Baroque and Mannerism: A Retrospect." In *Filologia y crítica hispánica,* edited by Antonio Porqueras Mayo and Carlos Royas, pp. 145–63. Madrid: Ediciones

Alcalá; Atlanta, Ga.: Emory University Press, 1969.

Shearman, John. "Maniera as an Aesthetic Ideal." In *Renaissance Art,* edited by Creighton Gilbert, pp. 181–221. New York, Evanston, and London: Harper Torchbooks, 1970.

_____. *Mannerism.* Baltimore: Penguin Books, 1967.

Smith, Robert. "Mannerism and Modernism." *Papers of the Symposium "Mannerism and the Manneristic Configurations in the Creative and Performing Arts,"* Canberra, Australia, June 1977. Published in *Miscellanea Musicologica* 11 (1980): 17–27.

Smyth, C. H. *Mannerism and Maniera.* New York: Augustin, 1963.

Spahr, B. L. "Baroque and Mannerism: Epoch and Style." *Colloquia Germanica* 1 (1967): 78–100.

Spencer, Harold, ed. *Readings in Art History.* New York: Scribner's, 1969.

Strinati, Claudio M. "Sulla storia del concetto di manierismo." In *Atti del congresso internazionale sul tema "Manierismo in arte e musica,"* Rome, 1973, pp. 13–31. Florence: Olschki, 1974.

Studies in Western Art: Acts of the Twentieth International Congress of the History of Art. Princeton: Princeton University Press, 1963.

Studing, Richard, and Elizabeth Kruz, comps. *Mannerism in Art, Literature and Music: A Bibliography.* San Antonio, Tex.: Trinity University Press, 1979.

Studi vasariani. Atti del convegno internazionale per il quarto centenario della prima edizione delle *Vite* del Vasari. Florence: Sansoni, 1952.

Sypher, Wylie. *Four Stages of Renaissance Style.* New York: Anchor Books, 1965.

Tafuri, Manfredo. *L'architettura del manierismo nel Cinquencento europeo.* Rome: Officina Edizioni, 1966.

Treves, Marco. "Maniera: The History of a Word." *Marsyas* 1 (1941): 69–88.

Ulivi, Ferruccio. "Il manierismo letterario in Italia." *Convivium* 35 (1967): 641–54.

_____. "La 'querelle' del manierismo." *Nuova antologia* 2062 (1972): 203–11.

Wanke, Christian. *Seneca, Lucan, Corneille: Studien zum Manierismus der romischen Kaiserzeit und der französischen Klassik.* Heidelberg: Carl Winter, 1964.

Weisbach, Werner. "Gegenreformation, Manierismus, Barock." *Reportorium für Kunstwissenschaft* 49 (1928): 16–28.

_____. *Die Kunst des Barock.* Berlin: Propyläen, 1924.

_____. "Der Manierismus." *Zeitschrift für Bildende Kunst* n.s. 30, 54 (1918–19): 161–83.

_____. "Zum Problem der Manierismus." *Studien zur Deutschen Kunstgeschichte* 300 (1934): 15–20.

Weise, Georg. "La doppia origine del concetto di manierismo." In *Studi vasariani.* Atti del convegno internazionale per il quarto centenario della prima edizione delle *Vite* del Vasari, pp. 181–85. Florence: Sansoni, 1952.

_____. "Maniera und Pellegrino: Zwei Lieblingswörter der Italienischen Literatur der Zeit des Manierismus." *Romanistische Jahrbuch* 3 (1950): 321–403.

_____. *Il manierismo: Bilancio critico del problema stilistico.* Florence: Olschki, 1971.

_____. *Manierismo e letteratura.* Florence: Olschki, 1976.

_____. "Sulla storia del termine *manierismo*." *Manierismo, Barocco, Rococò: Concetti e termini.* International meeting, Rome, 1960. Problemi Attuali di Scienza e di Cultura, quaderno 52, pp. 27–38. Rome: Accademia Nazionale dei Lincei, 1962.

Weitz, Morris. "Genre and Style." *Perspectives in Education, Religion and the Arts.* Vol. 3, edited by H. E. Kiefer and M. K. Munitz, pp. 183–218. Albany: The State University of New York Press, 1970.

Würtenberger, Franzsepp. *Mannerism: The European Style of the Sixteenth Century.* Translated by Michael Heron. New York: Holt, Rinehart and Winston, 1963.

Zerner, Henri. "Observations on the Use of the Concept of Mannerism." In *The Meaning of Mannierism,* edited by Franklin W. Robinson and Stephen G. Nichols, Jr., pp. 105–19). Hanover, N.H.: University Press of New England, 1972.

The Culture of Mannerism

SIXTEENTH-CENTURY SOURCES

Aretino, Pietro. *Lettere sull'arte di Pietro Aretino,* edited by Ettore Camesasca and Fidenzio
Pertile. 4 vols. Milan: Edizione del Milione, 1957–60.
_____. *Selected Letters.* Translated by George Bull. Harmondsworth, Middlesex: Pen-
guin Books, 1976.
Armenini, G. B. *On the True Precepts of the Art of Painting.* Translation of *De veri precetti
della pittura* (1587) by Edward J. Olszewski. New York: Burt Franklin, 1977.
Barocchi, Paola, ed. *Scritti d'arte del Cinquecento.* 3 vols. Milan-Naples: Riccardo Ricciardi,
1971–77.
_____, ed. *Trattati d'arte del Cinquecento.* 3 vols. Bari: Laterza, 1960–62.
Borghini, Raffaello. *Il Riposo.* Edited by Mario Rossi. Milan: Labor Riproduzioni e Docu-
mentazioni, 1967.
Bottari, Giovanni G., and Stefano Ticozzi, eds. *Raccolta di lettere sulla pittura, scultura ed
architettura.* 8 vols. Milan: G. Silvestri, 1822–25.
Clovio, Giulio. *The Farnese Hours.* Introduction and commentary by Webster Smith. New
York: Braziller, 1976.
Doni, Antonfrancesco. *Disegno.* Edited by Mario Pepe. Milan: Electa, 1970.
Gilbert, Allan H., ed. *Literary Criticism: Plato to Dryden.* Detroit, Mich.: Wayne State
University Press, 1940. Reprinted 1962.
Goldwater, Robert, and Marco Treves, eds. *Artists on Art.* New York: Pantheon, 1945.
Reprinted 1972.
Haydocke, Richard. *A Tract Containing the Artes of Curious Paintinge Carvinge & Buildinge.*
Oxford: Joseph Barnes, 1584. Reprinted 1970. Abridged translation of Lomazzo's
Trattato.
Holt, Elizabeth G. *A Documentary History of Art.* Vol 2. Princeton: Princeton University
Press, 1947. Reprinted 1982.
Klein, Robert, and Henri Zerner, eds. *Italian Art, 1500–1600.* Englewood Cliffs, N.J.:
Prentice-Hall, 1966.
Leonardo da Vinci. *Treatise on Painting.* Edited and translated by A. Philip McMahon.
Princeton: Princeton University Press, 1956.
Lomazzo, G. P. *Idea del Tempio della Pittura.* Edited by Robert Klein with French transla-
tion. 2 vols. Florence: Istituto Nazionale di Studi sul Rinascimento, 1974.
_____. *Scritti sulle arto.* Edited by R. P. Ciardi. 2 vols. Florence: Marchi & Bertolli,
1973–74. English translation of *Trattato dell'arte della pittura* by Richard Haydocke (see
above, under Haydocke).
Pino, Paolo. *Il dialogo di pittura.* Edited by Anna and Rodolfo Palluchini. Venice: D.
Guarnati, 1946.
Pozzi, Mario, ed. *Trattatisti del Cinquecento.* Milan: Riccardo Ricciardi, 1978.
Roskill, Mark W. *Dolce's "Aretino" and Venetian Art Theory of the Cinquecento.* New York:
New York University Press, 1968.
Vasari, Giorgio. *Lives.* Translated by George Bull. Baltimore: Penguin Books, 1965.
_____. *Opere.* Edited by Gaetano Milanesi. 9 vols. Florence: Sansoni, 1878–85.
Reprinted 1975.
_____. *Vita di Michelangelo nelle redazioni del 1550 e del 1568.* Edited by Paola
Barocchi. 5 vols. Milan-Naples: Riccardo Ricciardi, 1962.
_____. *Le vite dei più eccellenti pittori, scultori e architetti.* Edited by Licia and Carlo L.
Ragghianti. 4 vols. Milan: Rizzoli, 1971–78.

Vasari on Technique, Being the Introduction to the Three Arts of Design. Translated by Louisa S. Maclehose. Commentary by G. B. Brown. New York: Dover Books, 1960.

Weinberg, Bernard, ed. *Trattati di poetica e retorica del Cinquecento.* 4 vols. Bari: Laterza, 1970–74.

Zuccaro, Federico. *Scritti D'arte.* Edited by Detlef Heikamp. Florence: Olschki, 1961.

Modern Commentary on Mannerism in the Arts

The Age of Vasari. Catalogue of the Exhibition at the University of Notre Dame, South Bend, Indiana, and the State University of New York at Binghamton, 1970.

Anderson, Gordon A. "Mannerist Trends in the Music of the Late Thirteenth Century." *Papers of the Symposium "Mannerism and the Manneristic Configurations in the Creative and Performing Arts,"* Canberra, Australia, June 1977. Published in *Miscellanea Musicologica* 11 (1980): 105–10.

Barolsky, Paul. *Infinite Jest: Wit and Humor in Italian Renaissance Art.* Columbia: University of Missouri Press, 1978.

Baumgart, Fritz E. *Renaissance und Kunst des Manierismus.* Cologne: Mont, 1963.

Becherucci, Luisa. *Manieristi toscani.* Bergamo: Istituto Italiano d'Arti Grafiche, 1944.

Béguin, Sylvie. *L'Ecole de Fontainebleau.* Paris: Gonthier, 1960.

Bianconi, Lorenzo. *"Ah Dolente Partita:* Espressione ed artificio." In *Atti del congresso internazionale sul tema "Manierismo in arte e musica,"* Rome, 1973, pp. 105–30. Florence: Olschki, 1974.

Blunt, Anthony. *Artistic Theory in Italy, 1450–1600.* Oxford: Clarendon Press, 1940. Reprinted 1962.

Boase, T. S. R. *Giorgio Vasari: The Man and the Book.* Princeton: Princeton University Press, 1979.

*Burck, Erich. *Von Römischen Manierismus.* Darmstadt: Wissenschaftliche Buchgesellschaft, 1971.

Campbell, Malcolm. "Mannerism Italian Style." In *Essays on Mannerism in Art and Music,* edited by S. E. Murray and R. I. Weidner. West Chester State College Symposium on Interdisciplinary Studies, November 1978, pp. 1–33. West Chester, Pa.: West Chester State College, 1980.

Carapetyan, Armen. "The Concept of the *imitazione della natura* in the Sixteenth Century." *Journal of Renaissance and Baroque Music* 1 (1946): 47–67.

Carapezza, Paolo Emilio. " 'O soave armonia': classicità, maniera e barocco nella scuola polifonica siciliana." In *Atti del congresso internazionale sul tema "Manierismo in arte e musica,"* Rome, 1973, pp. 347–90. Florence: Olschki, 1974.

Chastel, André. "Le Maniérisme et l'art du Cinquecento." *International Center for the Study of Architecture* 9 (1967): 227–32.

Clements, Robert J. *Michelangelo: A Self-Portrait.* Englewood Cliffs, N.J.: Prentice-Hall, 1963.

————. *Michelangelo's Theory of Art.* New York: New York University Press, 1961.

Da Costa Kaufmann, Thomas. "The Problem of Northern Mannerism: A Critical Review." In *Essays on Mannerism in Art and Music,* edited by S. E. Murray and R. I. Weidner. West Chester State College Symposium on Interdisciplinary Studies, November 1978, pp. 89–115. West Chester, Pa.: West Chester State College, 1980.

Dahlhaus, Carl. "Musikalischer Humanismus als Manierismus." *Musikforschung* 35 (1982): 122–29.

L'Ecole de Fontainebleau. Exhibition at the Grand Palais, Paris, 1972–73. Catalogue published by the Editions des Musées Nationaux, Paris, 1972.

Evans, Robert J. W. "Prague Mannerism and the Magic Universe." *Rudolf II and His*

World, pp. 243–74. Oxford: Clarendon Press, 1973.

Fabbri, Paolo. "Tasso, Guarini e il 'divino Claudio.' " In *Atti del congresso internazionale sul tema "Manierismo in arte e musica,"* Rome, 1973, pp. 233–51. Florence: Olschki, 1974.

Federhofer, Helmut. "Der Manierismus-Begriff in der Musikgeschichte." In *Atti del congresso internazionale sul tema "Manierismo in arte e musica,"* Rome, 1973, pp. 37–50. Florence: Olschki, 1974.

Finscher, Ludwig. "Zur Problematik des Manierismus-Begriffes in der Musikgeschichteschreibung." In *Atti del congresso internazionale sul tema "Manierismo in arte e musica."* Rome, 1973, pp. 75–81. Florence: Olschki, 1974.

Forster, Kurt. *Mannerist Painting: The Sixteenth Century.* New York: McGraw-Hill, 1966.

Fubini, Enrico. "Il manierismo come categoria storiografica." In *Atti del congresso internazionale sul tema "Manierismo in arte e musica,"* Rome, 1973, pp. 3–11. Florence: Olschki, 1974.

Gallico, Claudio. "Aspetti musicali fra disposizione manierista ed età barocco." In *Atti del congresso internazionale sul tema "Manierismo in arte e musica,"* Rome, 1973, pp. 101–04. Florence: Olschki, 1974.

Göranson, Anna Maria. "Studies in Mannerism." *Kunsthistorisk Tidskrift* 38 (1969): 120–43.

Haar, James. "Classicism and Mannerism in Sixteenth-Century Music." *International Review of Music Aesthetics and Sociology* 1 (1970): 55–67.

_____. *"Maniera* and Mannerism in Italian Music of the Sixteenth Century." In *Essays on Mannerism in Art and Music,* edited by S. E. Murray and R. I. Weidner. West Chester State College Symposium on Interdisciplinary Studies, November 1978, pp. 34–62. West Chester, Pa.: West Chester State College, 1980.

_____. "Self-Consciousness in the Cinquecento Madrigal." In *Atti del congresso internazionale sul tema "Manierismo in arte e musica,"* Rome, 1973, pp. 219–27. Florence: Olschki, 1974.

Harran, Don. "Mannerism in the Cinquecento Madrigal." *Musical Quarterly* 55 (1969): 521–44.

Haskell, Francis. "The Moment of Mannerism." *Encounter* 35 (1970): 69–73.

Hayward, John F. *Virtuoso Goldsmiths and the Triumph of Mannerism.* New York: Rizzoli International Publications, 1976.

Hocke, G. R. *Malerei der Gegenwart: Der Neo-Manierismus von Surrealismus zum Meditation.* Munich: Limes, 1975.

Hucke, Helmut. "H. R. Hassler's *Neue Teutsche Gesang* (1596) und das Problem des Manierismus in der Musik." In *Atti del congresso internazionale sul tema "Manierismo in arte e musica,"* Rome, 1973, pp. 255–84. Florence: Olschki, 1974.

_____. "Das Problem des Manierismus in der Musik." *Literaturwissenschaftliches Jahrbuch* 2 (1961): 219–38.

Kenseth, Joy. "Bernini's Borghese Sculptures: Another View." *Art Bulletin* 63 (1981): 191–210.

Kirchman, Milton. *Mannerism and Imagination: A Reexamination of Sixteenth-Century Italian Aesthetic.* Atlantic Highlands, N.J.: Humanities Press, 1980.

Klein, Robert. "Judgment and Taste in Cinquecento Art Theory." In his *Form and Meaning: Writings on the Renaissance and Modern Art,* translated by Madeline Jay and Leon Wieseltier, pp. 161–69. Princeton: Princeton University Press, 1981.

_____. "The Theory of Figurative Expression in Italian Treatises on the Impresa." In his *Form and Meaning: Writings on the Renaissance and Modern Art,* translated by Madeline Jay and Leon Wieseltier, pp. 3–24. Princeton: Princeton University Press, 1981.

Kunisch, Hermann. "Zum Problem des Manierismus. Einführung." *Literaturwissenschaftliches Jahrbuch* 2 (1961): 173–75.

Lang, Paul Henry. *Music in Western Civilization*. New York: W. W. Norton, 1941.

Larousse Encyclopedia of Renaissance and Baroque Art. Edited by René Huyghe. New York: Prometheus Press, 1964.

Lee, Rensselaer W. *Ut Pictura Poesis: The Humanistic Theory of Painting*. New York: W. W. Norton, 1967.

Longhi, Roberto. *Cinquecento classico e cinquecento manieristico*. Florence: Sansoni, 1976.

McCredie, Andrew D. "Some Aspects of Late Cinquecento Musical Mannerism in Munich and Augsberg." *Papers of the Symposium "Mannerism and the Manneristic Configurations in the Creative and Performing Arts,"* Canberra, Australia, June 1977. Published in *Miscellanea Musicologica* 11 (1980): 154–71.

Mendelsohn-Martone, Leatrice. *Benedetto Varchi's "Due Lezzioni": "Paragoni" and Cinquecento Art Theory*. 2 vols. Ann Arbor, Mich.: University Microfilms International, 1982.

Monterosso, Raffaello. "Strutture ritmiche nel madrigale cinquecentesco." In *Atti del congresso internazionale sul tema "Manierismo in arte e musica,"* Rome, 1973, pp. 287–308. Florence: Olschki, 1974.

Murray, Linda. *The Late Renaissance and Mannerism*. New York and Washington: Praeger, 1967.

Murray, S. E. and R. I. Weidner, eds. *Essays on Mannerism in Art and Music*. West Chester State College Symposium on Interdisciplinary Studies, November 1978. West Chester, Pa.: West Chester State College, 1980.

Orgel, Stephen, and Roy Strong. *Inigo Jones: The Theatre of the Stuart Court*. 2 vols. Berkeley: University of California Press, 1973.

Ossola, Carlo. *Autunno del Rinascimento: Idea del Tempio dell'arte nell'ultimo Cinquecento*. Florence: Olschki, 1970.

Panofsky, Erwin. *Galileo as a Critic of the Arts*. The Hague: Nijhoff, 1954.

––––––––. *Idea: A Concept in Art Theory*. Translated by Joseph J. S. Peake. New York: Harper & Row, 1968.

Papers of the Symposium "Mannerism and the Manneristic Configurations in the Creative and Performing Arts," Australian National University, Canberra, Australia, June 1977. Published in the journal *Miscellanea Musicologica, Adelaide Studies in Musicology*, vol. 11 (1980).

Pevsner, Nikolaus. *Academies of Art Past and Present*. New York: Macmillan, 1940.

Piel, Friedrich. "Zum Problem des Manierismus in der Kunstgeschichte." *Literaturwissenschaftliches Jahrbuch* 2 (1961): 207–18.

Pope-Hennessy, John. "Nicholas Hilliard and Mannerist Art Theory." *Journal of the Warburg and Courtauld Institutes* 6 (1943): 89–100.

*Preiss, Pavel. *Panoráma Manýrismus*. Prague: Odeon, 1974.

Quartermaine, Luisa. "Vicino Orsini's Garden of Conceits." *Italian Studies* 32 (1977): 68–85.

Ravizza, Victor. "Manierismus—ein musikgeschichtlicher Epochenbegriff?" *Musikforschung* 34 (1981): 273–84.

Resnik, Solomon. "Conoscenza e creatività." In *Tiziano e il manierismo europeo*, edited by Rodolfo Palluchini, pp. 415–33. Florence: Olschki, 1978.

Rosci, Marco. "Manierismo e accademismo nel pensiero critico del Cinquecento." *Acme* 9 (1956): 57–81.

Samuels, Richard S. "Benedetto Varchi, the *Accademia degli Infiammati*, and the Origins of the Italian Academic Movement." *Renaissance Quarterly* 29 (1976): 599–633.

Schlosser, Julius von. *Die Kunstliteratur*. Vienna: Schroll, 1924. Amended, enlarged, and with appendix in Italian translation, *La letteratura artistica,* by Filippo Rossi. 3d ed. Florence: Nuova Italia, 1964.

Schrade, Leo. "Von der 'Maniera' der Komposition in der Musik des 16. Jahrhunderts."
    Zeitschrift für Musikwissenschaft 16 (1934): 3–20, 98–117, 152–70.
Shearman, John. "The Galerie François Premier: A Case in Point." *Papers of the Symposium
    "Mannerism and the Manneristic Configurations in the Creative and Performing Arts,"* Can-
    berra, Australia, June 1977. Published in *Miscellanea Musicologica* 11 (1980): 1–16.
Smart, Alastair. *The Renaissance and Mannerism in Italy.* New York: Harcourt Brace
    Jovanovich, 1971.
——————. *The Renaissance and Mannerism in Northern Europe.* New York: Harcourt Brace
    Jovanovich, 1972.
Spina-Barelli, Emma. *Teorici e scrittori d'arte tra manierismo e barocco.* Milan: Società Editrice
    Vita e Pensiero, 1966.
Steele, John. "Marenzio—from Mannerist to Expressionist." *Papers of the Symposium "Man-
    nerism and the Manneristic Configurations in the Creative and Performing Arts,"* Canberra,
    Australia, June 1977. Published in *Miscellanea Musicologica* 11 (1980): 129–53.
Summers, David. *Michelangelo and the Language of Art.* Princeton: Princeton University
    Press, 1981.
Sutton, Denys. "Mannerism: The Art of Permanent Ambiguity." *Apollo* 81 (1965):
    222–27.
Die Triomf van bet Manierisme. Catalogue of the Council of Europe Exhibition, Amsterdam,
    1955. *The Triumph of European Mannerism from Michelangelo to El Greco.* Translated by O.
    Salway, text by Sabine Cotté. Paris: Publications filmées d'art et d'histoire, 1968.
Il Vasari storiografico e artista. Atti del congresso internazionale nel IV centenario della
    morte, Arezzo-Florence, 1974. Florence: Istituto Nazionale di Studi sul Rinascimento,
    1976.
Venturi, Lionello. *History of Art Criticism.* New York: E. P. Dutton, 1964.
——————. *The Sixteenth Century, from Leonardo to El Greco.* New York: Skira, 1956.
Watkins, Glenn. "Carlo Gesualdo and the Delimitations of Late Mannerist Style." In *Atti
    del congresso internazionale sul tema "Manierismo in arte e musica,"* Rome, 1973, pp.
    55–74. Florence: Olschki, 1974.
——————. *Gesualdo: The Man and His Music.* Chapel Hill: University of North Carolina
    Press, 1973.
——————. "Gesualdo as Mannerist: A Reconsideration." In S. E. Murray and R. I.
    Weidner, eds., *Essays on Mannerism in Art and Music.* West Chester State College
    Symposium on Interdisciplinary Studies, November 1978, pp. 63–68. West Chester,
    Pa.: West Chester State College, 1980.
Whittington, Steven C. "The Two Faces of Mannerism." *Papers of the Symposium "Man-
    nerism and the Manneristic Configurations in the Creative and Performing Arts,"* Canberra,
    Australia, June 1977. Published in *Miscellanea Musicologica* 11 (1980): 97–104.
Williams, Carol. "Two Examples of Mannerist Notation in the Late Fourteenth Century."
    *Papers of the Symposium "Mannerism and the Manneristic Configurations in the Creative and
    Performing Arts,"* Canberra, Australia, June 1977. Published in *Miscellanea Musicologica*
    11 (1980): 111–28.
Wittkower, Rudolf, and Margot Wittkower. *Born under Saturn.* New York: W. W.
    Norton, 1969.
——————. "Individualism in Art and Artists: A Renaissance Problem." *Journal of the
    History of Ideas* 22 (1961): 291–302.
——————. "Michelangelo's Biblioteca Laurenziana." *Art Bulletin* 16 (1934): 123–216.
Wolf, Robert E., and Ronald Millen. *Renaissance and Mannerist Art.* New York: Harry N.
    Abrams, 1968.
Wölfflin, Heinrich. *Classic Art.* Translated by Peter and Linda Murray. London: Phaidon,
    1959.

Zerner, Henri. *The School of Fontainebleau: Etchings and Engravings.* New York: Harry N. Abrams, 1969.

Modern Commentary on Literature and Art

Adhémar, Jean. "Ronsard et l'école de Fontainebleau." *Bibliothèque d'Humanisme et Renaissance* 20 (1958): 344–48.

Argan, G. C. "Il Tasso e le arti figurative." *Torquato Tasso,* pp. 209–26. Milan: Marzorati, 1957.

Ariani, Marco. *Il teatro tragico del Cinquecento tra classicismo e manierismo.* Florence: Olschki, 1974.

Bayley, Peter, and Dorothy G. Coleman, eds. Foreword by Alison Fairlie. *The Equilibrium of Wit: Essays for Odette de Mourgues.* French Forum Monographs No. 36. Lexington, Ky.: French Forum Publishers, 1982.

Bensimon, Marc. "La Porte étroite: Essai sur le maniérisme (Le Greco, Saint Jean de la Croix, Sponde, Chassignet, d'Aubigné, Montaigne)." *Journal of Medieval and Renaissance Studies* 10 (1980): 255–80.

Berger, Harry J. "The Renaissance Imagination: Second World and Green World." *Centennial Review* 9 (1965): 36–78.

Bonnet, Pierre. "Montaigne, le maniérisme et le baroque." *Bulletin de la Société des Amis de Montaigne,* ser. 5, nos. 7–8 (1973): 45–58.

Borowitz, Helen G. "Michelangelo's Harsh Music." *Art Journal* 29 (1970): 318–25.

Braendel, Doris B. "The Limits of Clarity: Lyly's *Endymion,* Bronzino's *Allegory of Venus and Cupid,* Webster's *White Devil* and Botticelli's *Primavera.*" *University of Hartford Studies in Literature* 4 (1972): 197–215.

Burgess, Robert M. "Mannerism in Philippe Desportes." *L'Esprit créateur* 6 (1966): 270–81.

Campagnoli, Ruggero. "Su Jodelle e il manierismo." *Rivista di letterature moderne e comparate* 25 (1972): 5–49.

Carrara, Enrico. "Il manierismo letterario di Benvenuto Cellini." *Studi romanzi* 19 (1928): 171–200.

Cave, Terence. *The Cornucopian Text: Problems of Writing in the French Renaissance.* Oxford: Clarendon Press, 1979.

————. "Ronsard's Mythological Universe. In *Ronsard the Poet,* edited by Terence Cave, pp. 159–208. London: Methuen, 1973.

Chaney, Richard. "The Problem of Mannerism in Sixteenth-Century French Literature." *Papers of the Symposium "Mannerism and the Manneristic Configurations in the Creative and Performing Arts,"* Canberra, Australia, June 1977. Published in *Miscellanea Musicologica* 11 (1980): 28–48.

Clements, Robert J. "The Identity of Literary and Artistic Theory in the Renaissance." *The Peregrine Muse.* Chapel Hill: University of North Carolina Press, 1969.

Cousins, A. D. "The Coming of Mannerism: The Later Ralegh and the Early Donne." *English Literary Renaissance* 9 (1979): 86–107.

Daniells, Roy. "The Mannerist Element in English Literature." *University of Toronto Quarterly* 36 (1966), 1–11.

————. *Milton, Mannerism and Baroque.* Toronto: University of Toronto Press, 1963.

Darst, David H. "Mannerism in Sixteenth-Century Spanish Literature." In *Renaissance Papers 1981,* edited by A. Leigh Deneef and M. Thomas Hester, pp. 87–95. Published by the Southeastern Renaissance Conference. Raleigh, N.C.: School of Humanities and Social Sciences, North Carolina State University, 1982.

Demerson, Guy, ed. *Poétiques de la métamorphose de Pétrarque à John Donne.* Saint-Etienne:

Publications de l'Université de Saint-Etienne, 1981.

Dionisotti, Carlo. "La letteratura italiana nell'età del Concilio de Trento." In his *Geografia e storia della letteratura italiano*, pp. 183–204. Turin: Einaudi 1976.

Dobrez, Livio. "Mannerism and Baroque in English Literature." *Papers of the Symposium "Mannerism and the Manneristic Configurations in the Creative and Performing Arts,"* Canberra, Australia, June 1977. Published in *Miscellanea Musicologica* 11 (1980): 84–96.

Donaldson-Evans, Lance. "Two Stages of Renaissance Style: Mannerism and Baroque in French Poetry." *French Forum* 7 (1982): 210–23.

Dresden, Sem. "Montaigne maniériste." In *Mélanges de linguistiques et de littérature offerts à Lein Geschiere*, pp. 131–44. Amsterdam: Rodopi, 1975.

Dubois, Claude-Gilbert, ed. *La Poésie baroque*. 2 vols. Paris: Larousse, 1969.

Durán, Manuel. "Lope de Vega y el problema del manierismo." *Anuario de Letras* 2 (1962): 76–98.

_____. "Manierismo en Quevedo." *Actas del Segundo Congreso Internacional de Hispanistas*, 1965, pp. 301–08. Nijmegen, The Netherlands: Instituto Español de la Universidad de Nimega, 1967.

_____. "Manierismo en Quevedo." *Letras de Deusto* 10 (1980): 191–98. Reprint of 1965 article.

Elsky, Martin. "*La Corona:* Spatiality and Mannerist Painting." *Modern Language Studies* 13 (1983): 3–11.

Fowler, Alastair. *Conceitful Thought*. Edinburgh: Edinburgh University Press, 1975.

Gent, Lucy. *Picture and Poetry, 1560–1620*. Leamington Spa, Eng.: James Hall, 1981.

Gornall, J. F. G. "The Poetry of Wit: Góngora Reconsidered." *Modern Language Review* 75 (1980): 311–21.

Graham, Victor E. "Aspects du maniérisme et du baroque in littérature." *Neohelicon* 3 (1976): 361–74.

Greenblatt, Stephen J. *Renaissance Self-Fashioning from More to Shakespeare*. Chicago: Chicago University Press, 1980.

_____. *Sir Walter Ralegh: The Renaissance Man and His Role*. New Haven and London: Yale University Press, 1973.

Greene, Thomas M. "Image and Consciousness in Scève's *Délie*." In *The Meaning of Mannerism*, edited by Franklin W. Robinson and Stephen G. Nichols, Jr., pp. 25–36. Hanover, N.H.: University Press of New England, 1972.

_____. *The Light in Troy*. New Haven and London: Yale University Press, 1982.

_____. "Scève's *Saulsaye:* The Life and Death of Solitude." *Studies in Philology* 70 (1973): 123–40.

_____. "Styles of Experience in Scève's *Délie*." *Yale French Studies* 47 (1972): 57–75.

Hathaway, Baxter. *The Age of Criticism: The Late Renaissance in Italy*. Ithaca, N.Y.: Cornell University Press, 1962.

_____. *Marvels and Commonplaces: Renaissance Literary Criticism*. New York: Random House, 1968.

Hatzfeld, Helmut. "Literary Mannerism and Baroque in Spain and France." *Comparative Literature Studies* 7 (1970): 419–36.

Helgerson, Richard. *Self-Crowned Laureates: Spenser, Jonson, Milton, and the Literary System*. Berkeley: University of California Press, 1983.

Heninger, S. K. "Renaissance Perversions of Pastoral." *Journal of the History of Ideas* 22 (1961): 254–61.

Henniger, Gerd, ed. *Beispiele manieristischer Lyrik*. Munich: Deutscher Taschenbuch Verlag, 1970.

Hinkle, Douglas P. "Literary and Pictorial Mannerism in the Spanish Golden Age: A Question of Definitions." In *Studies in Language and Literature: Proceedings of the Twenty-Third Mountain Interstate Foreign Language Conference*, edited by Charles L. Nelson, pp.

257—61. Richmond, Ky.: Department of Foreign Languages, Eastern Kentucky University, 1976.

Howe, James. "Ford's *The Lady's Trial:* A Play of Metaphysical Wit." *Genre* 7 (1974): 342—61.

Hoy, Cyrus. "Jacobean Tragedy and the Mannerist Style." *Shakespeare Survey* 26 (1973): 49—67.

*Iser, Wolfgang. "Manieristische Metaphorik in der englischen Dichtung." *Germanisch-romanische Monatsschrift* 10 (1960): 266—87.

Jackson, Robert. *John Donne's Christian Vocation.* Evanston, Ill.: Northwestern University Press, 1970.

Jacobus, Lee A. "Richard Crashaw as Mannerist." *Bucknell Review* 18 (1970): 79—88.

Jehenson, Myriam Yvonne. *The Golden World of the Pastoral: A Comparative Study of Sidney's "New Arcadia" and d'Urfé's "Astrée".* Ravenna: Longo, 1981.

Jeuland-Maynard, Maryse, ed. *La Repréésentation du corps dans la culture italienne.* Actes du Colloque de 1980, Centre Université de Provence, 1981.

Johnson, W. R. *The Idea of Lyric: Lyric Modes in Ancient and Modern Poetry.* Berkeley: University of California Press, 1982.

Jones, R. O. "Renaissance Butterfly, Mannerist Flea: Tradition and Change in Renaissance Poetry." *Modern Language Notes* 80 (1965): 166—84.

Kennedy, William J. *Rhetorical Norms in Renaissance Literature.* New Haven and London: Yale University Press, 1978.

Kossoff, A. David. "Renacentista, manierista, barroco, definiciones y modelos para la literatura española." In *Actas del Quinto Congreso Internacional de Hispanistas,* 1974, edited by Maxime Chevalier, François Lopez, Joseph Lopez, Noël Salomon, pp. 537—41. Bordeaux: Instituto de Estudios Ibricos e Iberoamericanos, Universidad de Bordeaux, 1977.

Lanham, Richard A. *The Motives of Eloquence: Literary Rhetoric in the Renaissance.* New Haven and London: Yale University Press, 1976.

Le Coat, Gérard. *Rhetoric of the Arts, 1550—1650.* Berne: Lang, 1975.

Lee, Rensselaer W. *Poetry in Painting.* Middlebury, Vt.: The Fulton Memorial Lecture, 1970.

Levenson, Jill L. "Shakespeare's *Troilus and Cressida* and the Monumental Tradition in Tapestries and Literature." *Renaissance Drama* 7 (1976): 43—84.

Lott, Robert E. "On Mannerism and Mannered Approaches to Realism in *Un drama nuevo, Consuelo* and Earlier Nineteenth-Century Spanish Plays." *Hispania* 54 (1971): 844—55.

Lumières de la Pléiade. Neuvième stage international d'études humanistes, Tours, 1965. Paris: Vrin, 1966.

McGinn, Donald J., and George Howerton. *Literature as a Fine Art.* Evanston and New York: Row, Peterson and Company, 1959.

Margolin, J.-C. "La Découverte de l'Amerique dans une vision maniériste de Francastoro et de Stradan." *Renaissance, Maniérisme, Baroque.* Actes du XIe siècle: Sannazar et Belleau. Paris: Editions universitaires, 1974.

Monk, Samuel H. "A Grace beyond the Reach of Art." *Journal of the History of Ideas* 5 (1944): 131—50.

Montgomery, Robert L. *The Reader's Eye: Studies in Didactic Theory from Dante to Tasso.* Berkeley: University of California Press, 1979.

Moreno Baez, Enrique. "El manierismo de Pérez de Hita." In *Homenaje a Emilio Alarcos Garcia,* 2:353—67. Valladolid: Universidad de Valladolid, 1967.

Mourgues, Odette de. *Metaphysical, Baroque and Précieux Poetry.* Oxford: Clarendon, 1953.

Neill, Michael. " 'Anticke Pageantrie': The Mannerist Art of *Perkin Warbeck*" *Renaissance Drama* 7 (1976): 117—50.

_____. "Styles of Greatness: The Hero in English Mannerist Drama." *Papers of the*

Symposium "Mannerism and the Manneristic Configurations in the Creative and Performing Arts," Canberra, Australia, June 1977. Published in *Miscellanea Musicologica* 11 (1980): 66–83.

O'Connell, M. R. *The Counter-Reformation, 1560–1610.* New York: Harper & Row, 1974.

O'Regan, Michael. *The Mannerist Aesthetic: A Study of Racine's "Mithridate."* Bristol, Eng.: University of Bristol Press, 1980.

Pieri, Marzio. "Eros e manierismo nel Marino." *Convivium* 36 (1968): 453–81.

Pigman, George W. III. "Imitation and the Renaissance Sense of the Past: The Reception of Erasmus' *Ciceronianus.*" *Journal of Medieval and Renaissance Studies* 9 (1979): 155–77.

_____. "Versions of Imitation in the Renaissance." *Renaissance Quarterly* 33 (1980): 1–32.

Porqueras Mayo, Alberto, comp. *El prólogo en el manierismo y barroco españoles.* Madrid: Consejo Superior de Investigaciones Cientificas, 1968.

Praz, Mario. *Il giardino dei sense: studi sul manierismo e il barocco.* Milan: Mondadori, 1975.

Raymond, Marcel. "Aux frontières du maniérisme et du baroque." In his *Etre et Dire,* pp. 113–35. Neuchâtel: Baconnière, 1970.

_____. "La Pléiade et le maniérisme." In *Lumières de la Pléiade.* Neuvième stage international d'études humanistes, Tours, 1965, pp. 391–423. Paris: Vrin, 1966.

_____. "Ronsard et le maniérisme." In his *Etre et Dire,* pp. 63–112. Neuchâtel: Baconnière, 1970.

_____, ed. *La Poésie française et le maniérisme, 1546–1610.* Geneva: Droz, 1971.

Rebhorn, Wayne A. *Courtly Performances: Masking and Festivity in Castiglione's "Book of the Courtier."* Detroit, Mich.: Wayne State University Press, 1977.

Rizza, Cecilia. "L'Image de l'amant et son evolution entre maniérisme et baroque." *Travaux de Linguistique et de Littérature Publiée par Le Centre de Philologie et Littérature Romanes de l'Universiteé de Strasbourg* 20 (1982): 23–36.

Rodriguez Cepeda, Enrique. "Manierismo y barroco en el Siglo de Oro español." *Mester* 22.

Roston, Murray. *The Soul of Wit: A Study of John Donne.* Oxford: Clarendon Press, 1974.

Rowland, Daniel B. *Mannerism, Style and Mood: An Anatomy of Four Works and Three Art Forms.* New Haven and London: Yale University Press, 1964.

Rubin, D. L. "Mannerism and Love: The Sonnets of Abraham de Vermeil." *L'Esprit Créateur* 6 (1966): 257–63.

Saccone, Edoardo. *"Grazia, Sprezzatura* and *Affetazione* in Castiglione's *Book of the Courtier."* Glyph 5 (1979): 34–54.

Sacré, James. *Un Sang maniériste: Etude structurale autour du mot "sang" dans la poésie lyrique française de la fin du seizième siècle.* Neuchâtel: Baconnière, 1977.

Sayce, R. A. "Maniérisme et periodization: Quelques réflexions générales." In *Renaissance, Maniérisme, Baroque.* Actes du XIe stage internationale de Tours, pp. 43–54. Paris: Vrin, 1972.

_____. "Renaissance et maniérisme dans l'oeuvre de Montaigne." In *Renaissance, Maniérisme, Baroque.* Actes du XIe stage internationale de Tours, pp. 137–51. Paris: Vrin, 1972.

Scaglione, Aldo. "Cinquecento Mannerism and the Uses of Petrarch." *Medieval and Renaissance Studies* 5 (1971): 122–53.

Scrivano, Riccardo. *Il manierismo nella letteratura italiana del Cinquecento.* Padua: Liviana Editrice, 1959.

Smith, Gordon R. "Mannerist Frivolity and Shakespeare's *Venus and Adonis."* *University of Hartford Studies in Literature* 3 (1971): 1–11.

Socarrás, Cayetano J. "Fernando de Herrera (el rompimiento del equilibrio renacentista)."

In *Estudios de historia, literatura y arte hispánica ofrecidos a Rodrigo A. Molina*, pp. 299–315. Madrid: Insula, 1977.

Soellner, Rolf. *Shakespeare's Patterns of Self-Knowledge*. Columbus, Ohio: Ohio State University Press, 1972.

Soons, C. A. "Two Historical *Comedias* and the Question of *Manierismo*." *Romanische Forschungen* 73 (1961): 339–46.

Starobinski, Jean. "Montaigne et la polemique contre les apparences." In *Tiziano e il manierismo*, edited by Rodolfo Palluchini, pp. 389–413. Florence: Olschki, 1978.

Taddeo, Edoardo. "Il manierismo letterario nel Cinquecento." *Il manierismo letterario e i lirici veneziani del tardo '500*, pp. 11–35. Rome: Bulzoni, 1974.

Tannier, Bernard. "Un Bestiare maniériste: Monstres et animaux fantastiques dans *La Reine des fees* d'Edmund Spenser." In *Monstres et prodigues au temps de la Renaissance*, edited by Marie Thérèse Jones-Davis, pp. 55–65. Paris: Touzot, 1980.

della Terza, Dante. "Manierismo nella letteratura del Cinquecento." *Belfagor* 15 (1960): 462–66.

Tetel, Marcel. "Mannerism in the Imagery of Sponde's 'Sonnets de la morte' " *Rivista di letterature moderne e comparate* 21 (1968): 5–12.

Tuve, Rosemond. "Baroque and Mannerist Milton." In *Milton Studies in Honor of Harris Francis Fletcher*, pp. 209–25. Urbana: University of Illinois Press, 1961.

Ulivi, Ferruccio. *Il manierismo del Tasso e altri studi*. Florence: Olschki, 1966.

_____. "Tiziano e la letteratura del manierismo." In *Tiziano e il manierismo europeo*, edited by Rodolfo Palluchini, pp. 339–63. Florence: Olschki, 1978.

Ulivi, Ferruccio, and Rodolfo Macchioni Jodi, eds. *Prospettive e problemi. Antologia della critica letteraria e della civiltà italiana. Rinascimento e manierismo*. Vol. 4. Messina: Casa Editrice G. D'Anna, 1971.

Ullman, Pierre L. "The Surrogates of Baroque Marcela and Mannerist Leandra." *Revista de Estudios Hispánicos* 5 (1971): 307–19.

Ungerer, Gustav. "Bartholmew Yong, Mannerist Translator of Spanish Pastoral Romances." *English Studies* 54 (1973): 439–46.

Veit, Walter. "Mannerism and Rhetoric: Some Aspects of the History of the Concept in Literary Criticism." *Papers of the Symposium "Mannerism and the Manneristic Configurations in the Creative and Performing Arts,"* Canberra, Australia, June 1977. Published in *Miscellanea Musicologica* 11 (1980): 49–65.

Warnock, Robert G., and Roland Falter. "The German Pattern Poem: A Study in Mannerism of the Seventeenth Century." In *Festschrift für Detlev W. Schumann zum 70 Geburtstag*, edited by A. R. Schmidt, pp. 40–73. Munich: Delp, 1970.

Weinberg, Bernard. *A History of Literary Criticism in the Italian Renaissance*. 2 vols. Chicago: Chicago University Press, 1961.

Williamson, Edward. "The Concept of Grace in the Work of Raphael and Castiglione." *Italica* 24 (1947): 316–24.

Wilson, Harold S. "Some Meanings of 'Nature' in Renaissance Literary Theory." *Journal of the History of Ideas* 2 (1941): 430–48.

Index